UP TO MAMETZ
... AND BEYOND

TO THE MEMORY OF
PRIVATE WATCYN GRIFFITH
ROYAL WELCH FUSILIERS

'... I ddwys goffau
Y rhwyg o golli'r hogiau'

UP TO MAMETZ
... AND BEYOND

Llewelyn Wyn Griffith

Edited and annotated by
Jonathon Riley

Pen & Sword
MILITARY

First published in Great Britain in 2010
and republished in this format in 2021 by
Pen & Sword Military
an imprint of
Pen & Sword Books Ltd
47 Church Street
Barnsley
South Yorkshire
S70 2AS

Copyright © Llewelyn Wyn Griffith, 2010, 2021

ISBN: 978-1-52670-055-1

The right of Llewelyn Wyn Griffith to be identified as Author of this Work has been asserted by him in accordance with the Copyright, Designs and Patents Act 1988.

A CIP catalogue record for this book is available from the British Library.

All rights reserved. No part of this book may be reproduced or transmitted in any form or by any means, electronic or mechanical including photocopying, recording or by any information storage and retrieval system, without permission from the Publisher in writing.

Typeset in 11/13pt Sabon by Concept, Huddersfield, West Yorkshire.
Printed and bound in the UK by CPI Group (UK) Ltd, Croydon, CR0 4YY.

Pen & Sword Books Ltd incorporates the Imprints of Pen & Sword Aviation, Pen & Sword Maritime, Pen & Sword Military, Wharncliffe Local History, Pen & Sword Select, Pen & Sword Military Classics, Leo Cooper, Remember When, Seaforth Publishing and Frontline Publishing.

For a complete list of Pen & Sword titles please contact
PEN & SWORD BOOKS LIMITED
47 Church Street, Barnsley, South Yorkshire, S70 2AS, England
E-mail: enquiries@pen-and-sword.co.uk
Website: www.pen-and-sword.co.uk

Contents

List of Maps	vi
List of Figures and Drawings in the Text	vii
List of Photographs	ix
Foreword by Martin Wyn Griffith	xi
Editor's Introduction	xiii
Acknowledgements	xxvii

Part One – Up To Mametz

Chapter 1	Prentice Days	2
Chapter 2	Command	18
Chapter 3	Givenchy	34
Chapter 4	Mud	54
Chapter 5	Alarms and Diversions	72
Chapter 6	South	86
Chapter 7	Mametz Wood	96
Chapter 8	The Gleaning	123

Part Two – Beyond Mametz

Chapter 9	Salient	128
Chapter 10	ANZAC	150
Chapter 11	Kaiserschlacht	164
Chapter 12	Armistice	173

Appendix	187
Bibliography	199
Index	202

List of Maps

Drawn by Mr Steve Waites

Map No.		Chapter
1	The Western Front, 1914–1918	Introduction
2	The Givenchy Sector, 1916	3
3	The Somme Battlefield, 1916	6
4	Mametz Wood	7
5	The Trenches in the Yser Canal sector	9
6	The Battle of Messines, 1917	10
7	The Battle of Broodseinde, 1917	10
8	The German Offensive, March/April 1918	11
9	The Second Battle of the Marne, 1918 *(History of the 62nd (West Riding) Division)*	11

List of Figures and Drawings in the Text

All drawings are by David Jones, 15 RWF unless otherwise specified; the formation badges are from Wheeler-Holohan 'Divisional and Other Signs' unless otherwise specified.

	Chapter
The cap badge of the Royal Welch Fusiliers [Ministry of Defence]	1
'Salisbury Plain, 1915'	1
The crest of the 15th Royal Welch Fusiliers [RWF Trustees]	2
'Front line trench'	2
The badge of the British Fourth Army	3
Diagram of trench construction showing breastworks, from the General Staff pamphlet *British Trench Warfare 1917–1918*	3
Diagram of trench layout showing communications trenches, traverses, bays and dugouts, from the General Staff pamphlet *British Trench Warfare 1917–1918*	3
'Givenchy – a dug-out and a very big mine crater'	3
The Badge of XI Corps	4
'Somewhere in the Festubert sub-sector'	4
The shoulder title of 15th RWF	5

'Using a trench periscope'	5
The badge of II Corps	6
'Rouges Croix'	6
The badge of the 38th (Welsh) Division	7
'Forward dug-out'	7
The 15th RWF Memorial in the Inns of Court	8
The badge of VIII Corps	9
'Elverdinghe, North-west of Ypres'	9
'Brielen'	9
The badge of II ANZAC Corps	10
'Captured German machine gun'	10
The General Staff cap badge	11
The badge of XXII Corps	12
'Rats killed in an old dug-out'	12

List of Photographs

Llewelyn Wyn Griffith [RWF Trustees]
Llewelyn Wyn Griffith [Martin Wyn Griffith]
A newspaper cutting of 15th RWF in its earliest days at Grey's Inn
Captain W.A. Howells 15th RWF [RWF Trustees]
Major John Edwards, 15th RWF [RWF Trustees]
The Second-in-Command (Major H.V.R. Hodson) and the Adjutant (Captain L.N.V. Evans), 15th RWF [RWF Trustees]
2nd Lieutenant Noel Osbourne Jones, D Company 15th RWF [RWF Trustees]
WG and his company in tents. WG himself is facing the camera [family of John Bradshaw]
Soldiers of 15th RWF filling sandbags in the line [IWM Q8372]
Troops being fed hot rations in the line from dixies [IWM Q4843]
A field kitchen in a dugout [IWM E1219]
British trenches on the Western Front [RWF Trustees]
German trenches on the Western Front [RWF Trustees]
A communication trench in the Laventie sector [IWM Q17410]
A working party in trenches [IWM Q5092]
Men of 15 RWF resting before the attack (RWF Trustees)
An aerial photograph of Mametz Wood (RWF Trustees)
A German trench on the edge of a wood, such as that faced by 15th RWF during the assault on Mametz Wood [James Payne collections]
Brigadier Horatio Evans, Major Charles Veal and an unknown officer in Mametz Wood [IWM Q868]

GOC VIII Corps and staff [IWM Q736]
Winifred Wyn Griffith (Wyn) in 1916 [Martin Wyn Griffith]
Dugouts along the Yser Canal [IWM Q5947]
Infantry crossing a bridge on the Yser Canal [IWM Q2681]
Officers' rank badges as worn during the Great War
Arm bands of staff officers
A command dugout in the Ypres sector [IWM E690]
H Mess, Headquarters XXII Corps [IWM Q6938]
Australian troops, October 1917 [IWM E (Aus) 842]
King George V visiting Australian troops [IWM Q954]
The Battlefield near Soissons, 1918 [IWM Q57533]
GOC XXII Corps bids farewell to General Berthelot, 1918 [IWM Q9149]
Wyn Griffith, David Liddle and Major F.A. Pile at Mons, 1918 [Martin Wyn Griffith]
The Memorial to the 38th (Welsh) Division at Mametz Wood [RWF Trustees]

Foreword by Martin Wyn Griffith

It has been a pleasure and a privilege to work closely with Jonathon Riley over the last two years to bring back to life my grandfather's book *Up to Mametz*. I want to thank him for approaching my father and me with the idea of creating a new volume incorporating Taid's further insights and afterthoughts. I have been particularly struck by Jonathon's interest in exploring styles of leadership – both on and off the battlefield – and hope that these lessons will be of wider value.

Seeing my grandfather's words brought back to life has meant a lot to me. For a man who lost his younger brother in the battle at Mametz Wood and, a generation later, lost his eldest son in a bombing mission over Germany, these are words which carry behind them a heavy imprint of emotions held back, of losses too painful to magnify but also of hard toil borne of duty to one's country, to one's fellow man and to cherished principles of right and wrong that still resonate in modern times and in modern wars. This book serves as a reminder of a man and of a set of values that, in my generation, have been diluted by many diverse drivers over recent decades.

I came to know my grandfather well as a child. I was billeted in Berkhamsted for several long weekends and the occasional week when my parents needed to park me as they headed off for a break. I loved him and my grandmother dearly. Here was a man who taught me to drive his Austin 1100 in the car park at Cholesbury Common when I was fourteen: not the upright behaviour you would associate with a civil servant, a tax inspector even! Here was a retired man who did *The Times* crossword every morning in no more than thirty minutes, leaving time to write beautiful letters in his utterly consistent italic handwriting, whilst smoking one of his very many pipes. Here was a man who loved his wife deeply and cared for her in every way – did the shopping every day (and sneaked a half of Guinness in the pub opposite Waitrose en route), came home and cooked, did the gardening, organised everything. Here was a broadcaster, a man of letters and of art and music, who loved the German composers – Brahms, Beethoven, Wagner. A man who captained the Welsh team on BBC Radio's *Round Britain* quiz; who befriended and helped Ben and Winifred Nicholson in their early days as artists; who bought an early oil from L.S. Lowry for £25 when visiting Salford but admitted later that he never liked the picture!

He stood tall but was humble in his tastes, yet lived life to the full. His wife, my Nain, always said to me that she would outlive him. 'You'll see', she said, 'mark my words. I'll live longer than your grandfather'. And so it was that, once they were too weak to manage on their own, they came to live in a convent down the road from us in Bowdon, Cheshire and there they died – he first and then she, just three days later. She had no reason to live any more. We buried them together, in the family grave, in their beloved village of Rhiw in 1977.

Martin Wyn Griffith
August 2010

Editor's Introduction

Llewelyn Wyn Griffith's *Up To Mametz* has long been regarded as one of the classic texts of the Great War. Despite its low sales relative to some other works on the Great War when first published, it has had two successful re-issues and in terms of its literary reputation, it now ranks alongside the works of other Great War writers – of whom some of the most notable also served in the same Regiment as Wyn Griffith, The Royal Welch Fusiliers: Robert Graves, Siegfried Sassoon, David Jones, Frank Richards, Vivian de Sola Pinto, Bernard Adams, J.C. Dunn and the iconic Welsh Poet Ellis Humphrey Evans (Hedd Wyn) being the best known.

Wyn Griffith was born into a Welsh speaking family in Llandrillo yn Rhos in North Wales and attended Blaenau Ffestiniog County School, where his father taught.[1] When his father moved to become headmaster of Dolgellau Grammar School, Wyn Griffith went there. His father hoped that he would go on to Cambridge but instead he took the Civil Service Examination. At first he was employed in the Liverpool Tax Office of the Inland Revenue as an Assistant Surveyor of Taxes and it was in Liverpool that he met the girl whom he would later marry. In 1912 he was transferred to London where he embraced the cultural and artistic life available there with relish, attending the salon of Mrs Ellis Griffith, wife of the Liberal MP for Anglesey, where he met composers, artists, politicians and writers; it was at this time that his first essays in writing began. His father, who had inherited a modest sum of money, paid for him to study for the bar at the Middle Temple, while continuing his work with the Inland Revenue.

At the time of the outbreak of war he was twenty-four. On 4 August he was, like many people in Britain, on holiday, staying with his

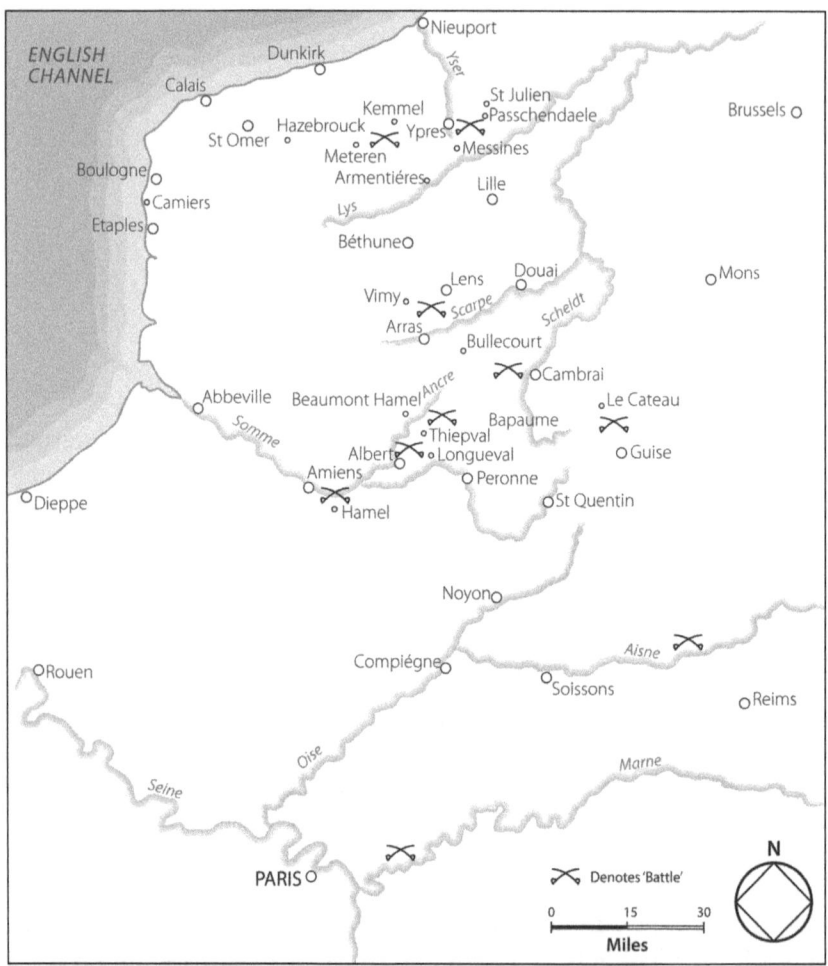

Map 1: The Western Front, 1914–1918.

parents at Dolgellau. He returned immediately to London with the intention of joining up but found to his chagrin that he was in a protected occupation and not able to enlist. It was not long, however, before the rules were relaxed; with a friend from his Liverpool days who had been an officer in the Royal Naval Volunteer Reserve, Wyn Griffith applied to join the Naval Division, an infantry division formed from men who could not be found employment in the Fleet. When his friend failed the medical examination, Wyn Griffith declined to enlist without him; both turned instead to the 7th (Merioneth & Montgomeryshire) Battalion of The Royal Welch

Editor's Introduction

Fusiliers at Newtown in Montgomeryshire, where the medical criteria proved rather more lenient.

Shortly before Christmas he received a letter from his friend Mrs Griffith telling him of the raising of the 15th (1st London Welsh) Battalion of the Regiment. He at once applied for a commission and was accepted in January 1915. 15 RWF had been raised in the Inns of Court as the 1st London Welsh Battalion of the Royal Welch Fusiliers as part of the raising of the New Army. The battalion was first inaugurated at a meeting of Welshmen in London on 16 September 1914, presided over by Sir Vincent Evans. It was officially recognised on 29 October 1914. Its headquarters were at the Inns of Court Hotel but most of the members continued to live at home during the early period. The Benchers of Gray's Inn lent the garden and square as a drill ground and it is here that, after the War, the battalion's war memorial was placed. The battalion left London for Llandudno on 15 December 1914 under the command of Lieutenant-Colonel W.A.L. Fox-Pitt of the Grenadier Guards and joined 113 Infantry Brigade, part of the 38th Welsh Division. It was here that Wyn Griffith joined them.

15 RWF and its home-service partner battalion, 18th (2nd London Welsh) RWF began by enlisting Welshmen living in London, as its name implies. Many of these were second or third generation exiles who, as Wyn Griffith notes in his recording of reported speech, sounded more Cockney than Welsh – but they still felt the pull of their homeland. A surprising number were Carmarthenshire families involved in the dairy business: Carmarthenshire, then as now, was Britain's biggest producer of milk and it was said that one scarcely met a dairyman in London who was not a Carmarthenshire Welshman. However, as with the bigger picture, the population could not maintain a sufficient supply of manpower to replace losses. The battalion was later filled up with drafts from all over Wales, many of whom were from rural North Wales. As well as Wyn Griffith, the battalion contained an extraordinary group of notable artists and writers: first, the writer, poet and artist David Jones, whose iconic work *In Parenthesis*, is based on his experiences with 15 RWF. Secondly the Welsh shepherd and bard Hedd Wyn, from Trawsfynydd in Merioneth, who was killed at Pilckem Ridge in 1917. He won the Bardic Chair at the Welsh National Eisteddfod in that year, and when called to take his place, it was announced that he was dead. The Chair was left empty, and draped in black.

Thirdly, Wyn Powell Wheldon, father of Sir Huw Wheldon (who served in The Royal Welch Fusiliers during the Second World War). Fourthly, W.A. (Bill) Tucker, author of *The Lousier War*, who later worked for many years on *The Times*, and helped launch *The Times Atlas of The World*. Last, Harold Gladstone (Bluey) Lewis, author of *Crow on a Barbed Wire Fence*.

David Lloyd George hoped that enough Welsh units could be raised to form a Welsh Army Corps, for national Corps are a powerful instrument in nation building, as the experience of Australia and Canada would show. However the population of Wales was not sufficient to raise two full divisions and all the corps units required – especially as the high command of the Army would not detach the regular Welsh infantry battalions from their parent divisions to these new ones, filled with temporary soldiers. Wales's contribution in terms of formations therefore rested on its two divisions – the 38th which served on the Western Front, and the 53rd which served at Gallipoli and in the Middle East. There was an additional problem in that immediately before the war, the big political issue had been Irish Home Rule, which had been shelved for the duration. Creating a Welsh national corps would have opened the door to similar formations in Ireland and Scotland and given the potential for awakening nationalism, no-one in Whitehall had any appetite for such a scheme.

38th (Welsh) Division was broken down into three brigades and its divisional units. 113 Brigade consisted of four RWF battalions – the 13th, 14th, 15th and 16th (Service) Battalions; 114 Brigade similarly had four battalions of the Welch Regiment – 10th, 13th, 14th and 15th; and 115 Brigade was a mixture of all three Welsh infantry regiments – 17th RWF, 10th and 11th South Wales Borderers, 16th Welch. The fighting strength of the division stood at around 18,500 but there was scarcely a man with any military experience aside from a few officers and NCOs brought back from retirement – 'dug-outs' as they were called and as Wyn Griffith mentions. Regular and Special Reservists were all mobilised into regular formations and the Territorial Army formed its own set of divisions – of which 53rd (Welsh) was one. The officers generally owed their position to the patronage of Lloyd George and others.

From January to August 1915 the division was spread around North Wales undergoing training with little equipment or transport. The highlight of the time here was probably the Review of Troops

EDITOR'S INTRODUCTION

held at Llandudno on St David's Day by Lloyd George himself. Thereafter, the division moved to Winchester: 15 RWF War Diary reports this as beginning on 19 August. On the South Downs, the training areas were better but equipment in no better supply. In late November the division was ordered to move to France. All troops had to fire a short course of twenty-four rounds on the rifle ranges before being pronounced fit to deploy; a regular soldier would have fired ten times that amount. More attention was paid to another review, this time by Her Majesty Queen Mary and HRH Princess Mary, at Crawley Down, on 29 November. On 1 December with a new Commanding Officer, Lieutenant-Colonel R.C. Bell of the Central India Horse, the division left Winchester for Southampton in pouring rain. It is here that *Up To Mametz* begins.

* * *

Up To Mametz was not published until 1931. It followed close behind three other great books about the war, all of which received immediate critical acclaim. These were Edmund Blunden's *Undertones of War* in 1928; Robert Graves's *Goodbye to All That* in 1929; and Siegfried Sassoon's *Memoirs of an Infantry Officer* in 1930. The delay in publication is explained by Colin Hughes in his introduction to the 1981 edition; he had written it immediately after the war but then 'Wyn Griffith ... wrapped the manuscript in brown paper and put it back on the shelf for his children to read in later years. Only when his friends Storm Jameson and Herbert Read[2] heard of it and read it did the process of publication begin.' When it was published, it was without doubt well received by both reviewers and the reading public, for it is well written, easy to read, and extraordinarily vivid. However it sold no more than a thousand copies. It is not until more modern times, coinciding with the anniversaries of the Great War and in particular, the unveiling of the 38th Division memorial at Mametz Wood in 1987, that its circulation has swelled through two new editions in 1981 and 1987.

* * *

Until June 1916, the 38th Division took its turn at the drudgery of trenches, learning its trade and being slowly turned from amateurs into something approaching competent ground-holding troops. I need say no more here for Wyn Griffith's narrative tells the story and I have supplemented it by explanatory notes wherever these

xvii

are needed to provide context, identify people or places, or explain technicalities. They were still, however, far from being capable of launching a major attack against well fortified German positions – the task given to them at Mametz Wood.

Allied war strategy for 1916 was formulated during the Chantilly conference in December 1915. It was decided that for the next year, simultaneous offensives would be mounted by the Russians, the Italians in the Alps and the British and French on the Western Front – thereby assailing the Central Powers from all sides. Shortly afterwards General Sir Douglas Haig had replaced General Sir John French as Commander-in-Chief of the British Expeditionary Force (BEF). Haig favoured a British offensive in Flanders, which was close to BEF supply routes through the Channel ports; and which also had the strategic advantage of driving the Germans from the North Sea coast of Belgium, from which their submarines were decimating British shipping. However, although there was no formal order of seniority, the British were the junior partner on the Western Front and had to go along with French direction. In January 1916, the French Commander-in-Chief, General Joseph Joffre, agreed to the BEF placing its main effort in Flanders, but after further discussions in February, the decision was reached to mount a combined offensive where the French and British armies joined, astride the Somme River in Picardy in August. During February 1916, while plans for the joint offensive on the Somme were still in the hands of the General Staff, the Germans launched their offensive against the French at Verdun. As the French threw all they had into defending Verdun, their ability to meet their commitments on the Somme was significantly reduced; the bulk of the burden was therefore shifted to the British with twenty divisions engaged against the French thirteen. Moreover, as the Battle of Verdun dragged on, the aim of the Somme offensive changed from delivering a decisive blow against Germany, to relieving pressure on the French army. The date of the offensive was brought forward from August to July. Tactically, there was disagreement among the British high command, between Haig and General Sir Henry Rawlinson, General Officer Commanding the Fourth Army, who favoured a 'bite and hold' approach – based on the Allies' inability to exploit breakthrough – rather than Haig's concept of a decisive blow. Much emphasis was based on the ability of artillery to destroy German field fortifications and allow the infantry to mop up: in reality, the

Editor's Introduction

bulk of the British artillery was still of light and medium calibres rather than heavy; nor had the developments in the fusing of shells which appeared later in 1917 and which allowed artillery to cut heavy wire entanglements yet come to pass.

The first BEF, based on regular forces heavily augmented with reservists, had been effectively wiped out by the battles of 1914 and 1915; the Territorial Force, which had entered the war in 1915, had also been badly depleted. The bulk of the BEF was now made up of the volunteers who had joined Lord Kitchener's New Army, which had begun forming in August 1914. Kitchener had formed the New Armies with the objective of having them ready for offensive warfare in 1917 yet because of the needs of Allied strategy, they were obliged to undertake a difficult offensive, having gained insufficient experience, and without a compensating weight of fire support.

With hindsight it is not surprising therefore that except in the south of the area of the offensive around Montauban, the objectives were not gained on 1 July 1916. Here, however, the 7th and 21st Divisions broke into the German lines around Fricourt and captured Mametz village. But as so often in the Great War until 1918, they broke *in*, but they did not break *through*. That evening, Haig decided not to try again where he had failed but to reinforce success by exploiting the advance around Fricourt and capture the German second line of defence at its closest point between Longeval and Bazentins. Rawlinson had little option but to attack this position, which was on a ridge commanding a view over the approaches, from the front. He decided to do so between two large woods, Mametz on the left and Trones on the right. The assault would be phased in order to provide the maximum weight of artillery fire in support of the assaulting troops. Mametz would be taken first, in order to secure the flank against the inevitable German counter-attack.

Mametz Wood was allocated to Sir Henry Horne's XIV Corps which would attack the wood from two directions. 17th Division was to attack from the west out of Quadrangle trench while 38th Division attacked across open ground from the east, out of Caterpillar and Marlborough Woods. This latter assault would be on a one-brigade front with 115 Brigade leading and it would take the troops on a route parallel to the German second line. Without suppressing artillery fire and especially smoke, the troops would be exposed to a flanking or enfilade fire from the German strong-points in Sabot and Flat Iron Copses. As Wyn Griffith records, the brigade commander,

Horatio Evans, thought the plan mad. The assault failed to close within 300 yards of the Wood not least because the supporting artillery fire did not arrive. A second attempt was ordered but Evans managed to get this called off. It resulted in him being invalided home after being wounded later in the attack, as he knew it would, and probably too sealed the fate of the divisional commander, Major-General Ivor Philipps.

With better fire planning and coordination, a second attempt a few days later succeeded in capturing most of the Wood but even so it was, as Wyn Griffith notes, 'a success that astonished all who knew the ground'. Given the tangle of undergrowth and the debris of centuries, made ten times worse by the constant fall of shells and lines of German tracer, the division could not generate enough momentum to clear the Wood completely. Even so, the fierceness of the fighting was too much for even the German Army. On the night of 11/12 July they evacuated their positions, leaving the largest piece of woodland on the Somme in Welsh hands. A few days later, Fourth Army captured the Bazentin–Longueval ridge although the Germans counter-attacked as they always did and High Wood remained untaken for two months. 38th Division was withdrawn, but left behind 4,000 officers and men killed and wounded. Among the dead was Wyn Griffith's nineteen-year-old brother Watcyn.[3]

* * *

This is where *Up To Mametz* ends. While sorting through the Royal Welch Fusiliers archives in preparation for a move to a new location, several incomplete narrative manuscripts came to light. Some or all of these were provided to Colin Hughes by the family when he complied and introduced the 1987 edition. These manuscripts were, like *Up To Mametz*, written for family consumption and pick up where *Up To Mametz* left off until the end of the war. Some of the material found its way into other published works, such as Wyn Griffith's essay 'The Pattern of One Man's Remembering' in *Promise of Greatness*, which was written especially for that work. I decided to edit and annotate the manuscript, which I tentatively called *After Mametz,* but it was very short, too short to make into a book in its own right, even when supplemented by another manuscript in which Wyn Griffith describes his return to civilian life. I then went to his surviving letters and diaries in the National Library of Wales and the Royal Welch Fusiliers Archives, the daily

Editor's Introduction

summaries and reports from formation staffs that he helped to write, and some material from his close contemporaries, and using these I have tried to ghostwrite what he called '... the book I had inside me [but did not write], a book that might have been of some value: the war and the regular soldier and the staff as seen through the eyes of a temporary soldier ...' This in due course became *Beyond Mametz*, which forms part two of this edition. I have made a major editorial decision with the backing of the Wyn Griffith family: when I studied Wyn Griffith's papers it seemed to me that there were two occasions in which he uses descriptions of people and events in *Up To Mametz*, which are actually drawn from later events. One of these is a description of his CO in 15 RWF, Bell, which I believe is actually a description of a later CO of the same battalion, C.C. Norman. The other is a description of Brigadier-General Price-Davies plaguing troops in trenches. In *Up To Mametz* this is used before the Somme offensive, to give a flavour of what the man was like and probably because Wyn Griffith felt that if he did not use it here it would remain unpublished. I believe however that it refers to a period in the Ypres Salient in 1917. I have accordingly restored these two short descriptions to their original owners, annotating both in the text. If any reader is offended then I ask their pardon.

* * *

The value of *Beyond Mametz* lies in its providing a record of the life of an officer on the staff – a species which came in for a good deal of adverse criticism both during and after the war from front line officers: '... a bloody nuisance, inefficient where it isn't actually crooked' as John Masters reported the common view; or more specifically

> The function of the staff is so to foul up operations, by giving contradictory orders and misreading their maps, that wars will be prolonged to a point where every staff officer has become a general.[4]

Beyond Mametz provides glimpses of a number of distinguished senior officers, and sketches of many people who achieved distinction in later years; but above all it gives the sense of how command was exercised at division and corps level at a time when almost all the ingredients of modern war were present except one: battlefield radio. Commanders of the time, and their staffs, were often criticised for what J.F.C. Fuller described as 'château generalship' – that is, for stationing themselves well behind the line and not sharing in the sufferings of the troops. In the 1930s and 1940s, the image of Generals was somewhat tarnished by this sort of mythology: there was a widespread feeling in the Army that at the higher levels of command during the war, a General, having made a plan and issued the orders, then frequently took no part in superintending the implementation or adapting it to changing circumstances: he merely waited in isolation for news.[5] This coloured the views of many of the next generation of senior commanders, and accounts for much of their behaviour during the Second World War. Slim, Montgomery, O'Connor, Horrocks and others were always at pains to be seen in the front line. This sort of thing prompted commentators analysing the lessons of the Great War to remark on the necessity of leadership by example at all levels: this, for instance, from a veteran of Gallipoli: 'War with impersonal leadership is a brutal, soul-destroying business ... Our senior officers must get back to sharing danger and sacrifice with the men, however elevated their rank ...'[6]

This is unfair on two counts. First, as a British General, you were far more likely to be killed in action during the Great War than during the Second World War, or at any time subsequently. Sixty-one British Generals were killed in action between 1914 and 1918,[7] as against only five between 1939 and 1945.[8] This despite the obvious reaction to the charge of château generalship, that made it such a point of honour for Second World War Generals to be seen leading from the front. The second count bears directly on this. In order to exercise command, a General had to be able to do three essential things: to find out what was going on; to communicate his intentions to his subordinates; and to communicate with the staff so that it could solve problems and implement decisions. In the absence of battlefield radio, the means of doing these three things were personal observation, telephone, telegraph, runner and despatch rider. The first always had value, but in a dispersed or extended battlefield it might be difficult to do, and might leave the General disconnected from his command for long periods. The others all indicate that the most complete information on which to base decisions would have been at the main headquarters. The simple truth is, therefore, that in those days, the closer a General approached

Editor's Introduction

to the front line, *the less he could command*. This argues for personal reconnaissance and visiting outside the periods of heavy fighting, and for remaining at the centre of communications when battle is joined. The decision about where to place himself, when, in order to command a battle is still one that every battlefield General must face. I know this from personal experience of the Balkans, Sierra Leone, Iraq and Afghanistan.

And what of the staff? It is this body that, on the General's behalf, exercises control of a formation and in doing so, plays a complementary role to the commander. Having evaluated workable courses of action, the General is in a position to decide, through a combination of objective calculation and subjective, intuitive, judgement, which one is most likely to be successful or, rather, which one has the greatest chance of success at least cost. Following this, the staff goes about developing the plan – the detailed co-ordination and control of activities to achieve the synchronisation upon which the course of action is based. Thus process has been engaged to confirm or discount what intuition tells the commander. And if time is short, the process can be abbreviated to a broad order staff check to expose any significant resource, environmental, or time constraints. The staff will also, by churning through the tedious but necessary calculations required to control an army, reduce the many uncertainties facing a commander's decision-making process. This is bound up with the General's function as manager of men and materiel, much of which, because of its complexity, has to be delegated to the staff. A management system there must be, and one that encompasses all the needs of an army: personnel management and documentation, training, intelligence gathering and processing, food supply, sanitation and drinking water, medical care, the maintenance of vehicles, weapons, animals, military justice and discipline to name but a few.

Thus the role of staff process is that of proving or disproving what the commander thinks intuitively; or of filling in detail in complex problems. Ideally it should be done ahead of battle as the basis of a plan, and to establish the intentions of an enemy, required resources, time-lines, decision points and their conditions, control measures, and so on. In doing this, process performs the valuable function of minimising risk – and thus gives a commander more freedom later when intuition will have to take over. John Masters, who served as both formation commander and staff officer in Burma during the

Second World War, reflected on this same subject of the interaction of commander and staff, of intuition and process. Although he did not use the same language, he is clearly expressing a similar view, developed in war:

> Staff work ... can be learned by civilians, for only a quick and accurate mind and a retentive memory are needed. A commander can do with less of these attributes, but he must add a quality easy to recognise but hard to define – a strength of character, a determination with no obstinacy in it ... The higher he stands the more he needs, too, another quality which cannot be taught by any quick means but is either there, by a stroke of genetic chance, or, more usually, is deposited cell by cell in the subconscious during the long years of study and practice. It is this quality that tells a commander, instantly and without cerebration, whether a plan is inherently sound or unsound. It is this that enables him to receive the advice of specialists and experts, and reach the proper decision ...[9]

But the staff has no command responsibility, although it has duties. It has no responsibilities because staff officers (unless specified by the General) have no powers of decision or command: they implement previously agreed control measures, such as timings, routes, boundaries, fire control measures and so on, in order to carry out the General's plan. The plan belongs to the General – not the staff. He will have led its development; he must lead its implementation. Therefore the General alone holds responsibility, and the staff must be absolutely clear on those decisions that must be referred to him, and him alone; on which decisions can be taken by subordinates; which must be referred to a superior authority; and which are really decisions relating to control measures and can be taken by the appropriate staff officer. If Generals do not obey this philosophy, then the personal factor in command is lost, and the staff system takes over. This is not to say that staff action should be regarded as somehow unsavoury, as Wyn Griffith's account makes very clear.

* * *

After his discharge from the Army, Wyn Griffith returned to the Inland Revenue in Liverpool. Later he moved to the office in Chester and eventually, around 1932, to London; he was one of the men

Editor's Introduction

who, under the leadership of Sir Paul Chambers,[10] launched the Pay-As-You-Earn (PAYE) system of income tax. He retired as an Assistant Secretary in 1952. Until his death in 1977 he filled many appointments in literary bodies: he was Vice Chairman of the Arts Council, Chairman of the Council of the Honourable Society of Cymmrodorion, and a frequent broadcaster – most notably at the Welsh end of the BBC Quiz *Around Britain* – and as the author of the script for BBC Wales's VE Day thanksgiving programme in 1945. He was made an Honorary D.Litt by the University of Wales and, in addition to the OBE, the Croix de Guerre and a Mention-in-Despatches from the war, he was made CBE in 1961.

Wyn Griffith was an outsider in the military system, with no axe to grind; indeed he could be brutally frank when he chose and there is no doubt that for every capable senior officer he encountered – like Plumer, Ellington, Godley or Grogan – there is a Hunter-Weston, a Philipps or a Price-Davies who 'waste men something shocking'. But in general his view of the system – the view of one who had been a regimental officer on the Western Front – is sympathetic. It should not be dismissed because it *is* sympathetic, even though that may go against much of the mythology of the Great War, of the 'lions led by donkeys' school of thought. This clings on, despite the more objective analysis of command on the Western Front begun by John Terraine's brave collection of essays in 1964,[11] and carried on by others like John Bourne, Gary Sheffield, Richard Holmes and Hew Strachan. Moreover it should not be discounted because it is personal, and because it is contemporary. By using his narrative, and fleshing it out with his letters and diaries as he himself considered doing, but did not complete, it may, in Wyn Griffith's own words, '[do] ... full justice to a much-maligned profession, and especially to commands or staff that were the target for all the many published war books.'

Jonathon Riley
Llanllwni, Carmarthenshire
2010

Notes

1. John Griffith (1863–1933), musician, teacher and scientist, was born in Rhiw, Lleyn, in 1863. He was educated at Botwnnog Grammar School and Normal College, Bangor. He was appointed teacher at Glanwydden in 1884 and in 1894 moved to Machynlleth. He returned to study at Bangor University and in

1900 took up a science teaching post in Blaenau Ffestiniog. He was appointed headmaster of Dolgellau Grammar School in 1905 and remained in the post until 1925. He edited the English section of *Y Cerddor* between 1930 and 1933 and was also chairman of the Harlech Festival for a period. He died at Bangor, November 1933.
2. Margaret Storm Jameson (1891–1986) wrote forty-five novels including three volumes of autobiography. She was a champion of pacifism and anti-fascism. Sir Herbert Read DSO MC (1893–1968) was an anarchist poet and critic of art and literature. He served on the Western Front in the Green Howards; his second volume of poetry, *Naked Warriors*, published in 1919, drew on his experiences in the trenches.
3. The story of Watcyn's death is told in the chapter 'Mametz Wood'. Wyn Griffith lived with that haunting memory for the rest of his life.
4. John Masters *The Road Past Mandalay*, p. 83.
5. J.F.C. Fuller *Generalship: Its Diseases and Their Cure*, p. 17.
6. Lt Col C.O. Head 'A Glance at Gallipoli' cited in J.F.C. Fuller *Generalship – Its Diseases and Their Cure*, p. 11.
7. Another nine died of wounds. This includes Brigadier-Generals, and among the Major-Generals were ten divisional commanders: Lomax, Hamilton, Capper, Wing, Thesiger, Broadwood, Feetham, Cape, Lipsett and Ingoville-Williams.
8. Barstow, Hopkinson, Mallaby, Lumsden and Tilly; four others died in accidents and six more in aircraft crashes.
9. John Masters *The Road Past Mandalay*, p. 199.
10. Sir Stanley Paul Chambers KBE CB CIE (1904–1981) was a noted economist and for eight years was chairman of ICI.
11. John Terraine *The Western Front* (London, 1964).

Acknowledgements

This book would not have been possible without the support and encouragement of the Wyn Griffith family, especially Hugh and Martin Wyn Griffith, and Mrs Margaret Dunn. I acknowledge with gratitude the help of the staff at the National Library of Wales, Aberystwyth; Brian Owen and Anne Pedley at the Royal Welch Fusiliers Museum and Archive in Caernarfon; Richard Sinnett, Nick Lock, and Peter Crocker, all of The Royal Welch Fusiliers. I acknowledge the help of the Department of Photographs at the Imperial War Museum and their ownership and copyright of the images reproduced with their permission in this book. I also wish to acknowledge various publications in which Wyn Griffith repeated material used here in various forms: 'The Pattern of One Man's Remembering' in *Promise of Greatness*, edited by George A. Panchiras (London, 1968); *Hiraeth* (Privately Printed, 1929) – the poems of which are to be found in his Army Book 136 in his personal papers and which he first put together in a bound typescript called *The Fading Years*, which also contains what may be an early draft of *Up To Mametz*; extracts from his writings in Richards's *Wales on the Western Front* (Cardiff University Press, 1994). Finally quotations or paraphrases, always acknowledged in the text, from Wyn Griffith's contemporaries: Wyn Wheldon, 'The Canal Bank at Ypres' in *The Welsh Outlook*, Volume VI, March 1919; and Emlyn Davies, *Taffy Went to War* (Knutsford, 1976).

In preparing this new edition of *Up to Mametz ... and Beyond*, with gratitude those who supplied additional material: Mr Lars Ahlkvist for biographical details of soldiers mentioned by Llewelyn Wyn Griffith; James Payne for the photograph of the German trench; Mr John Griffiths for the photograph of 15 RWF in camp and for additional details of CSM John Bradshaw; Martin Wyn Griffith for additional photographs and detail of his grandparents; Allan Poole for information on Emlyn Davies; and Patricia J. Evans for her research on Peter Jones Roberts and his sons.

Part One

Up To Mametz

Chapter 1

Prentice Days

Cap Badge of the Royal Welch Fusiliers

The evening had declined into night without any perceptible change in quality. A heavy fall of rain had covered the streets with a thin grey film, reflecting the lights in the shop windows and silencing the tread of all who walked the pavements of Winchester in their last hours of freedom. There was so little that remained to be done, so much to say. Minutes of silence dragged their way through the dark places of the heart: speech sought a neutral path in a vague reassurance, avoiding the unreality of optimism and the sharp outline of despair. Some talk of leave and of the joy of meeting again, promises of letters, all in a coward's effort to avoid the challenge of the morrow and to escape from the unescapable. To the very end of the last hour, and through the ritual of parting, strength and safety lay in this determination never to give shape in words to the spectre of loneliness.

Throughout the night the rain fell heavily, turning the clay into a heavy mud. We struggled down the slopes of the downs, loaded with burdens that weighed on mind and matter, and in the early hours of the morning, marched for the last time through the streets of Winchester and along the road to Southampton.

1 December 1915

PRENTICE DAYS

'Salisbury Plain 1915' by David Jones, 15 RWF. [Royal Welch Fusiliers Museum]

The day passed without change of mood, in an even drive of wind and rain, into a late afternoon that found us on a wet quayside, staring at a grey ship on a grey sea. Rain in England, rain in the Channel and rain in France; mud on the Hampshire Downs and mud in the unfinished horse-standings in Havre where we sheltered from the rain during the hours of waiting for a train. Rain beating against the trucks as we doddered through an unknown land to an unknown destination, and, late at night, as we stood in the mud of a station yard near St. Omer,[1] the rain was waiting for us, to drive us along twelve miles of muddy lanes to a sodden hamlet near Aire.[2]

Four days out of England, days and nights of fatigue and stiff-limbed weariness, nights of little sleep and days of little rest: a hundred hours of rain. Little wonder that, for me, England had resolved itself **5 December 1915** into a vision of a white face looking out of a window in Winchester on a wet December morning, while France lay unrevealed behind this curtain of rain.

Next morning the world changed suddenly. We found ourselves in a flat country of pollarded willows and long poplars, red brick cottages with dark thatches, green meadows and roadside ditches, with a mild winter sun as the chief author of the change. The Army produced its unfailing remedy for all self-indulgence, its antidote against the fever of memory, in the shape of an immediate task.

At the back of our farmhouse was a stone floored outhouse with a fireplace. A careful search in the cottages of the hamlet, and in the outlying farms, disclosed eight wooden washtubs, and after some negotiation, these were borrowed and carried into the outhouse. Three men of the company were told that so long as there was a continuous supply of hot water, they would be excused all parades. In an hour's time the enterprise was firmly established, and all day there was a steady changing of dirty men into clean men in clean clothes.

Next morning there came an urgent order from the Brigade[3] that all ranks must have a bath and a change of underclothing. Worried Company Commanders[4] were walking about the scattered hamlet in search of tubs, the Colonel was reputed to be cursing freely at the delay, but all in vain. 'C' Company had made a corner in wash-tubs. In the afternoon the Brigadier[5] visited us, and his surprise at discovering that his orders had been forestalled by a Company officer was undisguised. Words of blame flow so easily down the slopes of rank, calling for no rehearsal, but giving shape to praise without implying excessive merit is a harder task. The stumble of phrases about the virtue of taking a personal interest in the comfort of 'the men' sounded somewhat unreal to a temporary officer who had but recently ceased to be a 'man'. I record the incident in a spirit of vanity mingled with amusement, for sixteen months of soldiering had been as barren of praise as they were rich in condemnation, and the 'bubble reputation' had come to me from soapsuds.

The days passed in uneventful succession, and the smaller matters of life grew into vivid importance as we adjusted ourselves to the routine of a new existence. Suddenly it became the fashion to crop one's hair. All the officers sat down in turn under the regimental barber's clippers. We had little claim to good looks before this drastic shearing, but all the villainy latent in our faces stood out naked after a prison crop. In our simple and childish eagerness we felt that by so doing we had made ourselves better fitted for the life before us, with its unknown hardships; we saw in this act some shadow of an initiation into the great mystery of the trench world, and we were somehow proud of it. How innocent it seems at this interval of time! It was to be followed soon after by a vigorous reaction, by a desperate striving to maintain every detail of personal pride in one's appearance. Had all the Army maintained this Spartan simplicity, the makers of brilliantine in France would not have enriched themselves so greatly at our expense.

One morning the battalion transport brought to our farmhouse a strange load from a source known vaguely as 'Ordnance'. Bundles of sheepskin jackets, white, grey and black, were thrown down at the side of the road. We wore them under our equipment, with the fur outside. They were designed to keep us warm in the trenches, but they grew so heavy when caked with mud that they gradually sank back along the road from the front, from the infantry to the mounted men, from them to the labour battalions, until they faded away into the pit that engulfs the fashions of years gone by. They gave us the excitement of choosing the colour that pleased the most, and a slightly self conscious strutting about the hamlet: we were matriculating.

Shortly afterwards we were hurled violently along our course. A solemn conference at battalion headquarters sent us back to our billets with a feeling that our quiet farmhouses were no more than a stone's throw from the front line. Gone was that sense of comfort and

17 December 1915

security, and darkness fell quickly upon that December day. Early next morning buses would arrive to take us to the front, in itself a simple event, but bringing in its train a multitude of small domestic cares and worries about billets, equipment, rations, orders and counter orders that all but dwarfed into unreality the great transformation to be thrust upon us by the morrow. There was much to do before going to bed that night.

At eight o'clock on the morning of the 18th December, 1915, the company stood on parade in full marching order, pouches filled with ammunition, sheepskin jackets under the equipment, greatcoats rolled, and a cotton satchel containing a flannel gas-helmet slung over each man's shoulder. Half an hour later a fleet of London buses, painted grey, shook themselves clumsily along the muddy road. We mounted them with difficulty, fattened by our gear into unwieldy bundles, projecting rifles, entrenching-tool handles and mess-tins at unexpected corners of our bodies.

The morning passed quickly. We saw for the first time ammunition dumps, field hospitals, ordnance workshops and supply parks, every village bringing to our eager and excited minds some new embodiment of war. Outside Estaires we halted, on the La Bassée road. Here was a name we knew, part of the currency of war, and the very word, painted on a wooden signboard stuck on a house, seemed to throw us into contemporary history. In the moments that followed the impact of this new discovery, war suddenly came nearer to us, and thought would have travelled far but for the persistent intrusion of the task of the hour and place, the army's ancient cure for such indulgence. We dismounted and scattered ourselves along the roadside to eat our dinners of tinned stew – the unforgettable Maconochie.[6]

The day was fine, and the sky clear of clouds. An aeroplane buzzed high up above us, with little white flecks appearing from nowhere and disappearing again. This was our first seeing of war and of the intent of one man to kill another. It was difficult to translate this decorating of a blue background with white puff-balls into terms of killing. Had we ever truly believed that our military training was a perfecting of our power to kill, that we were of no value to the world unless we were skilled to hurt? I do not think so. However soldierly our muscles might be, however willingly the body accepted war, the mind was still a neutral. Through all the routine of training we were treading a path planned by others, looking to the right and to the left, sometimes looking backwards with longing, but never staring honestly into the face of the future. This is the damnable device of soldiering: confronted with an unending series of new tasks, trivial in themselves and harmless, full of the interest associated with any fresh test of skill and endurance, tempting even in their novel difficulties, the young soldier is so concerned to triumph over each passing obstacle that he does not see the goal at the end of the race. No one persuades him that drill is an exercise; that marksmanship is but a weapon; to him they are not means, but an end. If he perceived from the start that skill in the fulfilling of these daily tasks was destined only to help him to kill his fellow man, there would be fewer soldiers. The antiquity of arms is nowhere shown more clearly than in this evidence of its long practice in the art of war and its close understanding of youth.

Here, on the La Bassée road, the battalion broke up into companies, and the companies into platoons. We were to be 'attached' to a brigade of Guards,[7] to be taught by them the art and craft of trench life, and under the shelter of their greater responsibility we were to hold the line. The four platoons of my company were apprenticed to the four companies of a battalion of Coldstream Guards, so I marched off with a subaltern at the head of his platoon, guided by a Guardsman sent to meet us. Our masters were in reserve, scattered about in some ruined farmhouses a mile to the east of the La Bassée road. Falling dusk, flashes in the sky and the noise of guns, the stammer of machine guns, shell holes in the road, and a strange emptiness over the country, as if man had deserted it, all fused together into a gloom in the mind.

Some of the men turned off to a barn, and a little later we stopped at a group of battered cottages where my subaltern and I walked into a kitchen. This was the headquarters of the Guards company. The three officers greeted us in a manner benevolently neutral, showing neither cordiality nor resentment at the sudden burden of two thrown upon the company mess. Dinner followed, and a glass of port. What had we done to our hair? Why did we wear men's equipment and sheepskin coats? They smiled quietly, but not unkindly, at our answers, while we tried to learn as much about our task as question and answer could teach us. We were facing war, but they were turning away from it, tired in mind and body, as it seemed.

We slept upon some straw in an outhouse. I hesitated before asking whether I might take off my boots, but I was gravely assured that I might do so, as we were two miles behind the line. I was obsessed by the noise of our guns; they seemed to be firing over the cottage, shaking the floor and the walls. Through the broken corner of the roof I could see a star passing in and out through a dark cloud, and a distant rumble of transport brought a feeling that day and night were but arbitrary divisions of unending time; my period of rest was to another soldier the high noon of his activity. Thought swung uneasily from the known, with its clearly defined and pressing burden of practical worries, to the highly dramatized vision of the change that the morrow must bring into our lives. Less than twenty-four hours stood between us and the trenches; there were two kinds of men in the world – those who had been in the trenches, and the rest. We were to graduate from the one class to the other, to be reborn into the old age and experience of the front line, by the traversing of two miles over the fields in Flanders. Did one experience a sudden change of heart – would the fear of death overwhelm all else – could that fear be disguised, or must we suffer the humiliation of showing to others that for us, time was standing still? These thoughts were but clammy companions on a dark night in a strange place: reason could not drive them away, but fatigue triumphed over all in the end and brought sleep.

The day passed in inactivity: we were not to walk about more than was necessary lest we provoke a shelling of this quiet byway. In the evening we paraded on the road, carrying on our backs sufficient tackle to provide for all emergencies in a march from Flanders to the Rhine. The Guards were not so cumbered, and their greatest anxiety was to run no risk of a lack of firewood. We dared not imitate them, for our orders were stringent, and their officers would encourage no departure from the letter of our law, however unwise they deemed it in the light of their greater experience. There was little talking: we were anxious, and they were bored. The roll was called, and we set off east in separated sections – artillery formation, as it was called. Our destination was Fort Erith, a name that suggested a bastion fortified against all attack, to be held at every cost, wonderfully strong and secure, a key position, growing with every thought into an overwhelming importance as the pivot of England's struggle against Germany. So ran the mind as we marched along a narrow road with a low hedge on one side and a long-grassed moor on the other. The moon came out, and in its light we saw that the moor was only a derelict meadow. Lights were flashing in the eastern sky, strangely high up in this flat country; that was Aubers Ridge, said my companion. We broke into single file. A singing note drooped through the air – what was that? A stray bullet. Another followed, and another, and the sound grew ominous to me. Were we not conspicuously outlined against a white road in this moonlight – could not the enemy see us? No, not at this distance: it was very rarely that anyone was hit on this road. A sudden buzz of talking ahead, and the closer shuffling of our file showed that something had caught the attention of those who marched before us, bringing that slight slackening of pace that travels down the line like a concussion in a train of shunting trucks. Three men and a stretcher lying on the roadside in the shadow of the hedge – a wounded Guardsman greeting us happily and inviting us all to share in his delight at his good fortune. The whine of the next spent bullet became malevolent and full of danger.

We stepped down into a communication trench, and although we were so much nearer the enemy, there was a sign of safety in these muddy walls. The duckboards underfoot were unevenly set and covered with a slimy layer of mud, the trench turned right and left in a maze of windings, here deep and there shallow. What was this peculiar smell, so persistent in its penetration that the mouth tasted of it? Why was I so thirsty? Suddenly we found ourselves pushing past other soldiers leaning against the wall of the trench; we were in Fort Erith. The moon came out again, and I saw a wet straggling trench with bulging sides, uneven fire-steps and ramshackle dug-outs. This was the bastion, the wonderful fort of my imagining! A child had begun to build this mud castle and had tired of his play – were men to fight for this thing? Did it rank as a strong point? Was this a part of England's defence?

We stooped through a narrow doorway leading into a dug-out, and before I had removed sufficient of my equipment to allow me to sit down, the formalities of handing over the command of the fort were finished. Two tired men were bidding each other good-night – how tired they seemed, tired in mind and jaded. A sackcloth curtain covered a small window, another made a *portière* across the door, and a new candle stood in its grease on the middle of the table. I studied a plan of the redoubt, while its commander gave orders to a sergeant. We were in the trenches, a little behind the front line, but where was the great change, the rebirth that was to follow this initiation? Why was I not afraid? I was thirsty, but in no other way different from the man who had imagined an upheaval in his whole way of thinking, a warping of his direction now and for ever. The great transformation that I had so dreaded in advance had dissipated itself into a sequence of minute experiences, each in its turn claiming a concentration that forbade any remembering of its predecessor. A heavy pack, a pitted road, uneven duckboards in a trench, the steering of an awkward body past the projecting walls and its balancing on a slimy foothold – this was the sequence of problems, large in their moment, that had overshadowed the greater ordeal, dwarfing it into the insignificance of a dream.

I followed my companion round the circle of our trenchwork, listening to his orders and absorbing as much as I could of his general attitude as he gave his quick answers to questions that appeared to me to be of great moment. Four men were to go outside the parapet to fill sandbags for the rebuilding of one bay; to leave the shelter of this ditch seemed a desperate venture, to stand on top of the parapet an unjustifiable challenge, but they thought nothing of it. I jumped down from the fire-step, glad of a buttress between me and the bullets that could not fail to sweep that parapet the next second. Every second that passed in silence increased the possibility of danger in its successor, as I thought. I had stood for some minutes, head and shoulders exposed, in apparent unconcern, but seized with terror in anticipation of some calamity, and I did not attempt to ignore my secret relief at the end of this long waiting.

'This ain't so bad, this ain't,' I heard one of my men say. 'I wonder what it's like in the front line?' 'Wet,' answered a tall Guardsman. 'Rotten dug-outs.' He measured life on a scale of comfort and not according to the possibility of its extinction. Did one grow to rate comfort above safety? To me it seemed unbelievable that the edge of a desire for survival, so infinitely important to each individual man, could ever be dulled.

Dinner was ready; fried beef, boiled potatoes, and tinned fruit, followed by a cup of coffee and a glass of port. It was nearly ten o'clock, and I was hungry. Food brought with it a certain reinforcement, as if the mind had shared in the strengthening of the body; now I could believe that there was in reality a line of men between us and the enemy, that the night would not bring a sudden wild battle against a powerful foe. The three hundred yards that separated us from the front line became a measure of distance, not of nearness. I drew the Guards Officer into a discussion of the varying degrees of safety that characterized different parts of the line, in the hope of learning something of our own chance of safety; this was in reality but a disguising of my personal anxiety. I heard that the enemy rarely shelled this post unless our fires gave out too much smoke during the day.

The night was divided into three sections. From eleven until two we would keep joint watch, so that I might learn my duties; from two till four I was to take watch alone, and from four until stand-to the Guards officer would be on duty. We walked about as foremen of a building scheme, giving counsel here and criticism there. The night was quiet, and I learned the language of the various sounds of war – rifle-fire, machine-gun bursts, and light shell-fire, while from several points on the circumference of our post came the steady whack of a spade on the piled sandbags, rising from a dullish thud to a metallic and clear ring as the mud hardened beneath the blows. At two o'clock in the morning I was left alone to walk the decks of this vessel of war, proud of my responsibilities, but fearing to test either their extent or my powers of response. I walked from bay to bay, watching the men at work, overhearing strange and unfinished scraps of conversation from the dug-outs as I passed, content to be a presence, risking no exposure of my ignorance by any overt act of supervision. Time crawled, and the same thoughts recurred again and again – how long would this new life last ... Wyn[8] would now be fast asleep in Winchester ... when would they gazette my captaincy and let me draw the extra five shillings a day, a windfall to a married subaltern ... why did no one reset this sinking duckboard, by the very door of the dug-out?

At four o'clock I was to wake up my companion and to take my turn of rest, but when the time came I found a little pleasure in waiting, continuing my watch till half past four, and finding in this demonstration of a lack of haste a showing of my capacity to bear my burden. I turned into our dug-out and lit the candle, roused the sleeping Guards officer, and said that it was half past four; nothing had happened during the night. He got up slowly and stiffly, lit a cigarette and went out shivering. I stretched myself on the hard floor, making a pillow of my haversack, but I spent so much time trying to make myself comfortable, trying to keep warm, and trying not to listen to the noises of the night, that when somebody shouted 'Stand-to' I had nothing beyond a chill and aching stiffness in my legs to convince me that I must have slept. The dull grey dawn brought with it a greater intensity of cold and a hollow hunger. The garrison was stamping its feet in a lethargic attempt to remove the ache from its toes, some were swinging their arms or blowing upon their fingers, and all looked gaunt and grim. But of all the sights of that early December morning, the strangest was Fort Erith. A shabby, unfinished aggregate of mud, old sandbags, sagging posts and rusty wire, decayed and evil-looking, uneven parapets and bulging ramparts, pits of muddy water, stagnant and rank. A splintered stump of a tree trunk peered over the wall, ragged and black, a coil of barbed wire lay rusting on a fire-step, and an old ground sheet, torn and mud-stained, flapped stiffly against a staggered post. Grey desolation everywhere, till it was hard to believe that the garrison was alive. This mean ditch a fort? It was incredible that our lodging, with its appearance of a hastily improvised and quickly abandoned earth-work, should masquerade as a strong point in a system of defences. As the light became stronger, its imperfections grew out of a mass of detail into a total inadequacy of protection or of shelter; security and comfort were impossible of attainment. Surely the front line trenches were stronger and better planned, or else we had little safety!

We stood down and waited for breakfast. Fires crackled, and a smell of frying bacon made the post seem better fitted for habitation. A fried egg and three rashers, on a cold enamelled plate, half a loaf of bread and **21 December 1915** a tin of jam, a brown metal teapot, a tin of milk ... these became more important than any speculation about the ways of war. They brought with them bodily warmth and a sudden loss of the fatigue of the night, the power to talk naturally and without effort, and the good taste of a pipe of tobacco. Two days and nights followed, uneventful and uncomfortable, with a drizzle of rain to accentuate the feeling that war was mostly a matter of being wet, of struggling for a temporary mastery over mud. Late on the third night we were relieved by another garrison and we marched back stiffly to the ruined houses from which we had set out, years older in body and mind. Down the communication trench, along the Rue Tilleloy, and into the bare kitchen of an abandoned cottage, we walked in a crescendo of appreciation, caring less and less about the fortunes of the sector with every step that increased the distance between us and that servitude of mud. Three days ago this cottage was a poor place, low down in the scale of human habitation, but to-night it promised a glorious ease – so had we changed in this short time. To stand upright before a fire after stooping night and day in a cold dug-out, to walk about on a dry stone floor, to wear dry clothes with no down-dragging weight on the shoulders, to read a paper by candlelight with outstretched legs, to smoke a last pipe by the dying embers; all these, and many other ordinary things, became a high privilege and matter for thanksgiving. The long day ended in a lying down in a warm sleeping bag, on soft straw, and a sudden dropping into a heavy sleep. Our guns were firing, shaking the cottage as they did three nights ago, but their noise was now a thing of no significance – they were our own guns.

I woke up on the morning of Christmas Eve chilled to the bone and very stiff. As I turned over from one side to the other and tucked the upper blanket of my sleeping bag into my shoulder, I noticed that it was damp. A few seconds later I found that the whole of my sleeping bag was wet, the straw sodden, and that there were two inches of water on the floor. I reached for my boots and stepped out of my bag to find that the clothes in which I had slept were wet: a good beginning to this last day of rest. A few nights ago I had gazed at the stars through that hole in the roof, but now I wished that I had repaired it. Little wonder that I was cold and stiff. Had this happened two years earlier I would have waited for pneumonia, but all I did was to change my underclothing and allow the rest to dry upon me.

24 December 1915

Another day of inactivity faded into a dull evening, and shortly after dusk we paraded on the road. We were to go to the front line, there to spend our Christmas. Last year there had been much fraternizing with the enemy,[9] but this year strict orders had been issued that we must confine our goodwill not only to our fellow Christians, but to Christians of allied nationality. We were to remain throughout possessed by the spirit of hate, answering any advances with lead. This was the substance of the message read out to us on parade on Christmas Eve; it created no stir, nor did it seem in any way unreasonable at the time. Not one of us, standing on that road, had any desire to show cordiality to an enemy unseen and unknown, whose presence was manifested only in sudden moments of a great uprising of fear. Why should we cherish any thought of sharing with this impersonal cause of our degradation even one arbitrary day of peace? I do not say that we marched up the Rue Tilleloy inspired with a fresh determination to kill at every opportunity on Christmas Day, nor that we meditated a secret overthrowing of the orders that we had received. We reached the front line in a neutral mood, hoping rather for a quiet and uneventful spell of trench duty.

The night was fine and starry, with little wind. The front line trench was wet and poor, flimsier even than Fort Erith – technically speaking it was a breastwork, not a trench; if Fort Erith seemed unfinished, this could not be rated higher than half-begun, with its evil-smelling wet walls, undrained sump-pits and ramshackle dug-outs. There were five officers to share the watch, and when the company commander[10] allotted to me a two-hour period, from one in the morning till three, I felt proud to command a stretch of the front line on my first visit. At dinner that evening a bottle of champagne gave a spurious glow to an ordinary meal, if a first meal in the front line can ever be called ordinary. Towards midnight we heard voices from the German trenches and some snatches of song: they were making merry. The night was still, and its quiet was unbroken by rifle or machine-gun fire. The artillery on both sides sent over a few shells towards the rear of the lines. The firing could rightly be described as desultory, for there was little desire on either side to create trouble; some rounds must of course be fired, otherwise questions would follow.

The battalion on our right was shouting to the enemy, and he was responding. Gradually the shouts became more deliberate, and we could hear 'Merry Christmas Tommy' and 'Merry Christmas Fritz'. As soon **25 December 1915** as it became light, we saw hands and bottles being waved at us, with encouraging shouts that we could neither understand nor mis-understand. A drunken German stumbled over his parapet and advanced through the barbed wire, followed by several others, and in a few moments there was a rush of men from both sides, carrying tins of meat, biscuits, and other odd commodities for barter. This was the first time I had seen No Man's Land, and it was now Every Man's Land, or nearly so. Some of our men would not go, and they gave terse and bitter reasons for their refusal. The officers called our men back to the line, and in a few minutes No Man's Land was once more empty and desolate. There had been a feverish exchange of 'souvenirs', a suggestion for peace all day and a football match in the afternoon, and a promise of no rifle fire at night. All this came to naught. An irate Brigadier came spluttering up to the line, thundering hard, throwing a 'court martial' into every other sentence, ordering an extra dose of militant action that night, and breathing fury everywhere. We had evidently jeopardized the safety of the Allied cause. I suspect that across No Man's Land a similar scene was being played, for later in the day the guns became active. The artillery was stimulating the infantry to resume the war. Despite the fulminations of the Generals, the infantry was in no mood for offensive measures, and it was obvious that, on both sides, rifles and machine guns were aimed high.

A few days later we read in the papers that on Christmas Day, 1915, there was no fraternizing with the enemy – hate was too bitter to permit of such a yielding. Our men were wary enough to press as close as they might to the German wire in the hope of concealing from sight the weakness of our own defence. I could find no residue of tenderness towards the enemy as a result of this encounter, nor can I think now that any harm was done. The infantry hated the enemy artillery, and extended an impersonal hate to the opposing infantry if it interfered with the routine of trench life, but the infantry of one side never saw its opponents under the conditions of our soldiering except at times of battle or raiding. What was there of an enemy in an unarmed man clad in a different uniform, eager to secure something of ours in return for some little possession of his own? Let that man be armed, and intent to kill – all would be different, and lead and iron the only commodities for barter.

Turning into the dug-out in the late afternoon, I saw the company commander seated in the corner reading a book, to all appearances far away in another country. At my entry he looked up, and went on reading. Some minutes later I spoke to him as he put down his book.

'You are the first man I have seen in France reading poetry,' said I. He grunted a query.

'Do you read much of it?' I went on to ask.

'Yes ... do you?'

'I do, whenever I get an opportunity.'

'Now that is where you make a mistake,' he said; 'I make a point of learning by heart one poem a day, no matter where I am. It is the only way to keep sane. What are you reading?'

'I am trying to learn Browning's *Abt Vogler*,' I replied.

'Too long,' said he, 'try sonnets. I am learning one of Wordsworth's sonnets each day ... Well, I must go out to see what sort of a mess they are making of that new bomb store.'

I attempted later to renew our discussion of poetry, but I met with no success. He retired behind his customary cloud of reserve, speaking only of the numerous practical details of everyday life and sharing with me, in his quiet generous way, his long experience of trench management. I do not know what became of him, but I hope he lived to read his sonnets in better days.

On Boxing Night we were relieved by the Irish Guards. I have no experience of their military virtues, but they greatly enriched my life and enlarged my vocabulary; their oaths and curses were romantic imaginings after the banalities and repetitions of our English swearing, their voices a splash of colour against the grey mud. Back again to the same cottage, but this time by ourselves, for we had finished our apprenticeship. The Guards marched further west, into divisional reserve and rest, and as we said good-bye to them, they were kind enough to praise our discipline. We had approached the Guards a few days ago with some awe, but we left them now with a deep respect for their strong and sturdy self-reliance, and with some understanding of their pride in their regiment.

Green, my servant, was a devoted and untiring worker, and had, I believe, shown his worth as a successful manager of one of the multiple grocery shops in Cricklewood, but he was a poor cook. We sat down to a dinner of fried steak and mashed potatoes, washed down with rum and water, and all night I was very sick. I blamed Green, but it is possible that the water I drank in the line had delayed its ruthless action until that evening.

The next day we went away in buses to a little hamlet called Le Sart,[11] near the Forêt de Nieppe; here the battalion came together again, to talk of great doings in the trenches, and to enjoy the luxury of good billets.

Notes

1. The War Diary says that the battalion entrained at 10.15 p.m. for Blendecques.
2. The War diary gives this as Warnes in the Laventie sector of the Western Front.
3. The brigade is the basic all-arms formation of an army, the lowest command for a general officer – in this case, a Brigadier-General. In 1916 it usually comprised four infantry battalions, a signal company, a field artillery brigade, field engineer section, medium machine gun company, and a trench mortar battery. The history of the 38th Division, cited in the bibliography, shows that 113 Infantry Brigade consisted of 13, 14, 15 and 16 RWF. It was supported by 119 Brigade, RFA; a section of 124th Field Company RE; 113 MG Company; 113 Light Trench Mortar Battery; and a cyclist company from 19 Welsh. All administrative and logistic support was centralized at division level and above.

4. Wyn Griffith had taken command of C Company before embarking for France, although still a Lieutenant. He did not learn of his promotion to Captain for some time after it had appeared in *The London Gazette*.
5. Wyn Griffith's first brigade commander would have been Brigadier-General Owen Thomas, MP. Thomas raised and trained 113 Brigade but, because of his age, he was denied the chance to command in France. Three of his four sons were commissioned into The Royal Welch Fusiliers; all three were killed. Brigadier-General Llewellyn Alberic Emilius Price-Davies VC CMG DSO (1875–1965) had been commissioned into the KRRC and won the VC at the Blood River in South Africa in September 1901. A substantive major, temporary Brigadier-General, he commanded 113 Brigade from November 1915 to November 1917. He was the brother-in-law of Lieutenant-General (later Field Marshal) Sir Henry Wilson who was at this time commanding IV Corps.
6. Maconochie was a stew of meat, sliced turnips and carrots in a thin gravy, named because of its manufacture by the Maconochie Company of Aberdeen. The company produced it in large quantities after it became a standard food ration item for British soldiers when in trenches. Though the stew was tolerable when a soldier was famished, many hated it. As one soldier put it, 'warmed in the tin, Maconochie was edible; cold it was a man-killer.'
7. The Guards and the 19th Infantry Divisions held the line at this point. A Company of 15 RWF was assigned to 1st Scots Guards; B Company to the 3rd Grenadiers; Wyn Griffith's company, C, to the 1st Coldstream and D Company to the 2nd Irish Guards.
8. Wyn Griffith's wife, Winifred Elizabeth Frimston (1890–1977), also called Wyn. She was a distant cousin of Wyn Griffiths: the Frimston family, despite their name, were Welsh, and from St Asaph. They were Welsh speaking, although Wyn Griffith noted in manuscript notes that the girls 'did not speak it from choice'. This partly explains why his letters are in English, not Welsh; the other part of the explanation being that the censor would have required them to be written in English. The Wyn Griffiths were devoted to each other all their lives; Wyn Griffith died in the convent at Bowden on 27 September 1977, followed three days later by Winifred. They were cremated together in Altrincham and their ashes buried together in the family grave in Rhiw.
9. Wyn Griffith refers to the famous unofficial Christmas Truce of 1914. 2 RWF had taken part in this ceasefire and had played football with the Germans in No-Man's Land. A memorial to the event was unveiled at Freilinghen in northern France on 11 November 2008. The truce had extended over two-thirds of the British line and there were similar ceasefires in areas of the French and Belgian sectors. See the account in Malcolm Brown and Shirley Seaton *Christmas Truce* (London, 1994).
10. Captain Wilfred Allen Howells OBE, commissioned February 1915. He commanded A Company at Mametz Wood where he was wounded; however he survived the war.
11. This is close to the larger village of Merville.

Chapter 2

Command

15 RWF

We marched through Merville, Vieille Chapelle and Lacouture to Richebourg St. Vaast,[1] an empty shell of a village. Bombardment had driven away all its inhabitants and had left gaping holes in its red-bricked outline. **January 1916** The church was little more than a grey scree of stone, and as the buildings near to it had suffered more severely than those in the outskirts of the village, there was a progression of decayed brickwork visible to the eye. One wall had already become a heap of rubble tidily piled at a street corner so as to allow free movement over the cobbles; a little further back, what was once a house was now but a ten-foot ruin; behind this the curve rose to a house damaged but not disarticulated, with a part of the roof miraculously poised over its frame. Here and there a garden had run wild into long dark grass, and through an orchard on one side ran an aimless trench, now overgrown with weeds. We dumped our equipment in good corners of the most habitable rooms, staking a hasty claim, then finding a better pitch and abandoning the first found, but a burst of shellfire brought our explorings to a quick end.

The enemy had in all probability observed our march, or our entry into the village, and for an hour we were heavily shelled. A shell-burst, even in the soft mud of the trenches, seemed the greatest noise on earth, but when I heard a succession of 'five-nines'[2] hitting these houses I plumbed depths of terror hitherto undiscovered by me. I found it hard to maintain an appearance of unconcern while these monsters were stealing out of the silence into a hiss and a burst, reverberating in a rumble that lingered for some time as if it were loath to cease its echoing. I had begun to eat, but food dried in my mouth. I stopped and lit a cigarette, walked up and down the room, wondering whether it were better to remain indoors, risking a fall of brick, than to be outside, exposed to flying pieces of shell splinters. It did not seem to matter. A greater need was to find something to do, so I went from house to house talking to the small groups of men. In time of danger, the greatest burden of all is enforced inactivity. An hour passed incredibly slowly before the shelling ceased, and when we came to count the cost, we found that two men had been killed, and five seriously wounded.

At night we carried stores up to Richebourg l'Avoué, and there, a little behind the front line, we spent five hours digging a communication trench through the village cemetery – an evil task, even in winter. The next day we were so heavily shelled in our village that we were forced to seek shelter in the scattered trenches and in the ditches outside. That night we went into the front line at Richebourg l'Avoué, to take complete charge of a sector for the first time; the war was now surging round our feet, and it was hard to believe that less than a month ago we were wondering what a trench looked like. This trench was wet and ill-built; there were but few fire-bays where the water was not ankle-deep above the duckboards, and in most parts it was knee-deep On the extreme right of the company front the trench abandoned its useless struggle against the encroaching water and stopped abruptly, leaving rows of rusty barbed wire entanglements to keep a silent watch on the enemy. At night we sent out a patrol to make contact with our neighbours across the gap. The division we had relieved[3] left its artillery to cover our front – noisy fellows, easily stirred to strife, and much given to wire-cutting. There was water in our narrow dug-out, so narrow that I could not lie full length on the bench at the back of it. It was difficult to sleep, and the labour of wading through water added greatly to the fatigue of the four long days and nights. Our artillery bombarded the enemy's wire, his artillery shelled our trenches in retaliation: our guns, regarding this as an insult, doubled their fury, and the enemy responded to the challenge. The infantry sat and suffered, cursing all artillery, allied or enemy. What task was more pressing than the draining of wet trenches, rebuilding fire-bays, and making dug-outs sound enough to keep out the rain? A dug-out in this sector was not a hole in the ground; it was a child's clumsy effort to build a little one-roomed house, with sandbags full of viscous mud for bricks. It had no foundation, no frame, no structure. For a roof, some sheets of corrugated iron were laid on two or three timbers resting on the sandbag walls, and on the iron a course or two of sandbags. Most of the dug-outs were bullet-proof, certainly, but a direct hit with a light shell would destroy the best of them. If we improved one place, the enemy artillery, responding to our gun-fire, would bring our work to naught. Artillery was meant to cover or to stop an attack; if there was no attack, then let the guns fire at their own true opponents, the enemy artillery. Thus spake the infantry and I am quite sure that across No Man's Land, Saxon and Bavarian spoke the same words. At this time our guns were short of shells. If we asked the artillery to fire in retaliation for a drubbing of our line, the response did not equal the original offence, which increased our annoyance at what we thought to be wasteful shelling.

At night a trench mortar officer set his guns in a derelict trench about twenty yards behind the line and carried up his ammunition, heavy globes of iron with a little cylindrical projection like a broken handle.[4] In the morning I moved the men from the bays between the trench mortars and their target, to lighten the risk of loss from the retaliatory fire. A pop, and then a black ball went soaring up, spinning round as it went through the air slowly, more pops and more queer birds against the sky A stutter of terrific detonations seemed to shake the air and the ground, sandbags and bits of timber sailed up slowly and fell in a calm deliberate way. In the silence that followed the explosions, an angry voice called out in English, across No Man's Land, 'YOU BLOODY WELSH MURDERERS.'

The trench mortar team hurried away, pleased with their shooting – as they always were – and left us to wait for the shelling of our line. It did not begin immediately, as we had expected. An hour passed, then another, until the suspense became harder to bear than a bombardment. In the late afternoon, when we had decided that the enemy was going to swallow this insult and we had resumed our mud-building and irrigation, a sudden fury of shellfire turned our poor trench into a field of spouting volcanoes, spattering mud up into the air. The angry hiss of 77s,[5] the ponderous whirr of 5.9s, the dull empty whack of bombs and the whipping crack of shrapnel all merged into a sea of noise. Ten minutes of this drove us into a stupor of fear, and fear brought its terrible thirst; there was nothing to do but to sit still, half crouched against the wall of the trench, waiting, waiting. Every moment we expected to hear a shout of 'Stretcher-bearers at the double', but it never came. The storm ended as suddenly as it began; now was the time to count the cost. By some uncommon stroke of luck, not one man was wounded or killed, and in ten minutes we drank the best cup of tea ever made on this earth.

* * *

We found the cottage marked 'Company Mess' to be furnished a little better than its counterpart in other villages. There was a good lamp, a marble-topped sideboard, and one arm-chair upholstered in red plush. Madame was willing to lend us plates and cups, provided that we paid for any damage done. Two of our subalterns, stirred by this sudden luxury, had gone to Béthune to buy a gramophone, 'lorry-hopping' there and back. Two records had been broken on the journey home, but two had survived; one a song called 'Red Devon'[6], the other a song whose title was, I think, 'Galway by the Sea'. I have forgotten the words of both, and the tune of the first, but I shall never forget the melody of the second. It was an ordinary ballad, poor enough, and soaked in sentiment, buoyed up by the most conventional of chord sequences, but for me it is one of a few pieces of music that set in motion a whole complex of waves.[7] The waves of sound are the least important in this response; I see more than I hear. A shuttered room, an oil lamp throwing dingy shadows of a bottle of wine and a loaf on a table covered with yellow varnished American cloth[8]; maps and typewritten orders, a Sam Browne belt hanging over the back of a chair, Billy[9] sitting down with unbuttoned tunic, brooding silently, his young face clouded and morose, hearing in the simple tune a world of things he could not say; other good men who shared with me the hard days of war but did not live to look back upon them with a profound and unending feeling of miraculous deliverance. Music is a key that can open strange rooms in the house of memory. Some time after this, I rejoined my battalion in a village far behind the line.[10] I was at the very nadir of my military fortunes, having failed, for ever as I thought, to secure a prize so near to my hand. As I walked along the village street to the company mess, I heard a gramophone playing Chaminade's *Danse Créole*, and I can never hear it now without its accompaniment of failure and despondency.

After an evening and a day of listening to these two ballads, we began to wish for some variety of entertainment. The two broken records were in a lighter vein, we were told. A longing for any part of England must needs be set in a minor key of sentiment, but a yearning for the Southern States of America could find a cheerful expression. Another trip to Béthune brought into our repertoire a syncopated ditty with the ironical title of 'This is the Life'. Three lines of it have wedged themselves into my memory, possibly because of their vivid untruth:

> I love the cows AND chickens
> BUT this is the life,
> OH this is the life ...

The rest of the song has faded away, buried by that very life of which it sang.

In these days we went more than halfway to meet and welcome any diversion to the eye or the ear, or any colouring of the ever-moving but never-changing environment. It was this that made of a gramophone, and of Kirchner's drawings of thin-legged, silk-stockinged women,[11] not a luxury, nor a decoration, but furniture in every mess. The drawings were pinned on the dingy walls of country cottages whose womenfolk seemed of another species, not easily recognizable as contemporary, and in dug-outs where the silk stockings shone against the background of sackcloth. They pleased the eye, but a cynic might say that they offered nothing more than a liqueur to a man parched with thirst.

The company commander was reading the battalion orders, beginning with the duties of the morrow, passing through the local gossip and the much-travelled snippets of wisdom from GHQ, when he burst into laughter. The mess was lingering over a bottle of thin red wine of unknown derivation, and we looked up in surprise.

'Griff,' he said, 'you have got a job.'

'What is it?' I asked.

'Listen ... A Brigade class in cookery will be held at Battalion Headquarters – why, it's tomorrow – one company cook will be detailed from each battalion to report at ten a.m. – you've got to take command of the class.'

'I command a cookery class? Why, it's nonsense – what do I know about cooking? I'm going to see the adjutant now ... Hand me my belt.'

I disappeared, leaving behind me a cackle of laughter and much wit about the sick parades that would follow, and found the adjutant[12] finishing his coffee. I harangued him and argued with him, but to no purpose; it was a Brigade order, and the order said that I was to take command of the class. The only advice I could get was to stay up all night trying to rake together some semblance of knowledge, but I did convince him that the assistance of the battalion master-cook was essential to the success of the venture.

I traced the expert to an outhouse where he stood knife in hand, a grimy figure, flanked by enormous sides of bacon, pieces of cheese, and sacks full of bread.

'Sergeant, you've got to start a cooking class with me tomorrow morning.'

'Yes, sir,' he said calmly, as if this were a matter of no moment.

'You had better begin thinking hard what to do and say, for I'm blest if I know anything about cooking. You'll have to do the talking. The class is going to last for four solid days. How on earth are we to keep these fellows quiet for all that time?'

'Don't you worry, sir – we'll find 'em plenty to do ... I got'n idea, sir ... I was on a class myself once ... We'll teach them to make ovens and to make puddings.'

'Splendid,' said I; 'I like the "We".'

'Don't you fret, sir, I'll come round at nine o'clock tomorrow and we'll find a good place for to teach 'em.'

I walked back to the mess and burrowed in the depths of my kit-bag until I found that encyclopædia of military lore – Field Service Regulations.[13] There was sure to be something about cooking in this manual – indeed I had a dim recollection of drawings of ovens and neatly arranged pots and dixies.[14] I sat up late that night, fuddling my brain with technical terms until I felt confident of my ability to conceal my ignorance behind vague sentences full of the jargon of the craft. I had served long enough in the army to know the value of words. To throw a few 'bracketings'[15] into a talk with a gunner, or to introduce an odd 'revetment'[16] into a conversation with an engineer, was more than a friendly acknowledgement of the importance of his trade in your everyday life; it created an atmosphere of temporary equality, of unity of purpose, and a presupposition of vast reserves of undisclosed knowledge. Being infantry, we had no rich vocabulary of craft jargon, and we succumbed easily to the temptation to use other people's words, with a slight self consciousness in their handling.

In the morning Sergeant Smith came to my billet, looking strangely clean and fresh, so different from the stew-coloured figure of the evening that I stared at him.

'Put my best tunic on, sir, and I washed my overalls last night and put them in the cookhouse to dry.'

In his hand he held an unused notebook, a badge of his new office. We walked to a farmhouse where he had discovered a small unused barn, open on one side, with a wooden table: this was to be our laboratory.

'If you was to go to the Quartermaster Sergeant, sir, and ask him to save some currants and a bit of flour, I could show them how to make a pudding. He'd do it for you, sir, he would, and I could get a few things together here ready to start.'

I went obediently, and was promised currants, but there was no flour.

'No matter, sir, we'll show 'em how to make flour from biscuits.'

Four men arrived, dumped their rifles and kit in a corner, and stood in a row while I addressed them.

'The object of this course', said I, with an air of great wisdom, 'is to see what can be done to vary the diet, using only the rations that are issued. We think it possible to make boiled puddings, to roast meat, and to make rissoles with bully and biscuit.' Sergeant Smith nodded encouragingly. 'I'm sure you'll agree that it is worth going to a little trouble to get a change from stew and curried stew. Sergeant Smith will give demonstrations. Carry on, Sergeant.'

He carried on. He pounded biscuits into flour, made a currant pudding, using bacon drip for lard, tied the agglomerate in a flew sandbag, and boiled it in a dixie. I went for a walk while the pudding boiled, and came back to find five men eating it. I joined them. It was a plain unobjectionable pudding of the plum duff variety, very filling, but undoubtedly a pudding. The sandbag left a certain amount of fluff, but not enough to worry a soldier. Encouraged by this success, we made rissoles of bully, powdered biscuit and bacon drip – they were also very satisfying. Our greatest triumph was the conversion of two oil drums into an oven – I call this 'our' triumph because my ignorance of cooking did not prevent me from giving assistance in the solution of a mechanical problem. The ordinary field oven of the text-book was a hit and miss affair; you put a fire in your oven, raked it out and put the meat in, and when you took out the joint it was cooked – or not. Using two oil drums, we contrived to maintain a fire under the oven while the joint was being cooked, and we were able to open the oven to turn the meat.

One afternoon the Brigadier called to see us. He said he would sample our cooking, so we offered him a rissole and a slab of currant duff. He praised them highly, and bravely ate both. He already had the Victoria Cross. The class was a success, and he said that it was to be repeated on every occasion of our coming out of the line, and that I was to take charge of it. I walked with him towards the road.

'Do you inspect the men's rifles every morning?' he asked.

'Yes, sir,' said I, vowing to start the next morning.

'Where did you pick up your knowledge of cooking?'

'I haven't any, sir; all the cooking I have ever done is to make my own breakfast in Chambers in the Temple.'

'Well, you've got a good sergeant, which is equally to your credit.'

I taught nothing, but I learnt a great deal. When we went back to the line I gave permission to the company cooks to stay behind with the cooker on condition that the rations were supplemented every night by a boiled pudding or rissoles; if the supplement were lacking, they were to come up to the line next day. The supply never failed.

In our early days in the line, the multitude of small cares and the unbroken sequence of starting a score of new tasks in different places, all calling for constant supervision, brought with them a strange busyness. The body moved from bay to bay, tiring itself in the long hours of wading through mud and water. Four days in the trenches were four days and nights of walking and standing, with shoulders aching from the drag of wet clothes. To lie down for two hours on a plank, half sinking into a dream ridden sleep, half hearing every noise within the radius of audibility, imagining in every step that approached the dug-out a summons to return to the world of concentrated attention; this was little rest to body or to mind. On such a bed flesh was no protection to the bones; it was a small envelope containing a jumble of crossing nerves, warring with themselves, and raised to a state of red-hot sensitivity. Bone pressed down upon, and wood forced up against this thin cushion until the sting changed slowly into a dragging pain. Getting up was a process of re-assembling the members; arms were stiff, though near at hand, legs had travelled further from control, but feet were far away in a cold and distant land. A queer lightness in the knees enhanced the weight of the feet, making the leg a lever too fragile to bear such a load at its extremity. A waking man was a slack-stringed fiddle, to be tuned up peg by peg into the full tension of self-command.

There was always something to be done, involving a movement and a standing about. Digging, filling sandbags, building, carrying stores and ammunition, repairing the walls damaged by shell fire, scheming against the insidious attack of water, strengthening the barbed wire, resetting duckboards; an officer did none of these things with his own hands, or but rarely. He was there when such things were done, and being there demanded a presence of body and of mind. These tasks, in our early days, seemed to be of such importance that their supervision became an occupation capable of absorbing one's entire stock of energy. They filled the mind so fully that a bombardment became a troublesome interruption of the serious business of life in the trenches.

Later, however, the redistribution of mud took the second place, for the men knew what to do; the zeal of the beginner faded into the semi-drudgery of the journeyman. Days and nights passed by in an oscillation between a suddenly roused fear of instant death and a slowly increasing dread of the continuance of this life of atrophy. An enemy we never saw – no, not an enemy, for maiming or extinction came from a bursting of iron in a ditch, the result of a mathematical computation made some miles away, tragically wrong to us, while the arithmetician knew not whether his answer were right.

Across No Man's Land there were men sharing trouble with us, fighting the same losing battle against water, powerless before the sudden storm of bursting metal, and longing to be home again with their children. Were they an enemy? A scrap of song floating across at dusk, or a grey helmet seen for a moment through a periscope – were we to freeze into hatred at these manifestations of a life so like our own? An unrelieved weariness drugged us into a dullness of mind so overpowering that the brain declined a metaphysical battle on these issues. Everything was unreason, and it profited not to refine the ridiculous into the mad. On the other side of Aubers Ridge a German gunner twirled a few wheels into a new position, moved a bar of iron, and sent death soaring into the air; he went to his dinner.

While he was moving his wheels and dials, three Londoners were filling sandbags in a ditch on the plain, arguing about Tottenham Hotspur. A flash, a noise, and a cloud of smoke.

'Blast 'em, they've killed old Parkinson[17] – blown 'is 'ead off, they 'ave, the bastards.'

Blast whom? The unseen German, going to his dinner? The man who sang, over the way? No. Blast everybody and everything; blast all who contributed to the sending of this quiet middle-aged Londoner to die not in combat between men, but in a struggle between two sets of mathematical equations. Did we think out this bitter problem, or discuss the ways of bringing an end to this distemper? No ... we were too tired. Blast them, and back to the weary lifting of mud, this time passing a stretcher covered with a blanket hiding all but a thin trickle of blood. Four children, and his wife's name was 'Liz' ... must write to her tonight ... Oh, blast them!

While the mind was spinning slowly round a pivot of 'How long?' the muscles were carrying an aching frame back and fro along a wet and sour-smelling trench, finding each journey more difficult than the one before. How long must we wait for the relief? How long could one hope to live, after two months of daily escape? How long would it be before we could get leave? How long could this war last? This was the series of concentric circles of sentences passing through a deadened mind, each one repeated again and again, a new way of 'counting sheep', dulling the brain into a half-sleep. Four days in the line can be written down as a rapid fall along the slope of vitality into a stupor of weariness; on the path, some sharp crests of fear, but the end was overwhelming fatigue. Now that the war is half-forgotten, many men have described trench life, some with a wealth of remembered detail both of doing and of saying, rebuilding for the reader a day, a place and a people. Some clever writers have found in an early morning visit to the line material enough to furnish a vivid background for a long play of wit and character. But to most of us who served in the infantry, the thought of a trench brings back that long span of damnable tiredness, broken here and there by a sudden dry tongued spasm of fear. Cold nights, the discomfort of wet clothes, dragging minutes of anxiety on patrol, the sufferings of men ... these are all fading with the passing years, but nothing can efface the memory of that all-conquering fatigue.

Up To Mametz

The days were lengthening and February had filled the dykes to overflowing. There was a theory that the Germans, with the cunning of which they were the sole proprietors, had contrived to drain all the water from their trenches into ours. The men were convinced of its truth. It was easy enough to believe that Germany made no mistakes in any matter calling for the exercise of long-ranged scientific knowledge, and also to credit the enemy with a complete mastery over the material conditions of war. Wherever we had stood in a trench, the Germans were above us, looking down from some ridge upon our amateurish struggles on the plain.[18] We had not seen the enemy's trenches except through a periscope or a sniper's peephole, but among the men it was accepted as inevitable that these trenches should be dry, and full of safe and comfortable dug-out. We lived in a world of our own mistakes, compelled by the unsuccess of our commanders, as we thought, to inhabit a sodden and water-logged plain, failing to make a dry trench or a comfortable dug-out. We knew the crashing terrors of the enemy's 'five-nines', and the malignant punch of his 'seven-sevens', but we had not as yet been shelled by our own artillery, so we could not believe that our shell-fire equalled his in malevolence. Our guns might have been excellent weapons, but we were short of shells, and, one afternoon, a call for retaliation on the enemy's trenches brought seventeen rounds of 4.5s,[19] of which fourteen failed to explode. For our comforting we were told that there was an unlimited supply of ammunition to fire if the enemy attacked us; if his infantry left their trenches to advance, our S.O.S. barrage would be impenetrable. Our day-to-day firing, however, was severely restricted. Standing up to the knees in water, half ashamed of the weakness of our gunfire, it was easy to convince oneself that on the other side of No Man's Land dwelt a master of the craft of war, planning superhuman schemes for our destruction at the time of his choosing. Not that we thought the grey hatted infantrymen opposite to be one whit more able than ourselves to kill or to harass; the skill lay further back, in their commanders. Thus it came that hundreds of men believed that the water in our trenches was one of Germany's many weapons, and when one of our engineers strongly denied this possibility, his listeners saw in this denial another demonstration of our inferiority – in intelligence.

This great question of drainage remained unsettled when we left this sector, moving south towards the La Bassée canal to take charge

March 1916

of a marsh in front of Festubert. On our right the ground ran up to Givenchy, an ill-famed hillock where the pulse of war quickened to a restless exchange of shellfire and bombs. We were quiet enough in Festubert. Water had triumphed over man, and there was no front line to hold. The greater part of the battalion lived in a well-made breastwork some hundreds of yards away from the enemy, but my company held the Islands, a series of isolated posts in the marsh. Small groups of men spent the day lying down quietly in a short stretch of trench, with nothing whatever to do but to look through a periscope. There were no communication trenches leading up to these posts, and by day they were unapproachable from the rear or from their neighbours. There were frequent reliefs of the garrisons from the main body of the company, scattered about in bricked-up dug-outs made out of the ruins of the village. Visiting these posts at night was an eerie business, walking boldly above ground, across ditches and through the remains of barbed wire, past long-unburied corpses, up to the island posts. The wire in front was bad, and the loss of direction on a dark night carried a risk of stumbling into the German lines. A hard frost set in, and a heavy fall of snow added greatly to our troubles, making life a mere struggle to keep warm. At night we lit fires in braziers, but by day the smoke would draw shellfire upon our dug-outs, so we had to school ourselves to bear the ache of cold in inactivity, discovering in the process several new forms of stiffness. Our numbers were declining steadily with each visit to the line. On parade the company had shrunk to one half its original size, although we could not recall to memory any one day of large loss; the tree was shedding its leaves in its early autumn, and ever before us was the prospect of the gale of a battle that would strip us bare. The growing pressure of day added to day had made inelastic creatures of us all, incapable of reaction against good fortune or bad, dragging one foot after another upon the slow-moving treadmill of this weary life, torpid minds in unresponsive bodies. There was nothing new to talk about, one day was like another.

At last something happened to rouse us a little. We heard that a platoon of Bantams[20] was coming to us to serve an apprenticeship in the line. Were we already old enough in the ways of war to teach others? It was not difficult to persuade ourselves that we were veterans, for years seemed to have passed by since we 'came out of our time' with the Guards. A whole platoon of fresh men to help us in carrying and in digging was a great reinforcement. The

Bantams were small, but very sturdy and self-possessed; on parade they seemed to be all equipment, and on the march, walking bundles of gear. The Londoners gave them a great welcome, and I heard many a traveller's tale being told to the newcomers. This I overheard in a dug-out in Festubert.

'I tell you what, kid, the shells ain't so bad, nor the bullets ain't, nor the blarsted fatigues. It's the bleedin' rats as does it. When you're standin' on guard at night they runs abaht on the parapet and lashes out at yer with their bleedin' 'ind legs and if you ain't careful they knocks yer off the bleedin' fire-step back inter the trench.'

'And it ain't only that,' said another. 'Look what they did to Sergeant Tracy.[21] Now 'e was farst asleep in a dug-out, 'e was, and when 'e woke up, blowed if a rat 'adn't bitten off 'alf 'is blinkin' ear.'

''Ave yer seen the Cap'n's mackintosh?' asked a third. 'Just you look at the collar when 'e comes round tonight. You'll find one 'alf of it all gone, all chewed away by a rat when 'e was sleepin'. Big fat things they are, big as dogs, and fat as 'ell.'

The very first night the Bantams accompanied us to the line, the Germans opposite called out 'Cock-a-doodle-do' many times. There was no mistaking it: they knew perfectly well that the Bantams were with us. We on our part, in the infantry, did not know whether a Bavarian or a Saxon stood against us, so that this display of knowledge brought to us all an uneasy feeling that every movement we made was put down in some enormous notebook on the other side. Here was clear proof that the German High Command was omniscient, and there was a large increase in the supporters of the theory that their infinite cunning enabled the Germans to drain all their water into our trenches.

Four days of this hard weather were a severe trial of our powers of resistance. Hands and feet were sore when we set out on our trudge along the road to Gorre, the pack seemed heavier than usual, and the rifle made of lead. We started stiffly in small parties at five minute intervals, the Sergeant-Major and I walking at the rear of the last section. Traffic had turned the snow into slush, and men were staggering uneasily on the slippery road, sometimes falling into the drifts at the side, everybody silent, tired and sleepy. On along this never-ending lane, following a dark ribbon of trodden snow, bearing occasionally into the ditch to let pass by a limber wagon taking up supplies, regaining the crown of the road with increasing difficulty, and halting awhile to rest. At every halt it grew harder to restart this

'Front Line Trench' by David Jones. [RWF Museum Trustees]

toiling train of men. The Bantams were suffering severely, for their feet were not inured to the soaking, and their packs, equipment and rifles weighed nearly as much as themselves. The Sergeant-Major and I ended by driving these weary men like sheep, with curses and pushes, carrying several rifles, dragging back on to his feet every man who dropped down, allowing no one, upon any pretext, to rest. Cruel work, but kinder than letting men of low vitality drop into an endless sleep. Three hours after the first section of the company reached Gorre we brought in this tail of stupefied stragglers, pushed them into a barn and gave them a tot of rum; they were half asleep as they took off their equipment and dropped into the straw. I drank half a cupful of rum and began to nibble at a biscuit, but I was too sleepy to finish it.

Notes

1. 5 kilometres (3½ miles) north-east of Béthune.
2. The 5.9 referred to in many British war time reports was in fact a 15cm medium Field Howitzer manufactured by Krupp, which fired a shell of 85lbs to ranges between 6,000 and 8,500 yards.
3. According to the History of the 38th Division, this was the regular 19th Infantry Division.
4. Designed by Sir Wilfred Scott-Stokes (he was knighted for this work), the managing director of a mechanical engineering firm, Ransome & Rapier of

Ipswich, the *Stokes* trench mortar was designed to answer the need for a mobile and quick firing trench mortar. Scott-Stokes had a prototype ready by December 1914. Though highly thought of by the Army the mortar did not immediately go into production as it was still believed that the war would be short. Within a few months things had changed and the 3-inch *Stokes* Trench Mortar Mark I went into production in the spring of 1915. It was the ancestor of all subsequent mortars.

The gun was basically very simple. A 51-inch long, 3-inch diameter barrel was supported by a bipod, which sat on a base-plate. The Stokes was fired by dropping the 11lb shell down the tube onto the fixed firing pin at the base of the tube. This set off a cartridge which in turn ignited propellant rings attached to the mortar shell. The angle of the bipod could be adjusted to increase or decrease the range and the shell could be fired to a maximum range of 800 yards. The safe minimum distance was 100 yards.

5. The 7.7cm (3.1 inch) Field Gun was the 'whizz bang' of so many Great War memoirs. The nearest equivalent of the British 18pdr, the gun fired a 14.4lb shell up to 7,000 yards.
6. Wyn Griffith probably refers to the popular song *Glorious Devon*, composed by Sir Edward German and published by Boosey and Co in 1905. That he remembers it as 'Red Devon' is probably because of the words in the first verse:

> Coombe and Tor, green meadow and lane,
> Birds on the waving bough.
> Beetling cliffs by the surging main,
> Rich red loam for the plough.
> Devon's the fount of the bravest blood
> That braces England's breed,
> Her maidens fair as the apple bud,
> And her men are men indeed.

7. *Galway Bay* is the most likely candidate for this song. It was written by Francis A. Fahy who was born in 1850. The air is *My Irish Molly, O*. One verse, which may be what Wyn Griffith recalls, runs:

> Oh, grey and bleak, by shore and creek,
> The rugged rocks abound,
> But sweeter green the grass between
> Than grows on Irish ground.
> So friendship fond, all wealth beyond,
> And love that lives alway,
> Bless each poor home beside your foam,
> My dear old Galway Bay.

8. A cloth made of cotton with a glazed and varnished surface that could be wiped clean.
9. This is probably Lieutenant William John Rees who was commissioned in March 1915 and transferred to the Royal Flying Corps in 1916.
10. Wyn Griffith refers to his return to 15th RWF from the staff in late 1916, which is described in more detail in the new material in Part Two.

11. Raphael Kirchner (1876–1917) was an Austrian illustrator whose erotic pin-up sketches were popular with both Austrian and German soldiers, and with French, British and Empire troops. He produced around 1,000 postcards in his short life and was regularly featured in the *London Daily Sketch*. Born in Vienna, he was living in Paris at the start of war and moved immediately to New York.
12. Captain Lewis Noel Vincent Evans CB CBE (1886–1967), a founder member of the battalion in 1914. He was later Deputy Director of Public Prosecutions, a JP, High Sherriff and Deputy Lord Lieutenant of Merioneth.
13. *Field Service Regulations* had been issued in 1909 as a result of the Boer War. Part 1 covered operations and Part 2, organization and administration. It had been revised and re-issued in 1914 shortly before the outbreak of war and was the Army's doctrinal guide to every aspect of the business of life in the field. Contravening its specifications could be a matter for disciplinary proceedings.
14. *Dixie* was the name given to the 12-gallon metal containers used for cooking stew or tea in field kitchens.
15. Bracketing is the process of adjusting the fire of guns onto an unseen target by relaying the fall of shot indirectly by radio or telephone and ordering a series of adds or drops, left or rights, in gradually decreasing amounts of distance until the rounds fall onto the target.
16. Revetments are sheets of corrugated iron, or wooden pallets or woven matting supported by stakes and used to hold up the sides of trenches to prevent cave-ins.
17. 22193 Pte Sidney Arthur Parkington, enlisted at Holborn and killed on 11 January 1916 [Lars Ahlkvist].
18. The divisional history, however, says that 'During this period there is little to record except steady progress in obtaining an ascendancy over the enemy and carrying out several raids ...'
19. The Ordnance QF 4.5-inch Howitzer was the standard British Empire field howitzer of the war. It equipped some twenty-five per cent of the field artillery. It entered service in 1910 and remained in service through the interwar period and was last used in the field by British forces in early 1942. The weight of shell was 35lbs and the maximum range at this time was 6,600 yards. In 1914 the ammunition scale for 4.5-in howitzers was seventy per cent shrapnel and thirty per cent HE. New types of shell were introduced during the war. These were chemical at the end of 1915, incendiary shells in 1916 and smoke shells in 1917.

    At this period of the war, the British economy had not been brought fully onto a war footing: that had not begun until Lloyd George's appointment as Minister for Munitions during 1915; moreover the quality of mass-produced artillery rounds made in factories that had rapidly re-tooled, by a workforce that was inexperienced, was very poor as this account testifies.
20. For many years, the minimum regulation height for recruits into the British Army was 5 ft 3 ins. This requirement was lowered in 1915, to allow more men to enlist. They were recruited as volunteers in newly formed 'bantam' battalions. Over 50,000 under-height soldiers served in bantam battalions formed in a number of British infantry regiments and two Canadian infantry battalions.
21. Probably 222198 Sergeant Walter A. Tracey, an original member of the battalion [Lars Ahlkvist].

Chapter 3

Givenchy

The Badge of Fourth Army

Givenchy had a bad reputation. There were parts of the line that seemed to possess some quality of bitter enmity, seemed rather to be possessed by some demon of unrest, as if a battle once begun there had never ended. Each **April 1916** one stood, in the minds of all who knew it, as a focus of evil – a hearth whereon the fire of hatred had never died down to the ashes of a perfunctory showing of the daily discourtesies of the war. War, like other diseases, has its routine: the exchange of artillery-fire and rifle-fire at stand-to in the cold of dawn, followed by an interval of tranquillity while both sides broke their fast, then a definite programme of wire-cutting or trench bombardment by the artillery, fading into a slackening of gunfire during the night lest the flashes should disclose the positions of the guns. In the dark, both sides mended their broken wire and patrolled No Man's Land. This one might describe, not inaccurately, as the daily routine of trench warfare, and, like all routine in man's life, it was subject to cataclysmic upheaval from time to time, when orders came to the infantry to carry out a raid of the enemy's lines.

Nevertheless, there was a feeling that these disturbances were a passing fever, and that the routine would triumph over all. This conviction – for it was strong enough to warrant the name – would manifest itself in a personal resentment against the assumed authors

GIVENCHY

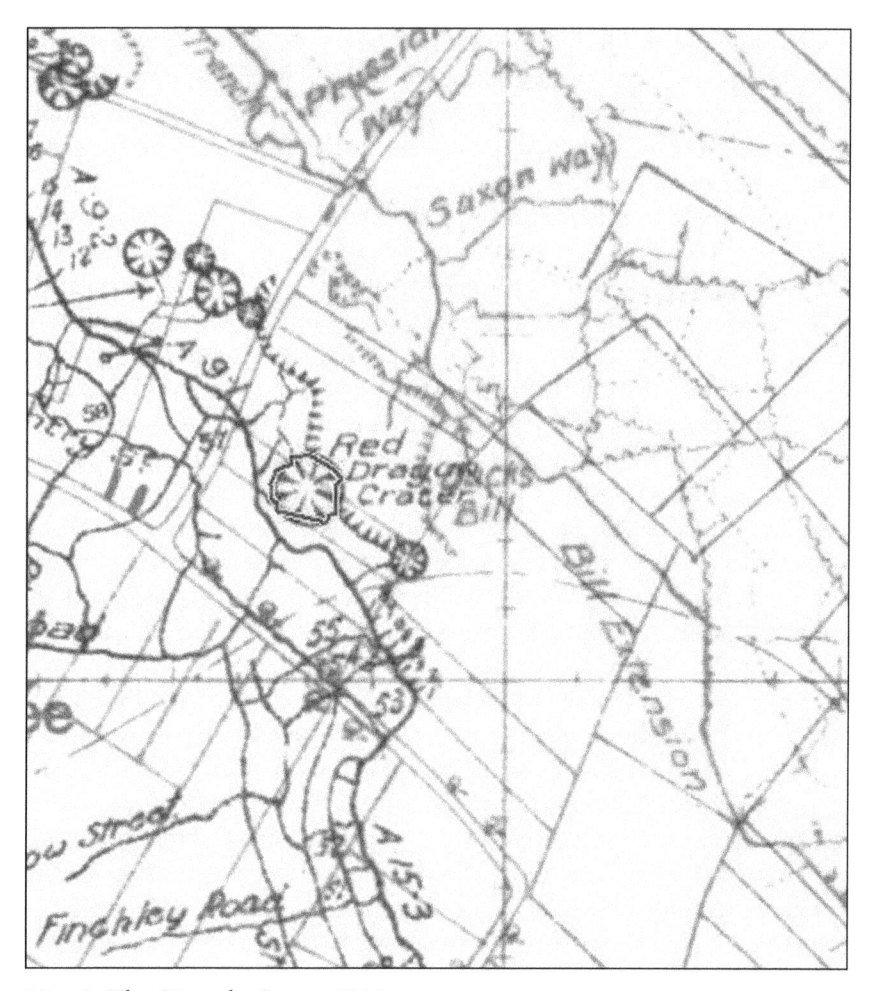

Map 2: The Givenchy Sector, 1916.

of this torment, invariably personified as some unknown pundits far removed from its dangers. We were in a state of war, admittedly, but the admission had to fight hard against an inborn desire for peace at the moment. At the time, and for long after, no opportunity was lost of impressing upon the minds and hearts of all that it was by means of such 'demonstrations' (as they were called) that the 'ascendency' over the enemy was gained. We were doubtful, sceptical even, at the time, for the balance of profit was not measured by our eyes. Twelve years have now gone by, and each year is strengthening the conviction that there was wisdom in the instinct of the humble soldier; I do not think that the theory of attrition has many adherents now, at any rate, not among those who served in the infantry. There was, in fact, a profound difference between sectors where routine triumphed and those whose quality took the form of a permanent manifestation of evil.[1]

The fire of bitter antagonism never died down to ashes in such places as Givenchy: the wind of every passing shell would fan the embers into a blaze of fury. Battle strode the air like a demon, and cast its shadow over this accursed hill, night and day, without respite; pillars of fire and clouds of smoke were here no signs of wonder. What I have called the routine of war may be likened to the mood of a man sullen in temper, but here man was in a rage. One could not believe that the mechanical processes of war determined the whole of this quality, that peace would brood over Givenchy as soon as the noise of the guns subsided. No such metamorphosis was credible, so strong was the feeling of the presence of malignant fate hovering above this hillock like a plain. It seemed rather as if nothing that man could do would ever succeed in bringing quiet to this village.

The eye could catch no promise in the landscape. In many places spring broke out into a riot of green hedges and blossoming orchards, a little further north one could look backwards from the line, over a small desert of destruction, into an abandoned garden struggling into life at the bidding of April. A small thing perhaps, but enough to stand for sanity to a mind obsessed with the greyness of the mud underfoot. Givenchy could not yield to this grain of comfort. Broken crucifixes, shattered walls, unmended roads, and splintered tree trunks – it was typical of the war as it was waged in our day. There was ugliness everywhere one looked, the ugliness of smashed new brick and new plaster, a terrible ugliness, inconceivable to one who has seen no ruins but those of aged walls, mellowed by sun, wind and rain.

Why does a new thing broken look so much older than a ruin of the Middle Ages? When the setting sun strikes the towers of Harlech Castle, it is easy to forget that cruel things have happened in its dark dungeons: it is indeed hard to believe fully that this house on the rock was ever a frame for the daily adventure of man and woman. It is difficult to imagine that the grey walls were linked with the life of man: in their long rest they have acquired another dignity, derived not from association with humanity, but rather from centuries of withdrawal from this contact. They dwell apart in a permanent retreat, they wear the sun in splendour and the mists with dignity. In the jagged outline and the broken walls of an old castle, the eye of the beholder sees only the fatigue of long years, and the simple, manly way in which such a noble creature grows old.

So have I seen many an old farmhouse, shelled into a formless jumble of brick, stone and tile, still retain a dignity of demeanour, as it quietly insisted on recognition. 'Wars come and go', it seemed to say, 'and men with them, but land must be tilled, and men will be wiser soon; when they have shed their distemper in an orgy of breaking of life and limb they will come back to me in penitence.' Man made these old brown dwellings, and they in their turn made men – man unmade them, but in the days to come they will once again make men. They gave shelter to the many generations of peasants who toiled to fill the sharp-roofed barns with food, they shook to the tramp of Spanish, French and British soldiers in the old forgotten wars, and suffered at the hands of many nations, but they were not long deflected from their stubborn purpose. An inherent nobility that never left them, even in their present hour of trial, gave to these broken walls an element of strength – it was as if they were looking forward into time, waiting to be restored to their proper usage when man had wearied of his rage.

But I have never seen a new house broken that did not chill the heart of the beholder with its air of unyielding futility. Some, with their ragged profiles, enlarged and gaping window-holes, looked like the faces of gibbering idiots, mad and meaningless, not in any way tragic. When the sun shone on full on these red masks they seemed to be laughing emptily, like a maniac who has no fear of evil. They could not stand silent, like a broken church, in a mute protest against the folly of war, they screeched their defiance of man's mastery over their poor and tenuous bodies. And yet it was but a few years since throbbed to the pulsing life within them. They were not built to store the yield of the fertile soil around, so that one generation should nourish another; they were brought into being to serve the present. But who can look at the shell of a new house where, a little while ago, man and woman began an era of joy in marriage, little children ran about and played, where happiness prevailed over every other mood – who can look at this newly-broken toy, even on a sunny day in early summer, with eyes that can for one moment forget the bitter folly that caused its breaking?

That battered frame of the Cloth Hall at Ypres never lost an air of grandeur, but the ruins of Givenchy village looked paltry, in spite of the many lives that were spilt to hold it as ours.

There was a curse on Givenchy village, a curse of blood and a curse of water. A mile to the north stood Festubert, where man fought more with water than with his fellow men; a mile or two to the south the trenches were dry, but on the Givenchy hill there was no respite from fire or flood, nor from that devil's volcano of a sprung mine. To stand in the trench was to wait to be blown up, without warning, from below, or to be struck down by some terror from the sky in the shape of a bomb, grenade or shell. We were spared the danger of bullets by the configuration of the ground while we were on the hill, but the approaches to it were swept with machine-gun fire, especially at night when reliefs and fatigue parties were moving. The feeling of waiting, waiting for sudden death all but overpowered a man, to be but half forgotten when he ate or talked. In a sector where there is no mining, an absence of shellfire brings rest to the mind for a while, until one begins to wonder when the shelling will start afresh, but mining puts an end to all repose.

More than a month passed in this slavery, and we were tethered to this hill by a rope that was never stretched far enough to allow us to forget its existence. One afternoon in early April I was standing in a trench on the hill, looking westwards over the parados towards Béthune and watching an enormous flock of starlings swaying back and fro in their peculiar mass formations. They were some miles away, black against a glowing sky, so like a half-deflated airship blown about by a gentle breeze that I did not laugh when a sentry asked me if that was a Zeppelin. I handed him my glasses, and believed him when he said that he 'Ain't never seed anythink like that before.' I walked down the trench towards the company dug-out, the first dug-out we ever dwelt in, for all the other shelters on the marshland were built up, not dug out. Tea was ready, and as we sat down to eat, a runner came stumbling down the wet steps with a message for me from Battalion Headquarters.

'You are detailed to attend a four-days' conference at Aire beginning at 10.00 hours on April 10th on Co-operation between artillery and infantry. You will proceed to the cross-roads in A 24 b^2 where a bus will meet you at 18.30 hours today April 9th ... Acknowledge.'

'Green!' I shouted.

'Coming, sir.'

GIVENCHY

'Get my kit together, all that I have with me here, and go down to the horse lines and get the rest of it. We've got to be at the crossroads outside Gorre at half-past six to catch a bus – mind you get the stuff there in good time. You are coming with me.' A clatter of enamelled plates and a 'So long, mate' showed that Green was off.

This was good news, for Aire was a pleasant town. Four days in good billets, dining in a hotel, shop windows to look at – no mud, no shells, no mines. As I left the dug-out it began to rain, but it did not seem to matter much; nothing mattered, for I was going away from those damnable trenches. I did not take any intellectual interest in co-operation between artillery and infantry – the artillery never satisfied the infantry, though at Givenchy it was admitted, grudgingly, that they shot well, considering. Considering what, I do not know, unless it be considering that they were not infantry! However, Aire was Aire, and the learned might talk as they liked.

There was no time to change my uniform or my underclothing, so I joined Green at the crossroads to wait for the bus. It was dark when we reached Aire. My orders were to go to the Town Major's Office[3] and to ask him for a billet. I entered his clerk's room cold and stiff, wet to the skin, unshaved and incredibly dirty, my clothes caked with mud.

As I was talking to his clerk, the Town Major, a bright-eyed and fresh-looking man of about sixty-five, evidently a retired officer, came out of his room.

'What is it you want?' said he, in a kindly tone of voice, casting his glance over my servant and me, and turning towards my kit and his rifle.

'I have been told to report to you for a billet, sir,' I replied. 'I am attending a course in Co-operation ...'

'Oh yes, I know all about that, What's your name?'

I told him.

'Where have you come from?'

'From Givenchy, sir ... I'm sorry I'm in such a mess, but I had to come straight down here from the line, and I have had no time to change.'

'Givenchy ... a bad place, especially in this weather.' He turned to his clerk and said:

'Send this officer to Number 11 in the Rue ... (I have forgotten its name) ... that's a good billet, isn't it?'

'Yes, sir, but Colonel Brown is going there,' said his clerk.

'Colonel Brown can go somewhere else – this gentleman has come straight from the trenches, and the infantry get the best billets in my town,' replied the Town Major.

To many people this will seem so obviously what ought to have happened that to call it a kind action would be an unnecessary underlining of one event in the daily routine of a Town Major's life, barely distinguishable from its neighbours in time. But the practice of war is the pursuit of a straight road, the search for an even way of mechanical progress that avoids a descent into cruelty as carefully as it forbears to rise into kindness; the aim is rather to decline battle with the feelings by confining thought to the impersonal aspect of every situation. It is so much easier at the moment to deal with units than to acknowledge the man inside the uniform. No word came oftener to the lips than 'men', as one would say, 'Send three men to Sap B, and tell them to hold it at all cost. They must throw two bombs for every one that comes over.' A 'man', in this usage, was no more than the temporary overseer of a weapon of destruction, the indispensible, but imperfect, servant of a potential gas asleep in a powder. Man, to a Town Major, was the envelope of a ration of food, the tenant of a bed. In this way, and in no other, lay sanity, for no man could escape madness who turned the impersonal and desiccated 'man' into a living creature with body to kill and soul to hurt. So it came that when the formula broke down, and an elderly man living in comfort in Aire saw before him a youth bearing on his body the outward marks of hardship and discomfort, and in his eye that dullness brought by danger and strain and lack of sleep, a mute and unformed protest took refuge in a kindly deed, long forgotten by the doer, but remembered by me to this distant day.

It was dark, and still raining, when I walked across the Grande Place, pursued by a memory of an earlier visit to this little town. So much had passed, so many events had stubbornly refused to pass, indenting for themselves a permanent depression in the roundness of the mind, that when my servant asked me if I had ever been to Aire before this visit, I thought that a 'No; would have rung as true as a 'Yes'.

'Yes, Green, I came here once, when we were billeted in Warne, to fetch some cakes for the Colonel's mess. I rode here on the water-cart horse, the first time I saw Aire, and the first time that I rode a horse ... No more war for four days, anyway, and by the time we finish here the battalion ought to be out of trenches and in rest billets, so we might have twelve days of comfort and civilisation.'

'Any chance of leave, sir?' said Green.

'None at all, as far as I can see – the married men with children are getting the first whack at the vacancies, so I hear.'

We halted at the door of a well-groomed town house standing obscurely in a cobbled street leading nowhere, and I rang the bell. I explained to Madame that I was billeted with her, and gave her a chit from the Town Major to warrant my presence. Through the open door I could see that the house was well furnished, with a look of polished cleanliness that put me to shame to think that man could be so dirty and tiles so clean. She was a woman of sixty, with a sad, quiet face and a gentle voice, and I felt at once that I must do something to atone for my condition. It was so obvious that her life was a battle against dirt, in which she triumphed, and that I was a loser in a similar conflict. I would not enter until I had scraped off my boots and my waterproof all that could be removed of that grey clinging mud of the Low Country, while she stood waiting in the hall, a still black figure against the dimly lit background.

'There is a room at the back where your servant can place your luggage until you require it,' said Madame, and Green passed through into some remote back-kitchen that I never visited, taking with him our dirty gear.

'Would Monsieur like to see his room? It is all ready, and there is a bathroom.'

'Could I have a bath, Madame?'

'Certainly, if your servant will carry up the hot water.'

'I'll look at my room, but I won't go into it until I have had a bath and changed my clothes.'

As we talked we went upstairs, and I saw a carpeted bedroom, with a four-poster bed, and linen so white that it seemed unreal. A carpet and a bed – the ordinary things of life, but not of the life of an infantry officer in France. W were invariably billeted in cottages and farmhouses, where the bedrooms had red-tiled floors and white-washed walls. I had spent five months in France, but this was the first time I had seen a carpet on the floor, and it was many months before I saw another. I thanked Madame, and in the simple words of a man stating the obvious I said how pleased and fortunate I was. Had she a bedroom for my servant? Yes, there was a room he could have, so we were both to revel in comfort.

I went to the bathroom and smoked a cigarette while I took off my dirty clothes and plied them in a corner. Half an hour later I was shaved and clean and hungry, and when I came downstairs I was invited to drink a glass of wine with Madame, while we discussed the war, the dearness of food, and the difficulty of getting meat. By this time Givenchy was far away, and I felt a man again; war had receded into a background of unreality, not to be revived until, a little later, on leaving the house to search for an hotel at which to dine, I could see in the sky the flickering glow of gun-flashes away in the east, bringing with it the thought of some poor devils standing in the mud and waiting.

A good dinner – for so it seemed – a bottle of wine shared with another infantry officer from the Bantam Division whom I had already met in the line, and early to bed. The poet who sang of the 'rough male kiss of blankets'[4] had strayed in his choice of emphasis, I felt, as I turned down the linen sheets and glided into their cool, clean embrace.

The four days that followed were spent in eating and sleeping, rioting in the glory of bearing no responsibility for anybody's actions but my own. Between meals I sat meekly at the back of a long room, where learned Artillery Colonels dwelt upon the possibilities of co-operation between artillery and infantry, while peevish Brigadiers and Colonels of infantry complained of the shortcomings of their own artillery. What artillery ever succeeded in pleasing the infantry? Either the artillery was too active, bringing retaliation upon the infantry, or it was too lethargic, inflicting no hurt upon the enemy infantry. I listened and made a few notes of matters mostly beyond my comprehension, knowing full well that nothing different would happen, however much we talked. My friend from the Bantam Division and I were the only junior officers present, and as was fitting, we kept silence, concealing our ignorance of the possibilities of artillery, and only revealing by an occasional mutual glance that we knew of its actualities.

I discovered the Town Major's name, and remembered that some friends of mine knew him well, so I called upon him and made known this common friendship. He was interested and pleased, and he invited me to dine with him at his mess. I do not remember much about the dinner, save that it was a quiet, gentlemanly and pleasant affair. It seemed to be another link with sanity, free from any fever of war, and free from any attempt to forget war; without aiming at distraction, it succeeded in giving a slight but noticeable deflection to the course of one's mind. I have forgotten what we talked about, but there remains this memory of a quiet precision of happenings from soup to the cheese, a sense of order prevailing in this one room, as if the neatness of the dinner were a symbol of a well ordered life. As a Town Major of a town not occupied by the headquarters of any high formation, he was all but omnipotent. Traces of the old Spanish occupation of the Lowlands were still visible in the buildings that framed the Grande Place, and traces of my host's love of order and his tidiness of mind were now to be seen in the carefully erected signboards, direction posts, and billet numbers; one military occupation superimposed upon another, at an interval of some centuries.

One morning as I was shaving, I scraped my chin too closely for comfort, and after breakfast I went in search of some cream to rub into my skin. There was never any difficulty in buying toilet accessories – not a village but you could buy brilliantine, shaving cream, razor blades, and tinctures of every colour and smell. The British Army must have consumed some thousands of tons of these commodities. I paid a franc or two for a pot of cream – I remember even now that it was a white china pot, that it was made by Roger et Gallet[5], and that it was called 'Crême Vera Violette'. Why this unimportant detail should remain in memory I cannot guess. I used it at once, but it was very highly scented, and it found its way into some corner of my kit-bag. There it stayed for some weeks until, when I was home on leave, my wife found the pot and seized it, counting it a great treasure not to be had in England in those days.

On my last day in Aire I said goodbye to Madame and went to the Town Major's office to discover where my battalion was to be found. It was out of the line, and at a little hamlet called Hingette. I found my way there, looking forward eagerly to finding a batch of letters, for I had had none in Aire, and it seemed a long time since I had heard from Wyn. On a warm and sunny spring day I reached the hamlet of Hingette, nestling in a spread of green meadows at the foot of a little hill, peaceful, and half hiding behind its poplars and fruit trees. I came to our company mess, in a clean and bare red-tiled room in a farmhouse, with its oilcloth-covered table and its rush-bottomed chairs. The officers were out, but on the mantelpiece I found several letters. I opened one from Wyn, to learn that her father was dead. To come back to a letter from her that was the nearest approach life held to coming home, and this was a sad homecoming. While I had revelled in four days of ease and rest, counting every moment of pleasure into a fund of profit against whatever losses the future might bring, she had borne days of grief, added to the daily burden of anxiety about me. All that I had won seemed lost at a blow, my comfort and content now stood as treason while she walked in the shadows and my letters from Aire, full of my own good fortune, were struck out of tune.

My next step was clear enough to me, and my immediate task was to persuade my superior officers to my way of seeing. I went to report to the Colonel, and found him at tea. After I told him what had happened, I asked him if he would support my application for leave. I was already due for leave, but there were more candidates than vacancies. He was sympathetic, and told me to apply, warning me that it would be many days before I could expect to hear the result.

On the next day we moved to Estaires, where we slept the night, and in the morning we moved nearer the line, but not into it. We did not go into the trenches again until five days had passed, and then we found ourselves making a quiet and uneventful journey into a moderately peaceful sector not far from Laventie. Our misfortunes began the next day: the rain came down so heavily and steadily that the side of our trench fell in. We were still in breastworks,[6] and the soil was so wet and marshy that digging was impossible. We

Diagram of trench construction showing breastworks, from the General Staff pamphlet 'British Trench Warfare 1917–1918'.

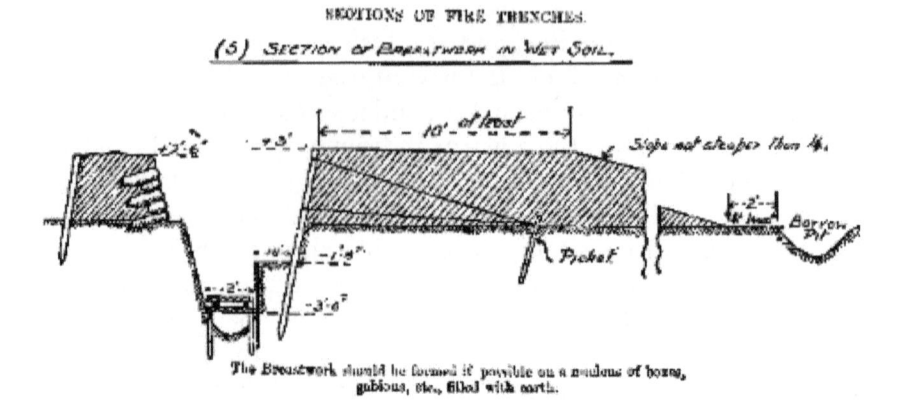

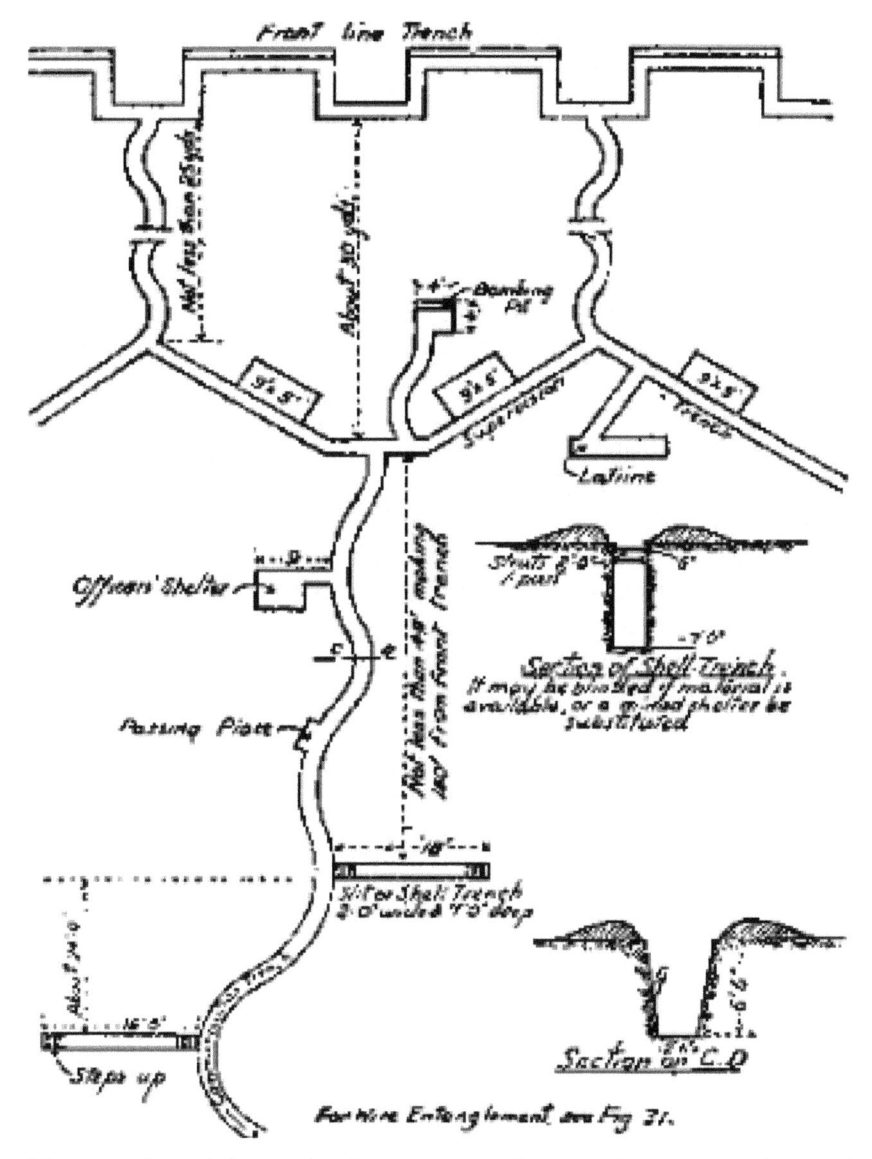

Diagram of trench layout showing communications trenches, traverses, bays and dugouts, from the General Staff pamphlet 'British Trench Warfare 1917–1918'.

lived behind a wall of sandbags filled with mud, with practically no protection from fire or water. Our rampart was not even bulletproof, and there was not one dug-out that could have withstood a light shell or a heavy shower of rain.

There was no lateral buildings of bays to localize the effect of a shell, and there was no parados at our backs. But there was water and mud in plenty, and as the rain fell continuously, the old and rotten sandbags burst, and all hands had to set to to rebuild the walls.

Unless the rain stopped, we were faced with four days of being wet through, and the rain did not stop. One subaltern of my company was ordered to join the Divisional Machine-Gun Company, another was wounded, so there were two fewer to walk the deck during the watches. The burden fell heavily on the survivors, and I was more or less continuously on duty. We had our share of excitement, for at seven o'clock in the morning, the enemy blew up a mine; the earth rocked, and all the artillery within reach started firing.

May 1916

Beyond the obvious fact that a mine had been sprung, there was no knowledge of what had happened, but there is an automatic response to all such challenges. I was strolling along the trench towards the dug-out where we ate and slept, wondering how soon breakfast would be ready. The men had been told to stand down and cook their food. 'Stand-to,' I yelled, and told them to pass the message up the line while I hurried down towards the evil spot; sergeants and corporals dashed away to see their sections, and the company sergeant-major joined me in my rush. It is never pleasant to run towards trouble, but to run into it is worse. Bullets from an enemy machinegun were ripping the air overhead, sweeping the line of the parapet to catch any heads that stood above it. Shells were bursting in plenty, but as far as I could see, they were doing little damage inside the trench. So we went on, giving a word or two of encouragement as we passed, but dreading all the time to find our progress stopped by a break in the line round the next bay. Soon after passing through the centre of the bombardment we came to the end of my company's sector, thankful that whatever had happened elsewhere, my line was not broken. There I found an officer of the next company and learnt that no damage had been done to his trench. A hurried glance over the parapet showed us the crater of the new mine. The enemy had misjudged the distance, and the crater was in No Man's Land, near an old one in our possession, instead of in our line. Two men had been wounded by shellfire, but not seriously, and as I passed them they made no attempt to disguise their glee at a prospect of a respite from war.

Givenchy

And so to breakfast, on our fourth day in the line. It was still raining, the walls were still falling in, and the water in the trench ran up to the knee. To move about was to wade through a grey-brown soup, feeling with the feet for the duckboards. To miss a duckboard was to dip into another eighteen inches of water. As you walked, your mackintosh trailed behind you and tapped against the corners of the bays; feet and clothes felt heavy, as if they did not belong to you. Another grey day went by, fading slowly into a greyer twilight logged with rain, without a gleam in the sky. About half-past five I was standing, looking towards the western sky and thinking of tea-time in England, an unfailing source of escape from the troubles of the moment, but bringing with it the sharp-toothed pain of longing.

A signaller came up to tell me that my leave had been granted, and that I was to go down at once to battalion headquarters to get my warrant for the journey. As I write them now, the words sound dull and ordinary, but in that wet and gloomy twilight they were highly charged. I hurried back to the company dug-out, rang up the adjutant, and he confirmed this message from another world. He did not know when the train left La Gorgue that evening, but he thought that it went early, so there was no time to dawdle.

I summoned the senior subaltern and handed over my command, making no attempt to disguise my hurry. My washing tackle was in a haversack in a corner of the dug-out; I picked it up, took off my revolver and handed it to my servant, and said goodbye to my company officers. I set off down the long, winding communication trench, down the road to England, as I said to myself. Although my feet were on duckboards, awash with water, my heart was already at home, and life had changed direction. In a few minutes there came a sudden reminder that my heart was too far in advance of my body, for the enemy started shelling the communication trench, thinking no doubt that ration parties would be on their way to the line. I confess that I was seized with panic – to be killed or wounded now, of all times, on my way home to Wyn! I ran, and as I ran I remember hoping that I would meet no one, for how could such an unmilitary progress be justified to the beholder? In my haste I turned too sharply round a corner, missed my footing on the duckboards, and fell into a pool of muddy water up to my waist. As I was already wet to the skin, this misadventure could not be said to worsen my condition, but it annoyed me intensely at the time, and I walked more warily. What if I slipped again and broke my leg?

I reached battalion headquarters and was given my yellow ticket. I had grace enough to thank the Colonel for his kindness, but I grudged every second that stood between me and that train. My mind was obsessed and my judgement warped: every shell that fell within two hundred yards drove terror into me. In my madness I felt sure that the enemy had concentrated the whole purpose of war into one determined attempt to break this journey of mine. War suddenly became real to me, and I was fighting an evil power. I did not dare to let my mind dwell on the prospect before me lest my thinking be made a challenge, to be answered by a sudden extinction. Every hazard was magnified into a valley of death. Reason did not triumph fully over this mad racing panic in my brain until I reached the high road, and saw in the groups of men setting about their tasks in a rational and unhurried way, a sign of comfort. They considered themselves to be in safety, so why not I?

Soon I reached houses not yet levelled with the ground, and I met transport going up towards the line with rations for the next day – none for me, praise God!

Then I passed an *estaminet*, and through the open door I could see groups of men talking and laughing. Poor devils, thought I, to find comfort in such trivialities, while I was treading the high road to England. I felt tired and hungry, but I did not dare to stop: it was past seven o'clock, and I could not bear to think of missing that train. I had no clothes for England, I was wet, dirty and unshaved; my shirt and vest were wet, and though I was warm with walking and excitement, I knew that I should be cold later on. Should I try to find the battalion transport lines and change my clothes? No – I might miss the train.

I must have walked eight miles before I reached the station at La Gorgue. My clothes felt heavy, and even leave sank before a dull sense of hunger and fatigue. It was eight o'clock when I walked into the Railway Transport Officer's office and asked his clerk at what time the leave train left for Boulogne.

'The leave train is cancelled,' said he. I cannot describe the next moment, but my clothes suddenly became heavier and I more tired and hungry. I was about to turn away when he said:

'There is an empty supply train going down to Boulogne at nine o'clock ... you can go in that if you like. It's only cattle trucks, and I don't know how long it will be on the journey. Go and tell the guard if you are going in it.'

'Is there a telegraph office anywhere near?' I asked. 'I want to send a wire to England.'

He told me where to find one, and I wired to Wyn to tell her to meet me at an hotel in London the next day. I was about to leave the station to search for a meal when I thought it would be better to interview the guard. He was a French civilian, and when I asked him how long it would be before his train started, he told me it was going to start that very minute. I climbed into an empty cattle truck and congratulated myself on my narrow escape; that train was worth more to me than any meal. He was wrong of course; it was nearly nine o'clock before we started. I walked up and down inside the truck trying to keep warm. It had stopped raining, and the sky was clear. The guard said that he thought it was going to freeze, but I did not believe him. If he was wrong about the time of our starting, he was right about the weather.

We started the longest journey I have ever known. We stopped at every signal and at every level crossing, but never at a station. I got tired of trying to keep warm and sat down in a corner of the truck, searching my pockets for chocolate, but none was to be found. There was nothing to do but smoke, and that soon palls on an empty stomach. I tried to sleep, but failed; I was too cold. We stopped and shunted, and started again, but never stopped at a station. About three o'clock in the morning my legs and feet began to get numb, while the rest of my body shivered, and I was desperately hungry and tired. It was freezing hard. I found that I could not move my legs – they did not belong to me. At one of our wayside halts I heard the guard passing my truck, so I hailed him. Were we far from Boulogne, or was it possible to stop at a station where we could find an *estaminet*? We were far from Boulogne, and there was no hope of an *estaminet*.

I told him that I had come straight down from the line after four days and nights of rain, that I had not a dry garment on me, and that I had had nothing to eat or drink since four o'clock the previous afternoon. I was afraid that my feet were becoming frost-bitten. He told me to wait a minute – he would be back soon. He returned, carrying a small box and his lantern, entered the truck and told me to take off my wet mackintosh and wrap it round my legs. Between my feet he put his lamp, and told me to sit still without moving until he came back.

In a few minutes the hot air from the lamp began to warm my legs, and I was soon in an agony of pain brought on by the returning circulation. In ten minutes I was comfortably warm and in my right mind, saved from frostbite, pneumonia, and many other evils, thanks to the kind ingenuity of my friendly guard. When I had thanked him, I suggested that if he would persuade the engine driver to stop at a station with an *estaminet* as soon as it was light, we might drink a cup of coffee at my expense. Soon after dawn we drew up at a small station, walked to the door of a café, and hammered at it till a sleepy head peered through a bedroom window to ask what we wanted.

'An English officer in danger of frostbite – come down and make us a cup of coffee.'

'But there is no fire!'

'Come and light it.'

Soon the door opened, and we walked into a musty room; a handful of straw in the stove, some wood, and the coffee pot was put on the fire. I called for some cognac, and the guard, driver, fireman, the landlord and I drank lukewarm coffee, with no sugar, but with plenty of cognac, in the early frost-bound dawn. Life seemed more under control, and the strong coffee dulled the sense of hunger: leave became a reality once more, and when we reached Boulogne at seven in the morning, the cold and discomfort of the ten-hour journey passed into the limbo of war.

I walked across the railway lines to the officers' club on the quay, washed and shaved, and ate an enormous breakfast. I tried to remove the signs of my slavery, but the mud was drying into my clothes, and the sum total of my exertion was merely to turn my khaki into a yellowish field grey. There was no help for it; I must wait until my mackintosh and breeches were thoroughly dry. My leave had begun, and I abandoned myself to a luxurious effort to catch every second of it, and to stamp every passing hour with an unmistakeable mark of its difference. In the heart a deep pedal note of joy, sustaining all passing moods of semi-anxiety; would Wyn get my wire in time to allow her to reach London tonight – would I be recalled from leave – was it possible that all sailings might be suspended and all ranks returned to their units? These were merely wisps of mist passing between me and the sun. There was no real and lasting challenge to the deep-laid melody of joy racing through my blood; today, indeed, Heaven lay before me.

Givenchy

I walked through the streets of Boulogne, finding a pleasure in its noise and bustle, in its shops, and in the rubbing of shoulders with people who went home to dinner and who wore slippers of an evening. War was no longer a pre-occupation, it was a disease from which I had recovered. Not even the sad significance of the universal black could penetrate my armour of content;[7] nothing could 'dim the mirror of my joy' that day. I wandered from shop window to shop window, seeking some little present for Wyn, deferring choice from sheer delight in the choosing, until it became a matter of necessity to decide unless I were to reach England empty-handed. I bought a bottle of eau-de-Cologne, finding something of a pleasing symbolism in its fragrance.

Shortly after, I shouldered my haversack and walked down the quay to the boat, forming one of a glad procession, strode up the gangway and went on deck. I met no-one I knew, but I did not feel any need of company – who could be lonely on his way home? I leant over the rails and watched the others crowding round the gangway, the soldiers struggling with kit and rifle, and I noticed one soldier carrying two rifles, one German. He was arguing with a sergeant at the foot of the gangway, protesting against the firm order that the German rifle must be left behind. It was a 'souvenir' that he had carried many miles. A Brigadier-General was leaning over the bulwarks and listening to the argument; for the moment it looked as if the soldier's obstinacy would cost him his leave. The General called out gaily, 'Tommy, hand me that rifle.' The soldier stepped to the quayside and handed the German rifle to the Brigadier. 'Go back to your place and get on to the boat.' The soldier saluted and went back to the foot of the gangway, and came aboard without further ado. As he stepped on deck the General hailed him and gave him back his rifle. 'Look out for me when we come alongside at Folkestone and I'll take it ashore for you.' 'Thank you very much, sir,' said the soldier, as he went away beaming.

It seemed as if we would never sail, but sail we did. As we neared Folkestone, England came in sight, and I realized why poets have sung of those white cliffs; years of my life had slipped away for ever in the five months I had spent in France, and I saw a new country; the train carried us past orchards in blossom; hedges had taken on a new beauty after my sojourn in the pollarded fens of Flanders. The country sang of peace, and every moment was bringing me nearer to Wyn; it would be strange if that journey were not stamped indelibly on my memory. It has now sunk deeper than memory; it has become a part of my being and of my way of thinking.

I reached London at eight o'clock in the evening. For a moment or two I stood outside Victoria station, watching the traffic and drinking in to the full the queer sensation of hearing English spoken by everybody, finding it strange that the inevitable should suddenly be the unexpected. I was in Victoria Street again, where, less than two years ago, I spent my days in a calm and uneventful way of life; I had nothing but memory to warrant my being the same person, and the sharp and bitter discontinuity of war had somehow weakened the belief in this truth. In all that mattered, I was not the same person, a different way of thinking and of feeling had overwhelmed the traces of the old life. The past had become an ancient monument, buried deep, and covered from the mind's eye by the mud of the Low Country. Were my present self to dig in this deposit, it would doubtless discover the remains of the life gone by, but the effort did not seem worth while; better to look forward from the hilltop on which I now stood than to seek the lowlands of 1914, so far away they seemed.

I turned into the hotel and enquired if Wyn had arrived: she had not reached the hotel, so I engaged a room and went upstairs. I called the chambermaid, showed her my clothes, and asked her if she could buy me a new shirt and a pair of socks while I had a bath.

'Givenchy – a dug-out and a big mine crater' by David Jones. [RWF Museum Trustees]

In twenty minutes I was clean, and reluctant to put on dirty clothes, so I got into bed and rang the bell. She had not succeeded in finding a shirt, but she gave me a pair of socks she had just finished knitting; I thanked her, and made a note of the number of the room, vowing that if I came back on leave again I would bring her a bottle of eau-de-Cologne to mark my gratitude. Many months after I fulfilled my vow. There was nothing to do but to dress again, and I went down to the lounge to wait for Wyn. Nine o'clock, ten o'clock, passed with no sign of her coming, and I was getting anxious, but at half-past ten she came in through the swing door, with shining eyes, looking pale and slight in her new black clothes. And so, with this meeting, I had reached my 'journey's end'.[8]

Notes

1. In many sectors of the line, an attitude of live-and-let live prevailed, especially where the trenches were very close together. Often, messages would be passed between the protagonists – sometimes by inert rifle-grenades, sometimes by voice – arranging for mutual toleration and inertia. In other areas it was a matter of policy by battalion and formation commanders to dominate No Man's Land or to make every effort to gain the initiative through aggressive behaviour. See the detailed explanation in Tony Ashworth *Trench Warfare 1914–1918: The Live and Let Live System* (London, 2000).
2. The map reference of the crossroads.
3. The Town Major was an officer – not necessarily a major – responsible for administration, route signing, traffic control, discipline and billeting arrangements in towns and villages behind the lines.
4. This line is from Rupert Brooke's poem *The Great Lover*, written in 1914.
5. The business was founded in 1806 in the Rue Sainte-Honoré in Paris, from where it served not only the Emperor Napoleon, but also many of the Royal houses of Europe. Roger et Gallet marketed the first round bath soap in 1879. The company is still trading today.
6. Breastworks were the first stage of fortification above ground in wet soil, as the diagram shows.
7. Wyn Griffith refers to the mourning clothes and black drapes which were evidence of the high casualty rate being borne by the French Army. The Battle of Verdun was at its height at this point in 1916.
8. Possibly a reference to the play of that name by R.C. Sherriff, first performed on 9 December 1928.

Chapter 4

Mud

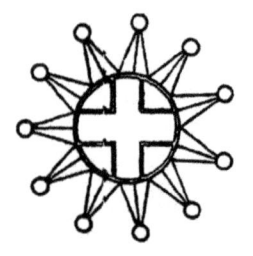

The badge of XI Corps

It was on the 5th May, 1916, that this ten days of delight was destined to end. Our last evening together we spent at some theatre; I have forgotten what we saw, but it is easy enough, even after this long interval of time, to remember the insidious growth of the canker of sadness, and to capture once again the struggle to turn the mind away from the morrow. Six months had passed since we sat in Winchester, on the eve of my first sailing overseas, oppressed by the same burden, and making the same effort to cast it off. Love grows rapidly in the forcing-house of war, and the dull ache of absence fosters a sensitivity and quickens response. The poets have taught us that to mortals endowed with their own delicacy of emotional structure, parting can become an agony of a death, but war, with its rude barbarian violence, had made even of us ordinary creatures, a regiment of sufferers. Common clay as we were, and far enough removed as we thought ourselves from the spun glass of the poet's imagining, we found ourselves betrayed into the very emotions they had sung. That the prose of war should prove the truth of poetry's tale of man's feeling – that it should now be easy to believe that some of those magic lines were indeed a reflection of the real thoughts of real men and women – that was an astonishing discovery. I had read a quantity of poetry, and had even tried to write it, but all with a sense of projecting my personality into an adjacent field of life. Here and now I was treading, at some remove, the very paths the poets had walked before me.

Shortly before eight o'clock in the morning the boat train steamed out of Victoria station, leaving Wyn standing on the platform, one of many women fighting each a lonely battle against a distant peril. Some were to know defeat, others triumph, but none was to escape the rack of doubt and suspense. I cannot tell her tale of that day; the return to an empty room, the quiet packing of a bag, and the cruel sight of other women looking into their husbands' eyes. I saw no beauty in the Kentish orchards that had delighted my eyes but ten days ago, and the flowering hedges were a mockery. If I survived the dangers of war I might once again come home on leave, but many months would have to pass. The 'life' of an infantry officer at the front in those days was very short; it worked out to a mathematical average of a few weeks, fatal or non-fatal wounds came quickly to a junior officer in a line regiment. I had seen many men come and go, and there was little comfort in the prospect before me. There were many officers on the train who were obviously better placed than I – some wonderful difference had raised them to the Staff, but I could see no endowment of mine that could ever serve to take me across the gap that divided the brains of the army from its brawn. My lot was pitched in the mud, and the less I longed for the fleshpots, the better would I be able to eat my bully beef and tinned jam. I had met but few of these higher creatures, nor had I tested their metal, so that it was easy to hold to a belief that my path would never cross their orbit of revolution round that mysterious centre where war was governed. Thus I thought at the time, but destiny was to take me into their midst and to make me one of them, after a close and painful realizing of their human limitations.

5 May 1916

On my way home to England, company was a superfluity, and now, on my journey back to France, it would have been an insult to the memory of the wistful glance that followed me overseas. I would go short of many things precious to have and to hold, but I had triumphed over war for ten days. Neither time nor turmoil could deprive me of such riches, garnered and housed, and for ever incorruptible within me. I held the 'perfect sum of all delight'.

In a waking dream I reached Boulogne and unhurriedly searched for my train, almost praying that it had gone. If I had failed to see beauty walking the fields of England that morning, there was little danger of the eye meeting pleasure in France. At ten o'clock I was at the railhead in Merville, and there I spent the night; I had no great desire to remember the journey, and I have forgotten where I slept. My mind was far away. Next morning I walked towards the line in search of my battalion, hoping to find it in reserve; anywhere but in the trenches. I met the transport officer who told me that we were in the trenches in front of Laventie, and that I had arrived just in time for a 'show' that very night. I had come down to earth with a thud, and I was seized with a wild rebellious fear. 'What a plague have I to do with a buffjerkin?' cried Falstaff, and so thought I. It was at such times as this that I pondered grimly on the strange fever that drove me to wrest from an unwilling Government Department permission to enlist in the army.

If any man says that he went into the trenches with indifference, you may brand him a liar. I hated the journey always, but never more than now. Coming straight from the ways of peace, it seemed that I had more to lose, for the deadening power of months of trench habit had been lifted from my mind, leaving my fibre bare to the weakest blast of war. I skulked along a quiet road leading to a few cottages still occupied by peasants, and there I met one of our company commanders.[1] From him I heard the full tale of the coming night. The Corps Commander[2] had decided that German prisoners must be taken, to identify the opposing forces in the sector. The Divisional Commander[3] had selected our brigade for the venture, and the mantle had fallen on him to lead the assaulting party. Men had been picked from the various companies, and a band of adventurers had been kept back from the line to rehearse their assault over a piece of marked ground. My part in the performance was limited. Just before the time fixed for the raid, the whole party would assemble in my company sector. Between the fall of dark and the striking of the hour, I had to see that 'lanes' were cut in our own barbed wire through which the raiders might pass. Our artillery would put down a barrage on the enemy trenches opposite me, to drive the Germans underground and to silence their machine guns. Their task done, the raiding party would dash back to my trenches and then down the communication trench to Battalion Headquarters, leaving me to bear the concentrated fire of the German artillery in the inevitable

Mud

counter-barrage and retaliation. Simple enough, but I wished that someone else were to play the host that night.

My mental equilibrium thoroughly upset by the prospect of a night of excitement, I took the road once again, steadily descending the scale of civilization from inhabited cottages to isolated ruins, now largely concealed by the budding foliage of May. Soon I came to a straight arrow of road, to all appearances untrodden by man, and all but conquered by the grass advancing from its verges; I had passed the eastern limit of transport, and, in sudden obedience to the bidding of caution I edged to the side of the road. Although I had not walked this way before, I knew well enough that my path would sink in a visible degradation from high road to ditch, and from ditch to an inconspicuous entrance into a communication trench. So it happened. In a few seconds my foot was on a duckboard, on my right hand and left a wall of sandbags, and as the duckboards swung to my tread there rose the unforgettable smell of Flanders mud. It struck chill into the heart, even on this sunny afternoon in late spring. Here and there a shell burst, with a black cloud in the blue sky to remain as a hideous sign of its menace. Sound, sight and smell were all challenged at once, and they must in concert submit to the degrading slavery of war, chained to a ridiculous chariot heading for utter destruction. Sense and soul were of no account; such ballast might have held the world to a course less futile, but in this mad runaway we had cast sanity to the winds. If ever war was meaningless, it was on this sunny afternoon in May, as I walked slowly on my winding way towards the line. Unheated by recent danger, untired by loss of sleep, judgment was keener and vision was normal; now, as never before, the unrelieved stupidity of this way of manifesting one nation's protest against another filled the mind. War's cruelty, its hideousness and its powers of destruction were today overshadowed by its irredeemable idiocy.

7 May 1916

Sullen in mood, with a dull dragging at heart, I reached the front line trench and walked along until I came to the company headquarters' dug-out. In a mechanical way I noticed that the sector was reasonably dry, and that the dug-out was better than the one I had left twelve days ago. I dipped my head, pushed in, and sat down at a table and greeted the officers. Ten minutes passed in exchanging gossip of the line and of London, then tea was brought in. Enamel plates, enamel cups, knives of every pedigree, and the same enamel teapot pouring the same acid tea; a tin of milk, slabs of close-knitted bread, and a tin of nondescript jam. There was little joy in body or mind at the sight of this first meal in the trenches. Within a short twenty-four hours I would succumb to the dull routine of life and would find in any meal a pleasant break, but at the moment I was too lately returned from England, where tea-time brought quiet intimacies by the fireside.

My second in command handed over the copy of battalion orders, and I drove my mind back to the business of the day.

'Have you sent off the situation report?' I asked.

'Yes, it went off an hour ago.'

'What was it?'

'Situation normal, wind south-west.'

I laughed. Those two phrases had become current coin in our intercourse with Battalion Headquarters and had, through long usage, acquired a certain momentum. The odds were that whatever happened during the preceding twelve hours, when the signaller came to say that the situation report was due to go, one would say, automatically, 'Situation normal, wind south-west.' I have written it out before going to sleep, and given it to the signaller with orders to send it off in an hour's time. I have also known the adjutant to ring up indignantly and demand to speak to the officer commanding 'C' Company. 'You say the wind is south-west; 'B' Company on your right say that the wind is north-east. Which is right?'

'Oh, just alter mine to north-east – I expect they are right.'

In theory, the situation report was intended to convey in brief summary the events of the day or night, and the direction of the wind would indicate whether a gas attack was probable. An integration of these reports should acquaint a Divisional Commander with the current history of his command, but I found later in my career that they became fuller as the distance of the writer from the front increased. A touch of east in the wind would cause alarm and despondency in the various commands, and the quick downward communication of such a mood brought irritation to us in the line. Gas-helmets must be ready for immediate use; flannel bags they were in those days, and damnable to wear. To our minds this was sheer fussiness.

It grew dark, and it was time to begin cutting lanes in our wire in front of the point of departure of the raiding party. Our artillery had been engaged during the day in cutting the enemy's wire, lest he should have any doubt where we proposed to attack him. Had we cut the lanes in our wire the night before, the daylight would have underlined our intentions. Soon there began a trickle of men into the trench, with blackened faces and hands, carrying weird weapons.[4] They and the junior officers were shepherded into their proper places with much whispering and shuffling, while the tenants of the trench endeavoured to pursue their normal occupations and to make the normal noises. There was a sense of strain in all, half covered by a spurious excitement. In a desperate silence they climbed over the parapet, hurrying over that small skyline lest the firing of a 'light' pistol[5] should reveal their motion, and taking care that there was no jangling of their equipment. They formed up in a line in No Man's Land, crawling slowly towards the gaps in the enemy wire. Last of all, the officer in command took with him a field telephone on which he could buzz signals back to the artillery liaison officer in the front line.[6] After an eternity of waiting, a buzz announced that the reconnaissance of the wire proved it to be passable, another buzz told us that the party was assembled and ready for the assault. It drew near to the appointed hour, and the seconds dragged unendingly. Watches had been synchronized most carefully.[7]

Zero,[8] a buzz, and then a wild tornado of shellfire. They were off on their journey, inside this three-walled screen of flame. We knew only too well that before many seconds the enemy would add a fourth wall of fire to this screen, and that his wall would rest with its foundation in our trench, but for the moment there was only one orchestra in play. Various coloured lights were sent up from neighbouring sectors of the enemy trenches, and his machine guns were enfilading No Man's Land. We could, however, hear the bursting of bombs thrown by our men, and we took heart at the sound; they must now be in conflict hand to hand. Then we knew that the enemy artillery had started his barrage, and for the next ten minutes we knew little else. It did not seem possible that any of us could survive this thunderstorm of bursting shells, but strangely enough we suffered little. The barrages and the machine-gun fire died down to spasmodic outbursts, and our men began to trickle back to our line – some of them, for many never came back. We could get no coherent account of what had happened, but it was clear that their visit was not unexpected. Two officers did not return. Now began an anxious and laborious task; we sent our patrols to scour No Man's Land in search of our wounded and dead. The search lasted all night, with diminishing success, and during the following day we scanned through our peep-holes and periscopes for any sign of our men, but we found none.

When the varying accounts of the survivors were collated and the final count was made, it became evident that we had paid dearly for the assault – no prisoner, dead or alive, came into our hands. Sadness fell upon us all, officers and men, for there were many friends we would never see again, and the reaction from the excitement of the night brooded over the whispering groups, assessing the ultimate value of the enterprise and finding it not worth the cost.[9]

In the evening we heard a shout from No Man's Land, and I sent out a patrol to investigate: they brought back one of our men, slightly wounded, who had spent the long day waiting for the night, but he seemed little the worse for his exposure.

This epilogue ended, we turned again to our daily task of unending displacement of mud. We filled sandbags with it, piled them up into a wall, beat them into a firm rampart, there to remain until a shell-burst undid our efforts. Then our damaged wall would sag and drop, and our labour in lifting mud three or four feet above its original resting place was made waste.

All our elaborate rearrangement of mud – for our task was nothing more than this – was born to be defeated; our triumph over mud was short-lived and highly localized. Here and there we used hurdles, but hurdles had to be carried up long and winding communication trenches, and there are few burdens more difficult to handle. On a dark night, with feet slipping on the slime-covered duckboards. If ever a party of men struggled up towards the line carrying these unwieldy loads, it was doomed to meet a descending file of fellow-sufferers bearing some ungainly and unmanageable freight. As infantry we were but hewers and drawers in any matter concerning trench architecture. The Engineers were our masters, and wisdom would die with them. When we had laboured all night to build a wall of sandbags, and had rammed hard at the middle to conceal a bulge that threatened to reveal our lack of science, a wise sapper would in the morning tell us that here, of all places, common sense would have indicated a hurdle. If we tried to turn this lesson to advantage and used hurdles in our next building, it was with no surprise that we heard that hurdles were useless in such emergencies. Whatever we did was wrong, or at best, it merited no more than the condescending recognition that as amateurs we could not in reason be held accountable to the standards of the sappers. The Engineers were large employers of labour, and we were the labour; they were capitalists, with their enormous stores of material, and we were the proletariat who had to carry these stores on our backs. How could they be loved of the infantry?

I wrote some doggerel verse that gained a considerable notoriety at the time, as it was reprinted in one of the illustrated weekly papers – it reflected the mood of the day. Here is some of it:

> Sing a song of sandbags,
> Fill them up all day,
> Build them up at nightfall,
> At dawn they slide away.
> When the sapper sees them,
> He'll have a lot to say,
> 'Why didn't you use hurdles?'
> 'Oh ... run away and play!'[10]

Day followed day with little to mark the eve from the morrow. Fear, boredom, boredom, fear – we swung from one to the other, with a growing fatigue as we drew nearer to the night of relief, and our minds became as muddied as our clothes.

When anything happened to revive our attention, it formed a topic of long discussion and minute examination. One day a German deserter came into our line. He was surrounded by eager questioners, but he could speak no English, and none of us knew German. His pockets were searched hurriedly by the curious, and I arrived in time to see that no letters or papers of any military value were taken from him: a few mark notes and some cigarettes were treasure enough for my company. Someone gave him a biscuit, another a slice of bully beef, and in a few minutes he had more cigarettes than he could smoke in a day. 'You're a lucky blighter, Fritz, not 'arf you ain't,' was the burden of their song. He seemed to be puzzled at this cordiality in a language he did not understand, as if he had expected hard words and blows. I sent him under escort to battalion headquarters, and saw him no more, but for many days I heard critical discussions of his clothing and boots, ending in unanimous recognition of their superiority over ours. His boots were better than ours, better fitted for trench life, but I could see no great merit in his clothes. There was endless argument, and his coming was no less a service to us than a betterment of his own condition.

We were not without other visitors, but they generally brought trouble in their wake. Every day, and sometimes more than once a day, the Colonel[11] would inspect his battalion front.[12]

In these days his great preoccupation was the removal of tins. All tins were to be buried behind the line, and woe to the company commander if the General found an empty tin in a trench – he was damned for the day. When the news of his coming sped before him, corporals and sergeants forsook the superintending of military tasks for a wild drive of forgotten tins into a hasty burial in the mud beneath the duckboards. Great was the urgency of concealing such indecencies if peace were to reign during his visit. Fundamentally he was right in his struggle for sanitation, but to us it seemed as if this admittedly worthy enterprise were of secondary importance compared to the strengthening of our protection against shellfire. Any improvement in the parapet, or parados when it existed, was sure to gain approval, but there was a queer reluctance to encourage the building of better dug-outs for our comfort and our safety at times when more war was waged against us than we were waging.

It seemed to us that our superiors did not inwardly admit that comfort was desirable, or that any one should seek to be in a dug-out if the enemy were shelling the line. I may be wrong. The real reason may have been that we were short of supplies, and not that the true British spirit of waging war was to scorn any perfectioning of our present position because we would in a day or two, according to the theory, be driving the enemy out of his trenches. We lost an army corps of men through inadequate protection from shellfire, and from diseases brought on by unnecessary exposure, but as they would in all probability have been murdered on the Somme, it might have made little difference in the sum of things. The enemy took great trouble to build strong and comfortable shelters for his men, while we were content with hasty improvisations but rarely rain-proof.

On rare occasions we were 'at home' to more distinguished visitors. The Divisional Commander, Staff Officers of the Division and Corps would move quietly and quickly through our trench in the early morning. We knew them not, save by their red tabs and badges of rank, but they asked no awkward questions and were easily entertained. They did not seem to belong to our army. We noticed that they were circumspect in their choice of day and time for such a venture, and we envied them their short sojourn in our wilderness. The lines that follow were written on one such occasion, and I see now that they are but a reflection of the immemorial contempt of the infantry:

> There they go round the company front
> To see the poor devils that bear the brunt
> Of ev'ry strafe and trench mortar stunt,
> On a dull and misty morning.
>
> What if the Hun should see them come?
> They'd vanish as soon as my tot of rum,
> But well do they know that the guns are dumb
> On a dull and misty morning.

When our four days in the front line came to an end, we marched to excellent billets in a little village called Laventie. The houses had suffered, and here and there were blotches of destruction, but several of the inhabitants had remained to trade with the soldiers. We had beds, and a comfortable mess-room in a small house with a pretty garden at the back, possibly the very garden that tempted Wyndham Tennant to write the poem called *Home Thoughts from Laventie*.[13] The name of this village has a music of its own. We found kindness there, rest and cleanliness. Another battalion of my regiment was near us, though in the line, and I met my young brother many times.[14] He was a private soldier, happy and proud of his task as battalion orderly and messenger. We were separated by the ocean of rank and discipline, but whenever I saw him in Laventie I smuggled him into the house, gave him a bath and a change of underclothing, and a tremendous meal followed by a cup of coffee – great luxuries to him, and now a cherished memory to me of brightness carried into a young life doomed to end so quickly.

The month of May drew towards its end with little to differentiate one spell of trench duty from another, but during one of our periods of rest I was selected by the Brigade to carry out a billeting reconnaissance. This took me four days to do, and though I have forgotten what I did, I still remember the feeling of self-importance that filled me as I started out on the task. Could it be that I was destined to use my brain in the service of our campaign, instead of my legs and arms? I could not say, and I dared not hope, but after six months of the trenches I would count any other service freedom. Some men found work to do where no danger shadowed them, where mud was not their master, so why not I? This was an uneasy ferment to lie in the mind of a company commander in the infantry; better for him to be content with a parapet for a horizon, to keep his imagination grey as the soil around him, and to indulge in no longing to join the aristocracy of war. No captain of foot could hope to survive the war if he were tied to the trenches day in and day out. His hope of salvation lay in a disabling wound, or in selection for work elsewhere, before the length of his days came to a sudden end.

I wondered how I had escaped from death or disablement in spite of six months' service at the front, but optimism was checked by the thought that we had not yet taken part in an open battle. That would come soon enough, bringing with it a quick assessment of my fate. I hoped, with many others, that I might find myself chosen to play a part of greater significance and of less danger than our daily drudgery. But I had no grounds for my hoping. I buoyed myself up with the thought that if I proved faithful in a little thing, such as a billeting reconnaissance, I might find greatness thrust upon me some day.

Shortly afterwards the adjutant fell sick on the eve of our going into the trenches, and I was summoned by the Colonel to take up his duties during his absence. Another stirring up of the fancy, and I saw in it a sign and a portent. Set down in cold blood, my claims to recognition as a budding staff officer were matter for laughter. First, and most mirth-provoking, I had organized and carried out a Brigade cookery class: second, I had made a billeting reconnaissance for the Brigade: third, I was chosen by the colonel to replace the adjutant during the latter's absence. More metal than this was required to forge a staff officer! But I did not allow this to diminish my present joy in the work of a locum tenens. I took pride in adding every new experience to my equipment, and I learnt with some surprise that the amenities of life at Ebenezer Farm – the strange name of our battalion headquarters – were more pleasant than our reports had suggested. There was a tablecloth and crockery, and the meat was properly cooked. In the line our meat was fried to a uniform toughness, made palatable only by the sauce of our hunger.

Closer acquaintance with the Colonel ripened my respect for him: I saw him at his ease, writing letters to his wife, vexed because the post had brought him no letters from England, grumbling at the shortage of butter – I saw him as a man with other men. I heard him argue with the Brigade Major,[15] defending the battalion against some threatening calumny, and I learnt that his peace was as open to interruption as that of any company commander. It may be said that any man of imagination should have known this, even if he did spend his days in the mud, but I can only answer that we did not exercise our imagination beyond the boundaries of our small parish in the trenches. There may have been junior officers who studied the course of the war at large, but I was not of their number. There was evil enough on my company front to satisfy my curiosity, and a certain callousness would permit a man of ordinary humaneness to show no concern at the afflictions of his neighbour company. Now, however, I had to enlarge my mind to the conception of a battalion of four companies; education was being thrust upon me. I was soon to relapse to my parochialism, for the adjutant recovered and returned to duty, and I reverted to my old and narrow task. My second in command probably felt a similar shrinking in his world when he went back to his platoon on my coming. I found my company in reserve billets at Riez Bailleul. It is enough to say of this hamlet that we slept between sheets, and that it seemed pleasant to the feet to tread upon a hard road, free from the downward tug of mud. It was nearly eleven o'clock at night before the company was safely tucked away in the big barns. A hundred men are a hundred possibilities of error to a company commander: naked lights, lost equipment, tomorrow's programme, men to go away to attend courses, wiring parties for strong points behind the line, fuel for the cooker – these and a score of other matters are projected on to the screen of the mind as slides from some powerful lantern, demanding each its quota of time and attention from a tired brain. Tomorrow the pack of men will be reshuffled; zealous corporals will discover better dwelling places for their sections, and the farmer's wife will be protesting with vigour against some proposed encroachment upon a storing place reserved for farm use, quoting the 'Etat Major' and threatening us with the 'Maine',[16] but tonight there is no desire strong enough to conquer every man's craving for rest and sleep.

The Company Sergeant-Major[17] and I turned at last to the farmhouse and walked through the kitchen into the little room beyond. The shutters are drawn, and a hanging oil lamp throws a yellow light on the faded walls. The stained and hacked American cloth nailed down on the top of the three-legged wooden table looks bright and clean tonight, and the red tiled floor shows here and there a glow of colour between the piles of equipment, gas-helmets and raincoats thrown carelessly upon it. Enamelled cups on the table, and a half-finished bottle of whisky, letters and newspapers to show that the mail has arrived, two subalterns sitting astride rush-bottomed chairs with jackets unbuttoned and Sam Browne belts hanging over one shoulder, reading their letters and opening parcels, one of them young enough to be eating sweets at this time of night. The sergeant-major shuts the door leading to the kitchen, and we both sit down wearily.

In private life he is a London school teacher: tall and thin, with a firm mouth and a determined eye, untiring and unmovable. The war seems to hold no surprises for him, either good or bad, and it is as if its plan were revealed to him, leaving him powerless to do aught but to acquiesce in its slow unfolding. If two words sufficed to make clear his meaning, to add a third would be to court confusion, so his words were few. His face showed plainly his amused tolerance of the idiosyncrasies of impetuous or lethargic subalterns, and I felt that in his thinking there were but two men in the company not entirely bereft of common sense, and that I was the second. Our life thrust us close something out of the ordinary give-and-take of trench bombardment was afoot grew into conviction that an attack was in progress. As it began to grow dark I walked out along the road and saw the ripple of flashes in the eastern sky. Suddenly a bugle sounded the Alarm.

I ran back to the farmyard to find everybody tumbling into equipment and picking up rifles, while the non-commissioned officers hurried back and fro from the barn to the alarm-post, shepherding the men into order and calling over the rolls of their sections. There was so much to be done at the moment that there was little time to think. Had every man got his gas-helmet, his bandoliers of ammunition and his iron ration of food? Had the bombers bombs, and the Lewis Gun section their spare drums of ammunition? Who left that light burning in the barn? Parade by platoons on the road, two deep and well to the side. The cooker could follow later, with the transport ... the adjutant wants to speak to the company commander ...

Gradually order triumphed over the welter of things to be done, each more urgent than the other, and in less than fifteen minutes the company was on the road, ready to move, while at the door of

Mud

the farmhouse stood the civilian inhabitants, stolidly wondering why this moil had broken in upon their evening of coffee selling. The moon rose over the tall poplars, and the bark of a dog sounded sharply against the background of whispering in the ranks.

There was now time to think, and to speculate on the hundred possibilities of the night. To plod our way back to the trenches we left twenty-four hours ago, to lose three whole days of peace in this quiet hamlet, to form up in some half-derelict breastwork before launching a counter-attack – whatever else the night might bring, it could not fail to bring us these. Was this the beginning of a new German offensive, and were we to be thrown haphazardly into a torrent that could not carry us anywhere but to destruction? Why could not the men in the trenches hold their own? We had called upon no one while we held the gate ... devil take them! Not a man felt that this was his time to give another stroke for his country, nor that his road would lead him to help a hard-pressed comrade. Walking up and down in front of the double line of men, I could hear nothing but grumbling. The flashes were still rippling across the eastern sky. Some vowed that the disturbance was well to the south of our divisional sector, others were equally confident that the Duck's Bill crater was the centre of the struggle.

The Colonel arrived; his first words were lost in the noisy jumping to attention and shouldering of arms, but I gathered that the adjutant was still trying to find out why we were in this state of alarm.

'Have your Lewis Gun men got their spare drums and their ammunition?'

'Yes, sir.'

'I've just found out that the battalion's spare drums are empty. Empty, d'ye see? Dam' bad business, dam' bad. What's the name of that corporal?'

'Brown, sir.'

'Damned untidy fellow!'

'Are we to stay here till orders come, sir?'

'Yes, stay where you are, but send an orderly to battalion headquarters to bring any messages ... The men can stand easy ...'

An hour passed, while we waited impatiently for some sign, but none came. We grew cold and weary, and our equipment began to pull down our shoulders in spite of all the hitching up, we began to feel hungry, and eager discussion about the unpleasantness of our immediate future gave way before the rising tide of our present discomfort. Better anything than this endless waiting. Suddenly an orderly dismounted from his bicycle, saluted and blurted out, 'Colonel's orders, sir... breath and a quick swallow. Company is to stand down and go back to the billets. Parade tomorrow morning as usual.'

I turned round to the subalterns, gave the order to dismiss by platoons and walked away, back to the farmhouse. So this was the end of that eternity of waiting! We never found out exactly what happened to cast this stone into our quiet pool; all that we could glean was that a very heavy bombardment of our trenches had caused our commanders to see in it the prelude to a large scale attack. We had lost more than an evening's quiet: gone for ever was that sense of inviolable security that had hitherto brooded over our days of rest in reserve. The hand of war had left the trenches to pillage our bedroom, an outrage we found hard to forgive, a breaking of a gentleman's bargain. There were trenches, and there were rest billets, and the rhythmic alternation between one and the other had emphasized their difference into an absolute cleavage. The era of systematic and determined long range shelling had not yet begun, neither was there any aeroplane bombing of back areas, so that two or three miles were sufficient to separate war from peace. We

'Somewhere in the Festubert sub-sector', by David Jones. [RWF Trustees]

were to look back later upon these months of early 1916 as a time of peace, marked by a gentlemanly observance of the decencies of life at the front, when the western end of a communication trench was the beginning of the eastern outposts of civilization, but this night we went to sleep in an angry mood of resentment at such a disturbance of our privacy.

Notes

1. Captain Goronwy Owen, an original member of the battalion since its inception. Owen (1881–1963) joined the staff later in the war, was awarded the DSO in 1916 and rose to the rank of Lieutenant-Colonel. He was distantly related to Lloyd George by marriage, which may account for his rapid rise. After the war he had distinguished careers in both business and politics. He became the President of British Controlled Oilfields; and was Liberal MP for Caernarvonshire from 1923 to 1945.
2. The 38th (Welsh) Division was under the command of XI Corps. The Corps Commander was Lieutenant-General Sir Richard Cyril Byrne Haking GBE KCB DSO (1862–1945).
3. Major-General Sir Ivor Philipps KCB DSO (1861–1940) commanded the division from January 1915 until July 1916.
4. For close quarter fighting in trenches soldiers often carried weapons that looked remarkably medieval: knobkerries, spiked clubs, loaded canes and sharpened shovels were favourites. Pistols were also used and grenades were thrown to cover an entry or withdrawal – more indiscriminate uses would be as likely to inflict casualties on one's own side as on the enemy and would be unhelpful if prisoners were required. In one battalion of the Royal Welch Fusiliers, the Commanding Officer, Lord Howard de Walden, commissioned and paid for an issue of short, leaf-shaped, Welsh swords of the sort used by Welsh archers during the Hundred Years' War.
5. In the British Army this would have been the *Very* pistol, which fired a one-inch phosphorus cartridge giving a few seconds' illumination. Its equivalent in the German Army was the *Hebel* 1894 flare pistol. Uses included light signal, light parachute signal, star cluster signal, whistling shell signal, smoke signal, and eventually an explosive projectile. The flares burned for about seven seconds in the air and a further five seconds on the ground.
6. Before the introduction of tactical radios, this would mean that a signaller or more likely two would accompany him, reeling out communication cable from the front line to the telephone.
7. This was to ensure coordination between the supporting fire of machine guns, artillery or mortars and the action on the ground, again before the introduction of tactical radios simplified the problem.
8. Zero Hour, the time set for the operation to start, now called H Hour.
9. The divisional history, however, says that this was '... mentioned in General Headquarters' despatches as being the third best raid carried out so far by the British Army'. The Battalion War Diary records that '... the raid was carried

out at Laventie on the night of 7th May by a party of fifty, under Captain Goronwy Owen, with 2nd Lieutenants N[oel]. Osbourne Jones and [Herbert] Taggart in command of the right and left respectively ... The raiding party while in No-Man's Land came across an enemy wiring party just finishing their work. Captain Owen altered his plans on the spot and with his raiding party quietly followed the German party into their line and then set upon them. The enemy were taken by surprise and about sixty were killed or wounded whilst trying to get grenades out of a grenade store. The party lost four killed and died of wounds and ten wounded. Unfortunately 2nd Lieuts Osbourne Jones and Taggart were both killed and their bodies remained in the hands of the Germans. Capt. Owen received the DSO; Cpl D.W. Bloor, Ptes P.F. Witten and S. Heeson the DCM; Sgt G.P. Downes the MM, the latter award being posthumous.' Osbourne Jones (1895–1916) had been a founder member of the 15th Battalion; Taggart (1894–1916) had been attached from the 11th (Service) Battalion; both are listed in *Officers Died in the Great War* as killed in action on 8 May 1916.

10. The draft of this poem is in Wyn Griffith's Army Book 136, now in his personal papers at the National Library of Wales. It was later printed with some minor variations in the collection *Hiraeth*. Subsequently, Griffith also wrote and published *The Barren Tree And Other Poems*. (Penmark Press: Cardiff, nd [1947]), a small volume of fifteen powerful poems which are not all about Griffith's War experiences but *The Song is Theirs* follows the progress of the Great War ending at Mametz Wood.

11. Wyn Griffith means the Commanding Officer of the battalion, Lieutenant-Colonel R.C. Bell DSO, who had assumed command in November 1915. Richard Carmichael Bell (1868–?) had been commissioned into the South Staffords in 1887 and served with the Central India Horse from 1891 until, like many experienced Indian Army officers, volunteering for service on the Western Front in order to stiffen the amateur New Army divisions. He was awarded the DSO in the New Year's Honours, 1917.

12. Two descriptions follow, which appear in Wyn Griffith's later, 1917, diary and evidently apply first, to the then Commanding Officer, Lieutenant Colonel C.C. Norman. I have therefore removed it from this chapter and restored it to its original owner in a later chapter. The second describes the Brigade Commander and records an incident in trenches; I have likewise restored that to the correct date and place.

13. The poem was composed in March 1916 by Lieutenant the Hon Edward Wyndham Tennant of the 4th Battalion Grenadier Guards. Tennant was killed in September 1916, aged 19. The first stanza runs thus:

> Green gardens in Laventie!
> Soldiers only know the street
> Where the mud is churned and splashed about
> By battle-wending feet;
> And yet beside one stricken house there is a glimpse of grass –
> Look for it when you pass.

14. Watcyn Griffith, who was killed aged 19 during the battle for Mametz Wood and to whom *Up To Mametz* was dedicated.
15. Captain R. Bently, who was Brigade Major from October 1915 until August 1916.
16. These terms were used to refer to the senior officers or staff of any formation.
17. 25149 W.O. II Henry Charles Ford. He was awarded the MC in the New Year's Honours for 1917 and a bar in *The London Gazette* 13 September 1918, for conspicuous gallantry during a night attack. He was commissioned and by 1918 was a captain in 13 RWF [Lars Ahlkvist].

Chapter 5

Alarms and Diversions

The shoulder title of 15 RWF

FLUELLEN: *Tell you the duke, it is not so good to come to the mines, for, look you, the mines is not according to the disciplines of the war: the concavities of it is not sufficient; for, look you, th' athversary, you may discuss unto the duke, look you, is digt himself four yard under the countermines, by Cheshu, I think a' will plow up all, if there is not better directions.*

King Henry V, iii, 2.

Early in June we went back to the front line, to the sector we knew so well. A warm and sunny day had dwindled to a quiet evening when we paraded on the roadside, a day of little work and much lounging. Many letters had been written and censored, the barns had been tidied, and the last of the stray tins was now in the incinerator; while the men stood gossiping in the ranks, the Company Sergeant-Major and I tramped silently in and out of the barns and the farm buildings on our final tour of inspection. We could find no sign of damage in our tenancy, but our hostess would follow with keener eye, and there would doubtless be a claim for some petty deterioration of an all but derelict

June 1916

farm. There was little need to talk, for there was nothing new to say. Twilight came, and the dusk, bringing with them a minor third into the key of our mood, while the tramp of feet on the road rang like the ticking of a clock to mark the slipping away of wasted time, hours that might have added to the true wealth of life, sunk instead into a morass of futile slavery. Every stride took us away from the simple pleasures of our local peace, of our temporary escape from the degradations of mud: the faint glow in the sky and the brooding stillness of the green earth conspired to sharpen the ache in each man's heart.

Our line strung out as we broke into sections, then into file, until we found our feet shuffling over the duckboards of the communication trench. It was dark, but the occasional firing of a Very light threw its unreal and harsh glare over the pitted landscape. We reached the line, and were greeted eagerly by the tired men who were waiting for us, waiting to return to the very barns we had left. There was little warmth in our answer. I had walked ahead of my company, and I pushed past the small groups in the fire-bays until I came to the dug-out where the officers sat, fully dressed and ready to cut to the shortest of words and time the formalities of handing over the command of the sector.

'I'm leaving you this candle, Gruff, and there's some rum in this bottle.'

'Thanks for the candle, but why didn't you get rid of your own rum! You know what a nuisance and a responsibility it is to have so much of it about ... Goodnight! I hope we have as quiet a time as you did. How's the Duck's Bill crater?'[1]

'Just as it was – quiet enough ... Good luck to you!'

We began badly. One of my subalterns took out a patrol to scour the slopes of the crater, to make sure that the enemy had not secured a hiding place on its eastern face. The message was passed along the line: 'Patrol going out to the Duck's Bill from one o'clock till two,' and all was quiet save the stammer of a Lewis Gun firing at the enemy's rear lines to conceal our lack of activity. Soon we heard a bomb bursting in No Man's Land, then many more in quick succession: the enemy did not fire, neither did we, lest the wrong men be hit. All was darkness, for the same reason. The flashes showed that the tussle was pitched near the crater, but after a dozen bombs were thrown, silence came again. There was nothing to do but wait until our patrol returned: ten minutes, twenty minutes passed slowly by with no whisper from the other side of the barbed wire, although most of the men were on the fire-step, peering and listening. I became uneasy in my mind and decided to go out in search of our patrol, taking one man with me. Revolver in hand, I crept out of our trench and felt my way through the wire, crawling in the direction of the crater and halting frequently to listen for any sound of our returning patrol. The night was very dark and still, magnifying every rustle of our clothes against the long grass into a malevolent hiss. We came to the crater, but found no challenge to our progress, so we clawed our way up its clayey side and stared into the cavity. Nothing seemed to move within this cauldron, and all was silent. Just as I stepped over this little sky-line, the enemy fired a Light pistol. From an enveloping blackness I broke into a world of light: my shadow seemed enormous as it crawled in the wake of the falling star above; my body grew into that of a giant as I stood still, watching my shadow, the target for every bullet within half a mile of me. I was terror stricken: I was naked to all the peering world. Would that light never flicker and fail? Why had I not been shot? My breath came quickly, and my mouth grew dry in an instant. I dared not move, not an arm nor a leg, although there seemed a paradise of security in the hollow at my feet. As a statue I might live; if I moved, I was dead. Dead, dead – the evil thought rang as a tolling bell in my head, and there would be a wild crash of pain. Now, at this instant of my thinking, there was a finger on a trigger, and a yard of steel moving slowly to choose the very point of my agony. The long seconds dragged themselves to an end, and the ball of fire dropped to the ground with a hiss: darkness rushed in to drown this will-o'-the-wisp, and I threw myself over the edge of the crater into safety. A few minutes later we crept through a sap into our own line, now become a blessed protection against the dangers lurking beyond this sand-bagged wall. My first question was a sign that I was back again in my normal world of responsibility for others.

... Yes, it had returned, after a bombing scrap with an enemy patrol, with no losses or hurt.

Just as a parent scolds a child who has narrowly escaped hurt, relieving his own anxiety by pointing a moral, and disguising his inward relief in reproof, so did I curse my subaltern because he did not return immediately to the line to report the result of his encounter. I my heart I was cursing that unknown German sentry who had fired a 'light' pistol at the very moment of my crossing a miniature hilltop, but my words were hurled at my subaltern. I damned all craters and all the devices of mining, drank half a cupful of rum, and stretched my legs on the floor of the dug-out for my two hours of sleep.

If the enemy digs a mine, we must dig another, and if we can dig below him and blow up our mine before he is ready to spring his, we have done well. If we can delay our springing until his is charged with explosive, our victory will become a triumph. A miner, though he works unseen, cannot conceal his work. The spoil that he carries from his mine has a clayey blueness easily distinguishable from the mud of the surface, and the sound of his pick travels through the ground into the tunnel where his rival is listening, and is magnified by a geophone – a kind of stethoscope – into clear audibility. The entrance to our mine stood at the end of my company's sector, just outside its boundary. An Australian Tunnelling Company[2] was responsible for this enterprise, easy prey to bantering queries from our men as to how their mothers were getting on down below, and when they were coming back from leave. Its commanding officer frequently walked along my sector on his way to the communication trench, and I learned from him, with much relief, that there was no suspicion of any mining in my territory, and with equal relief, that it would be some time before our mine would be ready for springing. I had suffered from mines at Givenchy, and I wished them all to the devil that prompted such inhuman and murderous devices.

On our second day in the line, a keen-eared sergeant reported that he had heard suspicious sounds in a certain fire-bay midway along our sector; he was a South Wales miner, and he was convinced that the sound was that of a pick at work underground. The adjutant decided to join us in our investigation, so we went to the threatened fire-bay to sit down and listen. I could hear nothing, but the adjutant thought that he could, so we listened again with our ears on the duckboards. There was a faint recurring sound. I went to the adjoining sector to look for the expert, and when I returned with the Australian subaltern, he also thought that there was a suspicious sound.

This was a disturbing business: we had no mine near this spot, and before we could countermine, the enemy could blow us up at his own choosing. I was ordered to move all the men out of this fire-bay and the bays on either side, to post a Lewis Gun team on each side of the threatened area, and to occupy a half-derelict trench some thirty yards to the rear with a garrison strong enough to repel any attack when the front line had been blown up. We spent a dismal night waiting, and I admit that I hurried through this deserted part of our front line during my patrolling of our sector. The time most favoured for touching off a mine was at stand-to in the early dawn, when the whole garrison was under arms and filling the bays, and this cargo of clay could take with it to destruction the greatest number of lives. Dawn broke slowly this morning, but the day came at last, and we saw in a thin column of smoke rising from the German trenches a sign of safety. He was cooking his breakfast; if he could start the day in normal fashion, so could we, and we turned to our ordinary tasks, relieved for another twenty-four hours from this wearying burden of anxiety.

In the afternoon I met the commander of the tunnelling company, and we sat down on the duckboards in the fire-bay, listening carefully. There was undoubtedly a faint noise, not unlike the echo of a distant tapping, somewhat hollow, and irregular in rhythm. He listened with his geophone, tapping the walls, and the floor of the trench, and the fire-step, in his endeavour to localize the origin of this mysterious sound. The instrument did not seem to magnify the noise. We were all confounded, and there was much discussion of technical matters beyond my comprehension.

I walked about, thinking. If the geophone did not magnify this throbbing, the sound must have an origin above ground. But there were no wires, nothing to make an Æolian harp; besides, the sound was low in pitch. I stood in one corner of the bay, leaning against the sandbagged wall of the trench, pondering idly while the tunnellers were investigating. Below my left hand, resting on the fire-step, there was an empty rum jar. Suddenly a thought flashed through my mind with all the vividness of an inspiration.

'Can you hear the noise now?' I asked.

'Yes, faintly, but quite definitely.'

'So can I,' I answered.

I changed my position slightly, and in an inconspicuous and apparently aimless way, I put the palm of my hand on the mouth of the rum jar, stopping the orifice.

'Can you hear it now?' said I.

'No, I don't think so – keep still a few moments while we listen... No, I can hear nothing.'

I agreed – I could hear nothing. I took my hand away, and the noise recurred. On some pretext or another I caused the experiment to be repeated, until I was satisfied.

'Here is your mine,' I said, pointing to the rum jar. They looked at me in astonishment, frankly incredulous. We all bent our heads and listened carefully, crowding round the rum jar: a faint and hollow booming was clearly heard, but when I put my hand on the mouth of the jar, it stopped abruptly. I placed my lips near the mouth and blew across it; the faint and hollow sound grew into a recurrent booming, and as I blew more strongly, gave place to the deep note of the jar. I picked up the jar and placed it in the next fire-bay, in the same position. There was silence in our bay, but a faint sound in the next. The wind, as it came round the corner, blew across the mouth of the jar, and the gusts made the sound recur.

We went away laughing, our anxiety dissolved into ridicule, and the 'rum jar mine' became a regimental joke. All that remained to be done was to cancel our elaborate precautions for the defence of the sector, and in an hour the fire-bays were once more inhabited; the empty jar was broken and buried with mock solemnity in a shell hole. This 'mine' at any rate, was not 'according to the disciplines of the war'.

Delivett[3] carried with him, even into the crowded warren of the trenches, a silence that made him seem a stranger. He had served with the battalion from the start, but he was little given to any conversation beyond the need of the moment. He had no tales to tell in billet or in dug-out. No one knew his age, no one knew whether Delivett was his real name. In spite of the figure standing opposite his name and regimental number, describing him as thirty-four in 1914 it was obvious that he had forgotten his first fifteen years when he gave that answer to the Recruiting Officer. He said that he had not served in the Army prior to the War, but there were times when his carriage brought a doubt to the mind.

Short in stature, and stockily built, with a smile weaving in and out of the lines of his face, never actually smiling, but always on the point of giving way; even when he slept there was a curious curving of the corners of his mouth, as if he were struggling not to laugh. I have forgotten what occupation he claimed in civil life, but it was so impossible to reconcile with his bearing that no one cared to question him about it. He wrote no letters that came to the officers to be censored; he may have found a Field Service Postcard with

'I am well', an ample link between him and his kin. Perhaps the occasional issue of a green envelope for uncensored letters, too rare an issue for most men,[4] was frequent enough to satisfy him. He strutted along the duckboards, pipe in mouth, head in the air, hailed by everybody as he passed, and slowly removing his pipe to spit before he threw over his shoulder some quiet monosyllabic reply.

Towards the end of May, a dozen recruits joined the company, young reinforcements, boyish and slight. Early one morning the enemy began to shell the trench with whizz-bangs[5]; it was a sudden angry storm, too fierce and too localized to last long. I had just passed the fire-bay in which Delivett was frying a rasher of bacon, with five of these lads watching him and waiting their turn to cook. I stopped in the next bay to reassure the others. Suddenly a pale and frightened youth came round the corner, halting indecisively when he saw me, turning again, but finally going back reluctantly to his fire-bay in despair of finding any escape from his trap. Between the crashes of the bursting shells a high-pitched sing-song soared up.

'You'll 'ev 'em all over,' ... *Crash* ... 'All the milky wuns.' ... *Crash* ... 'All the milky coconuts ...' '... You'll 'ev 'em all over ... All the milky wuns.' ... *Crash* ... 'Ther-ree shies a penny ... All the milky coconuts ... You'll 'ev 'em all over' ... *Crash – and then silence*, for the morning hate ended as suddenly as it began.

I walked to find Delivett still frying bacon, and the five youths smiling nervously, crouched below the fire-step. I sent them away on some improvised errand and faced Delivett.

'That's a fine thing you did then, Delivett,' I said. He looked up, mess-tin lid in his hand, saying nothing, but the lines round his mouth moved a little.

'You saved those lads from panic – they were frightened out of their wits,' I added.

'Yes sir, they was real scared,' he replied. 'Delivett, you've spent a lot of time on Hampstead Heath.'

'Yes sir ... I ran a coconut shy there once ...' With these words a man and an environment fused into a unity, satisfying and complete in itself here at last was a credible occupation for this quiet stranger.

'I'm going to tell the Colonel all about this,' I said. Delivett thought hard for several seconds, and put his bacon back on the fire.

'Well, sir,' he said, diffidently, 'if it's all the same to you, I'd much rather you made me Sanitary man.'

'Do you mean that you'd really like to go round with a bucket of chloride of lime, picking up tins and ...'

'Yes, sir, I'd like that job.'

'You shall have it here and now. You are made Sanitary man for valour in the field, this very moment.'

In half an hour Delivett was walking round with a bucket, his head a little higher in the air, spitting a little more deliberately than before, as his new dignity demanded. He had found a vocation.

The signallers were always with the company, but never of it. They did no fatigues, they carried nothing but their leather-cased instruments and odd lengths of wire, they dug no trenches. They spent most of their time sitting down in dug-outs, buzzing their telephones, disappearing occasionally down a trench with one finger on a wire, following that wire round corners, across ditches and over fields. They were a clan within our tribe. Their dug-outs were, as a rule, close to the company headquarters, and day and night, when not actually telephoning, testing or signalling messages, they talked, they sang, and they whistled. At three o'clock in the morning, or just after standing down at dawn, when all the world was quiet, and an officer relieved from trench duty was trying to concentrate twelve hours sleep into the brief two hours allotted to him, a voice from the next dug-out rasped in a whining drawl:

'You left ba-hind a bro-ken do-oil.' ... 'Beer emmer, beer emmer, beer emmer[6] ... 's that you, Bill?'

'I say, you remember that estaminet just beyond the crossroads, well, I asked Madame ...'

This was too much. I yelled out to them.

'Look here, you signallers, why can't you keep quiet? There are no messages coming through, are there?'

'No sir, we were only testing,' they replied. 'Well, shut up then, and let me go to sleep while the Boche is quiet.'

'Yes, sir.'

There was a dead silence for ten minutes, and then a whispered conversation rising with the energy of contradictions into a full-flavoured argument about the price of coffee in that estaminet. I got up to attend to this.

'Why the hell can't you fellows keep quiet? Of all the damned chattering magpies I've ever come across, you are the worst.'

I was angry, and much profanity followed, real hard cursing, of a sharp-edged variety that rises so easily to the lips in the early morning. I had lost an eighth part of my sleep, and nearly all my temper. As I turned away from the door of their dug-out and went back to mine, I heard a cheery and unabashed voice saying quietly:

'Old Gruff can't 'alf curse, can't he?'

After that there was silence.

We left the trenches and marched back to our billets at Riez Bailleul[7] late on a summer night. There were many rumours, all of untraceable origin, that this was to be our last spell in the trenches for some time. Circumstantial evidence was freely put forward to prove each conflicting theory, quartermasters and post-corporals were fathered with definite statements of our ultimate destination that, had they been true, would have indicated a remarkable acquaintance with the minds of our commanders. We were content to know that we were going back to our quiet farmhouse in Riez Bailleul, and from the wild variety of forecasts we found enough material to justify the belief that the Division was to be relieved by another division in the same Corps.

The customary number of days in reserve went by with no sign of another visit to the trenches. Rumours sprang up again – we were going to Ypres, we were to join the Belgian Army, the French Army, the British forces near Arras, the Division was to be disbanded and remade into battalions of miners and tunnellers, into Engineers, into Pioneers, we were to go south to be trained for open warfare. Of all these tales, the truth was in the last surmise, and we were warned that the battalion would start on a long march to the south.

On our last evening in Riez Bailleul, the Sergeant-Major came to the Company Headquarters to say that the men were anxious to give a concert. A piano had been found, and for a small fee the owner was willing to allow us to take it to the orchard for the evening, provided we kept a tarpaulin over it to 'keep out the damp'. Would the officers come, and would I persuade the Adjutant to play the piano?

A man of undoubted administrative ability, with a knowledge of one half of the world of the day that made backwoodsmen of us all, added to a large acquaintance with its more prominent citizens, he had sauntered through many occupations before attaining a large measure of success as a journalist. Through all his varying moods there ran one thread that gave a continuity to his changeful personality, and that was his love of music. He was an attractive pianist, not of the highest order of technique, but endowed with a capacity to make others share in his own delight in playing. Yes, he would play, and he would accompany the songs.

We assembled in the orchard in the dusk, a hundred and fifty men lying about on the trodden grass, talking and smoking. A thin haze of tobacco smoke hung as a pale blue shadow against the darkening sky, and two candles in the piano sconces gave a round blur of yellow light. The air was still, and in the distance a rumble of far-off shellfire served as an echo to the thunder of a limbered wagon passing along the road. We sang a chorus or two to unstiffen the minds of all, to weld us into a unity of mood.

Some forms had been lashed together to make a precarious platform, and on this the Sergeant-Major, by virtue of his office, president and prime mover of such an enterprise, stood to announce that Corporal Jackson 'would oblige', following the time-honoured formula, by singing a song. Corporal Jackson was greeted enthusiastically by all as he stepped up. At some time or another he had been on the stage, according to the best informed of the company – 'made a lot of money in 'is day, 'e 'as, an' 'e carn't 'arf dance'. He walked across to the piano.

'Music?' said the Adjutant, with a smile.

'No sir, got no music.'

'What are you going to sing?'

'*Don't Stop Me*, sir.'

'I don't know it – what's the tune?'

Jackson bent down and hummed into the Adjutant's ear.

'Right you are, Corporal ... Carry on.'

'Will you play a few bars of introduction first, sir, and then play the tune for the dance after each chorus?'

Corporal Jackson walked to the centre of the stage and gave an expert shuffle with his feet to test its stability. 'Mind them boots, Corporal, the Quarter's looking,' shouted some irrepressible member of the company. It was a third-rate song, sung by a fourth-rate singer, followed by a second-rate clog dance, but in the remoteness of that green orchard in Flanders, far from any standard of comparison, it claimed and held approval for its own sake. The words of the chorus still remain, wedded to a jerky tune, both trailing an air of days long passed away:

> Don't stop me, don't stop me,
> I've got a little job to go to,

'Using a trench periscope' by David Jones. [RWF Museum Trustees]

> Twas advertised in ninety-eight,
> If I'm not there I'll be too late.

Another corporal, fat and tenorish, sang *Thora*,[8] hanging precariously on its sentimental slopes, curving his mouth into a wonderful vowel fantasy over the:

> Noightin-gales in the brenches,
> Stawrs in the mej-jic skoy.

A good hard-working Corporal, though his belt was a perpetual worry to him in his convexity.

But the evening grew to its grand climax when the stern-faced Sergeant-Major stood grimly on the stage, thin-lipped and hawk-eyed, to sing a ballad of Northern Lands. Every line in his face, and every contour in his spare body, gave the lie to his opening words:

> Oh, Oh, Oh, I'm an Eskimo,
> And I live in the Land of Snow.

The rest of the song has faded, but that sense of contradiction is still vivid. He had to sing it twice because he could remember no other.

Private Walton[9] hunched his shoulders and adjusted the weight of his body carefully from one leg to another until he found a position of stable equilibrium, mental as well as physical. From his pocket he pulled out a mouth-organ, wiped it carefully on the underside of his sleeve, shook it and tapped it gently against his palm, presumably to remove any crumbs of tobacco or biscuit, and suddenly burst into a wild harmonic frenzy. From the welter of common chord and seventh there rose a recognizable tune, emphasized by the tapping of his foot, and he stimulated the whole company to song. When the audience had gathered sufficient momentum, he stopped to wipe his mouth organ.

The next performer was Signaller Downs[10], who roused the community to a long-drawn-out sequence of 'Nev-vah Mind' in Gertie Gitana's undying song[11], a song that declined in speed as it grew in sentiment. The moon rose in the blue-grey sky, mellowing the darkness and deepening the shadows under the trees, turning the orchard into a fine setting for a nobler stirring of the spirit. Over the subdued chatter of many voices and the noise of an occasional lighting of a match came the silvery spray of notes from the piano. The Adjutant was playing quietly to himself, meditating in music. The talking ceased, and men turned away from their comrades to listen, until there was dead silence under the trees to make a background for the ripple of the piano.

The silence broke in upon the player and he removed his hands from the keyboard for an instant. The world seemed to plunge into a deep pool of silence, rising again to hear a supple cascade of showering notes as he played one of Debussy's *Arabesques*. When he finished there was a second or two of silence before the applause began, enough of a gap to show that his listeners had been travelling with him into another land. He played it again, and as he turned away from the piano he whispered to me, 'I told you that they could appreciate good music if they got the chance.' A summer night in an orchard, with a moon low in the sky, and in the heart of each man a longing – if music could not speak in such a setting it were not music.

Notes

1. This was the remains of a 3,000lb mine blown under the German positions on 15 June 1915 by 176 Tunnelling Company RE during the Second Battle of Givenchy.
2. In 1915, eight Tunnelling Companies of the Royal Engineers were formed; these were usually composed of men recruited from coal or other mining – usually a protected occupation. Mining and countermining was a universal activity on the Western Front wherever the water table was low enough to allow it. The objective was to drive a shaft below the enemy's trenches, pack it with explosive, and then blow it up as the prelude to an assault. The most famous example was the multiple mining of the German line on Messines Ridge in 1917. On occasions, one set of miners would break through into the oppositions' mines and vicious hand-to-hand fights with any weapon at hand would take place in the darkness. See A. Barrie *War Underground 1914–1918* (London, 1964).
3. Probably 22745 Pte George Delivett, a former hawker born in 1880 in London. When 15 RWF was disbanded he transferred to 14 RWF, was wounded in the leg in September 1918 but survived and was discharged in 1919 [Lars Ahlkvist].
4. The Field Service Postcard was a standard form available in unlimited quantities that carried a choice of messages. It could be sent home at frequent intervals to reassure families or when there was no time for writing letters, or by men who were illiterate or semi-literate. All other letters had to be presented in unsealed envelopes to an officer in each headquarters or unit designated as the censor, who would make sure that nothing which could be of use to the enemy was revealed, if a letter found its way into the wrong hands. For more senior

Alarms and Diversions

officers there were green envelopes which carried letters of a sensitive nature, or contained information which the censor himself might be too junior to see.
5. Although the term was used widely by Allied (most often British and Commonwealth) soldiers to describe any form of German field artillery shells, the 'whizzbang' was originally attributed to the noise made by shells from German 77mm (3.1-inch) field guns. In all cases however the name was derived from the fact that shells fired from light or field artillery travelled faster than the speed of sound. Thus soldiers heard the typical 'whizz' noise of a travelling shell before the 'bang' issued by the gun itself. Whizz-bangs were consequently much feared since the result was that receiving infantrymen had no warning of incoming high-velocity artillery fire in the way that they had from enemy howitzers or mortars.
6. This refers to the phonetic alphabet then in use for line or wireless transmissions when it was necessary to spell words out letter by letter. A similar system is still in use, although the phonetics have changed and become standard across NATO. In 1916, A was 'Ack', B was 'Beer', C was 'Charlie', D was 'Don', E was 'Emma' and so on.
7. About one-and-a-half miles north-west of Aubers in the Laventie sector of the Western Front.
8. This song was published in 1913; the music was by Steven Adams and the words by Fred Wetherby.
9. Possibly 22476 Pte Samuel Walton, killed on 10 July 1916 at Mametz and buried in Flatiron Copse Cemetery; he was, however, serving with 13 RWF at that date [Lars Ahlkvist].
10. Possibly 22507 Pte Israel Downs, from Staffordshire, awarded the MM in *The London Gazette* 2 June 1916, shortly after his death of wounds on 13 May 1916. He is buried in Merville Communal Cemetery [Lars Ahlkvist].
11. Gertie Gitana (1887–1957) was a music hall entertainer from Stoke-on-Trent who was the Forces' sweetheart in the Great War. Her best known songs were *Nellie Dean* and *When I See the Love-light Gleaming*.

Chapter 6

South

The badge of II Corps

In the morning we began our long trek south.[1] We did not know our destination, nor the time we were to spend on our journey; as company officers it was enough for us to know the length of the day's march and where we were to sleep that night. For some reason unexplained to us, we marched through the heat of the June day, and after seven months of trench warfare we found the early stages troublesome until our feet were hardened. We spent a night at Merville, a town of good billets, and then two nights at a village called Gonnehem, a village rescued from oblivion by two memories, one of its fine old church, the other of its womenfolk – the dirtiest slatterns we had seen in France. Then up to the hills at Auchel, a mining village, with its men in blue smocks and leather hats, a long straggling street of indeterminate beginning and end.

11 June 1916

After so many months in the plain it was good to stand on a hill. For fourteen days we had been out of the trenches, clean and comfortable; body and mind were quickening again, early summer in the land, and a late spring inside us. The marching in good air was leaving its mark on us all, and we were gaining a release from the humiliating burden of mud that had clogged our pores and had turned our thoughts into its own greyness. We walked with a swing,

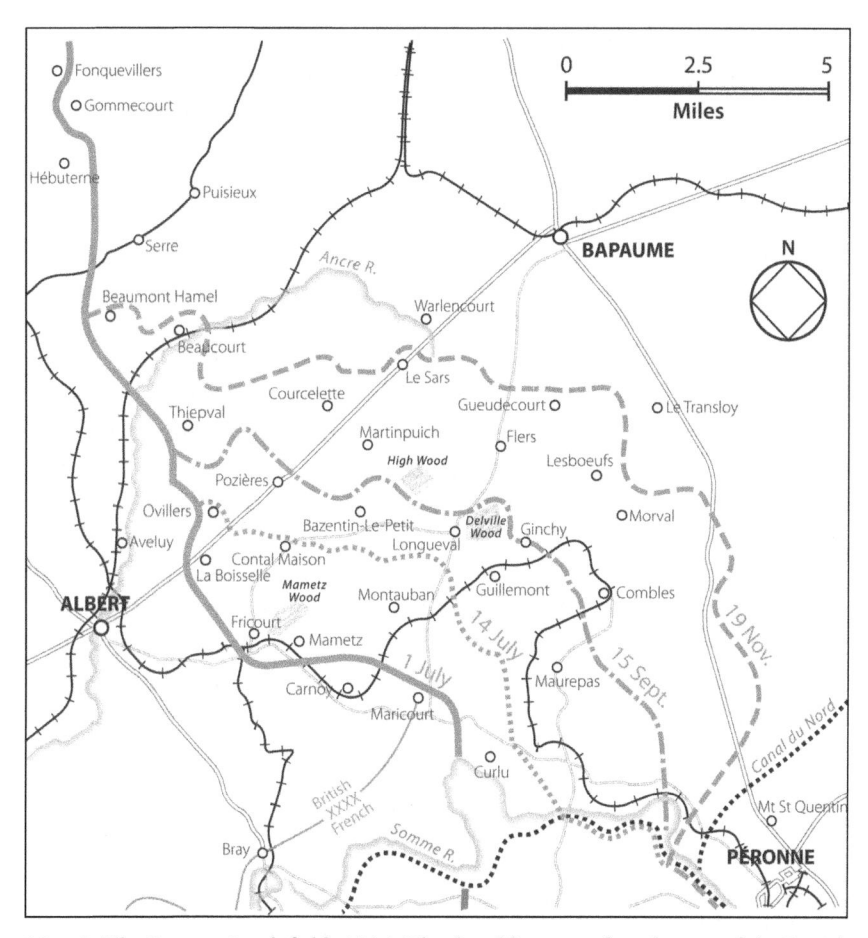

Map 3: *The Somme Battlefield, 1916. The dated lines are the advance of the British front line.*

we sang on the march; men began to laugh, to argue and even to quarrel, a sure sign of recovery from the torpor of winter. We were going into a battle, true enough, from which few of us could hope to return, but at the moment we were many miles from war, and the hedges were rich with dog rose and honeysuckle; we were seeing the old flowers in new country.

This emancipation brought with it a rekindling of our self-respect, showing itself in a more upright bearing, and in a shedding of the clod-hopping, farm labourers' shuffle of the feet, the last physical relic of the tyranny of mud. A month ago the Company was a disintegrated body of men, tired and dull, dragging the day into the night and the night into the day, with a horizon bounded on all sides by that damnable, evil-smelling and unnatural soil. Now we were above ground, welded into a free-moving unit, handling its arms with its old vigour and precision, no longer 'climbing up the rifle to the slope'. It was strangely easy to forget that this revival would be of short duration to most of us.

On our way out of Floringhem we found ourselves in a country of downs and wooded hills, small streams and high-hedged lanes – Hampshire again, and our first meeting with beauty in France. At one of our halts the officers were standing in a group in the road, smoking and talking, when the second-in-command of the battalion[2] rode up to join us. After some desultory conversation about our last billets, he turned to me and said, 'By the way, I hear that you are going to another Brigade to be trained as a Staff Officer – many congratulations!' With this he rode away.

To me, these were words of liberation, they opened the door of my prison. Seven months of shelling, of mud, discomfort, and the deadening, un-escapable routine of trench life, months of watching other men being killed and maimed, of dry-mouthed fear and racking fatigue; a time of waiting for the end, hoping that the end might be a bruising and not a sudden drop into darkness. All this weight of disharmony ran above one never-ceasing pedal note of 'No infantry officer can survive this war unless he is happily wounded.' Until this background is etched into the mind with the acid of experience, it is not possible to understand the full import of this message. For me, life had suddenly changed direction. Comparative safety, interesting work, a reasonable chance of survival without mutilation, and the elation that accompanied the knowledge that someone had chosen me to do something; the possibility of leave and of promotion, more pay and a richer housekeeping for my wife – this was the new country upon which I gazed through the suddenly opened door of my prison. A deep-lying thankfulness permeated the whole of my being, gaining strength from the knowledge that soon, very soon, the news would release some of the burden of anxiety that pressed down into a uniform greyness the days and nights of one whose life was linked to mine, who lived in daily dread of that baleful telegram from the War Office. A mad impulse came over me, not strange to one born in the mountains, to build a cairn on the roadside, marking the spot where I heard these words of freedom, but a whistle blew,

'Rouge Croix' by David Jones. [RWF Trustees]

and the battalion resumed the march down south. I was back in my Company, but with a difference.

When the mind has run riot for a few hours over the prospect of release and opportunity, there comes a certain pleasure in dwelling upon the greyer side of the picture. I was to go to another brigade as a stranger, possibly unwanted and half-suspected, to live day by day with a General, unable to conceal my ignorance, liable to be found out in a short space of time and returned to my battalion in disgrace. In a few days I would be turning my back on C Company, on the men I lived with and loved, leaving them a little while before their great hour of trial, deserting them, in fact. So it was ordained, and for my betterment; I was to stand my trial, with no influence or authority over my judges, merely an infantry captain, temporary, with no relations or friends in high places, a man of no importance to powers military or civil. The reward of success was advancement in the army, and enough pay to lift me clear of the margin of anxiety here and at home; failure meant a reversion to the trenches, so there must be no tottering.

Several days passed before I received orders to go, days of some anxiety lest there should be a hitch in this fateful affair, but days of pleasant marching in country lanes, of long evenings in good billets in villages far removed from contact with the strident clash of war. The inhabitants of the cleanly kept cottages lived a life into which we could not enter. Our coming roused an excitement that died away with our going, and we never saw them at their daily struggle to prevent the army's intrusion from growing into an occupation. Farms, houses and inns undamaged by shellfire suggested a prosperity and a strength alien to the provinces further north and east, but as we never penetrated into any intimacy with the villagers, we could not tell how they were faring.

My arrival at Brigade Headquarters[3] created no stir. I had walked to the Château at Chelers,[4] leaving my servant to bring my kit in the battalion cart. Never before had I entered a château, and there was a thrill in the thought of living in such magnificence. It was a newish house, standing in a small park, clean and white in the hot sunshine of June, decorated with a turret at every possible corner, and dominating the small village at its feet. It was half withdrawn from sight, yet eager not to be overlooked and ignored.

20 June 1916

I met a soldier and asked him if this were the Brigade Headquarters, and I was somewhat taken aback when he said that it was not; it was the General's billet, and the Brigade office was in the small house near the church. I turned back, consoling myself for the loss of this magnificence by the confident hope that as the Brigade staff would be well housed, I should find myself in a good billet, even though it were not a château.

I entered the Brigade office and made myself known to an elderly Major sitting down at a table covered with papers. He said that the Brigade Major[5] was on leave, and that he was merely deputizing for him; the Staff Captain[6] would be in shortly and would find me a billet. When the Staff Captain arrived he extinguished all my expectations of comfort and dignity by announcing that I could sleep in a bell tent in the garden, as there was no billet to be had in the village. A little later we all walked to the château for tea, and I was introduced to the Brigadier.[7] He said little, but whenever I looked in his direction I met his eye, and I felt that I was being assessed and valued. He was some sixty years of age, physically strong, with a hard and clear face, and the bearing of a man who has lived wisely. In the jargon of the day, he was a 'dug-out', a retired regular officer who had rejoined the army on the outbreak of war. The gossip of my old Brigade described him as a glutton for work, somewhat snappy in the early morning, sensible, and willing to listen even to a subaltern. At table he spoke as a man among men, and in my experience I found it hard to believe that he was a real General, own brother to the rest of his rank who walked the trenches in search of disappointment and of tasks undone, demanding an output of construction from tired men, wet and short of sleep, that would have staggered Henry Ford himself. He asked me no questions, but I felt that it was only because he had decided that there was no need to dissect a known specimen.

I spent the rest of the day in making myself as inconspicuous as possible, sitting in a corner of the office, reading orders and listening to the conversation of my companions, trying to penetrate unobtrusively into the life around me. It did not occur to me that as a company officer I had as much to impart to them as they had to teach me. In the evening I walked through the village and talked to some of the regimental officers I knew, keeping a watchful eye for my young brother, for his battalion was billeted in the village and belonged to my new brigade.[8] I found him, and in his obvious delight at this turn for the better in my fortunes, I recovered some of my own, and conquered that feeling of utter loneliness and unimportance that assails every individual at the time of his first joining a strange unit. He was merely a boy who had come straight from school into the ranks, and it was a matter of pride to him that his brother should shine in the reflected glory of the Brigadier, as if he felt that things could not fail thereby to prosper.

After breakfast next morning the General asked me if I could ride. In sheer cowardice I said that I could, for I did not dare begin my career by announcing my limitations. He told me to get the Machine Gun Officers' horse and to accompany him on a visit to the battalions at the training ground. My heart quailed within me when I saw the great black beast standing uneasily on the road, enormously tall, and as I thought, very fierce looking. I had neither spurs nor stick nor leggings, so I had tied my puttees cavalry-fashion[9]. I clambered up on to the back of this unwilling creature, feeling extremely insecure at so great a height above the road. We started off, and to my good fortune, the General did not trot his horse. He questioned me about my experience and training, both in the ranks and as a commissioned officer, told me to learn everything that came my way, and to ask him questions about what I did not understand. He shook his rein and trotted, and I followed, taking pains to keep behind him, as was fitting to my lower rank, and as my lack of horsemanship made essential if I were not to advertise my deficiencies.

I have no illusions whatever about my appearance on this occasion, but I take pride in having kept my seat. We rushed down the banks of sunken roads, and rushed up the other side, to the great danger of my nose; we jumped over trenches, and added to all my anxiety about my equilibrium was the determined effort to keep behind the General. When all was over and we reached Brigade Headquarters, the General turned to me and said, with a smile in his eyes:

'Next time I ask you whether you can do a thing, say so outright if you cannot.'

I answered timidly that, at any rate, I had not fallen off.

'No, but why you did not is more than I can say ... How much have you ridden?'

'This is the second time in my life I have ridden a horse, sir,' I replied.

'Good Lord, you might have broken your neck ... don't do things like that again.'

When the day is divided between an attempt to conceal ignorance of the things that are common knowledge to your colleagues, and a struggle to acquire familiarity in unobtrusive fashion, dreading to make lack of learning, and the desire to learn, equally a source of embarrassment to others, the day passes quickly enough. I cannot say that I was taught to do anything, but there were ample opportunities for imitating others in what they did, and if questions were asked with a due regard for the niceties of time and place, they were answered. More than this could not be expected of men who worked hard enough, but had little gift or inducement to explain their daily tasks. With such men, all the world over, there is more to be earned from their negations than from their assertions.

To my fresh eye, the work was divisible into two categories – issuing orders, and seeing that those orders were carried out. In the nature of things, I had little to do with issuing orders, but enquiry into their fate and reminder of their existence seemed to involve a considerable running about. And here, as everywhere in the army, there was a fresh vocabulary to learn, a new craft jargon, another weapon of verbal equipment. The Staff Captain's activities were multifarious, and at first all but incomprehensible owing to my ignorance of the language. There was, and presumably still exists, a scheme of words and phrases that may be called a verbal shorthand for dealing on paper with matters as diverse as a court martial and a shortage of incinerators, an Esperanto of the army. How it arose is to me a mystery, but I can only surmise that someone once made an index, in alphabetical order, of all the commodities and occasions involved in war, and that the descriptive phrase in this index became a sacred title to be used henceforth and for ever in all writings. There is much to be said for the practice, as for a universal language, and the eye soon accustoms itself to 'Waggons, G.S.'.[10] After a few weeks of army shopkeeping, the G.S. becomes a part of the waggon as integral as its wheels.

The British Army is, in some respects, an army of brothers, and every man above the rank of private is his brother's keeper. Every commander must know what his command is doing at the moment, and his superior officers must know what it did yesterday, and what it intends to do tomorrow. This concern, this anxiety, and interest, minute and unceasing, are as characteristic of the British Army as their non-existence is typical of other armies. It can be harassing, and it often is, but it is omnipresent throughout the hierarchy of the command and the staff. A soldier, short of some article of equipment, mental or material, is a matter of concern to many functionaries far removed from contact with him. Private Smith, in a fit of temper, may by his delinquencies set in motion a long chain of Captains, Majors, Colonels and Generals, further removed from him geographically as they rise in rank, but all in some way concerned with his destiny.

Notes

1. Orders had been received on 10 June for the 38th Division to move south in preparation for the forthcoming Somme Battle. The Givenchy sector was handed over to the 61st Division that night and the division moved to the St Pol area for training.
2. Major Harry Vivian Robert Hodson (1881–?), a founder member of the battalion in 1914. He had been commissioned into the North Staffords in 1900. Hodson went on to command the 14th Battalion after the Battle of the Somme as a Lieutenant-Colonel, until June 1917. He was awarded the DSO and MiD in 1918 and survived the war.
3. Wyn Griffith had been sent to 115 Infantry Brigade, which comprised 17 RWF, 10 and 11 SWB and 16 and 19 Welch. Its supporting units were 121 Brigade RFA; 115 MG Company of the 38th Battalion MGC; 115 Light Trench Mortar Battery; and 131 Field Ambulance RAMC.
4. No château of this name can be found.
5. The Brigade Major was Captain Charles Lewis Veal, of the Welch Regiment. The elderly Major is unidentified. The role of the Brigade Major, whose only assistant was the Staff Captain (in this case, Captain Harold Virgo Hinton, late of the Welch now General List) [TNA WO 95/2560 115 Inf Bde War Diary], was defined in *Field Service Regulations* as being:

    i. To assist [his] commander in the execution of his functions of command.
    ii. To assist the fighting troops and services in the execution of their tasks.

    This rather general guidance was supplemented by specific responsibilities laid on the G, or General Staff, branch, to which the Brigade Major's post was assigned. These were laid down in the *Field Service Pocket Book* as:

    i. To obtain and communicate information about our own troops, the enemy, and the theatre of war.
    ii. To prepare plans and issue orders for operations.
    iii. To arrange for communication, cipher, censorship. The provision and distribution of maps, secret service, guides, interpreters and propaganda.
    iv. The organisation, training and efficiency of troops. To draft dispatches.

6. No name is given and the divisional history gives none.

7. Colonel (Honorary Brigadier) Horatio John Evans (1862–?) had commanded No. 4 District of Western Command – i.e. Wales and the West Midlands – before mobilisation in 1914.
8. This was the 13th (Service) Battalion of The Royal Welch Fusiliers.
9. The puttee was a form of leg covering binding the ankle boot to the breeches, picked up by the British Army in India and much cheaper to produce than high boots or leggings. The puttee consisted of a 9-foot strip of cloth about 5 inches wide, wound round the leg and fastened with tape. In the infantry, the puttee was wound from the ankle to the knee and fastened at the top; in the cavalry it was wound from knee to ankle and fastened at the bottom in order to prevent the puttee riding up the leg when in contact with a moving horse's flanks.
10. General Service.

Chapter 7

Mametz Wood

At seven in the morning,[1] Brigade Headquarters was to 'close down' at one place and to 'open' at another. This has a sound of the impossible in it, but it is easily resolved into a problem of telephone communication. If there is a telephone at the new headquarters, giving a means of speech backward to Divisional Headquarters[2] and forward to Battalion Headquarters, the command of the brigade can be as well exercised from the new hole in the ground as from the old. For in this war, a telephone wire was not only the outward sign of command, but the life-blood of its existence, a General without a telephone was to all practical purposes impotent, a lay figure dressed in uniform, deprived of eyes, arms and ears.[3]

7 July 1916

All through the night the signallers had worked at their task of picking and choosing the right wire from the tangled mass of tendrils that wound round post and trench in this desperate jungle, following the wire across country, testing it in sections, until the welcome sound of the right voice in response brought an end to their search. A chance shell, or the unlucky stumble of a passer-by, might cut the wire and send weary men out again on their search.

In the stuffy darkness of the old German dug-out an orderly lit a candle and roused us to say that it was half-past four. I swung my

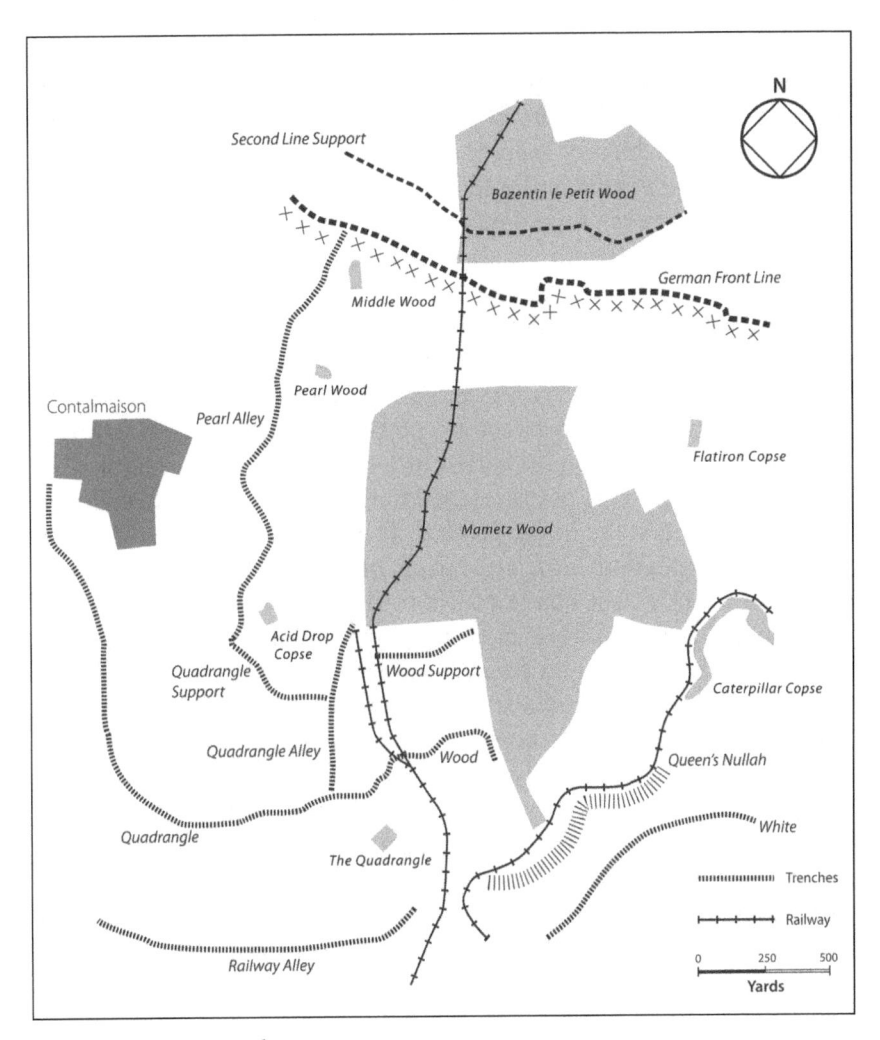

Map 4: Mametz Wood.

feet over the side of the wire-net mattress and stumbled up the stairs into the thin chill of the dawn, stupid and less than half awake, conscious chiefly of the difficulty of keeping my eyes from closing, and of a clammy, bitter-tasting thirst, a legacy from a short and too heavy sleep in a musty dug-out. Shivering and stretching, stamping my feet on the duckboards, swinging my arms like a cab-driver, I walked along towards the sound of a crackling wood fire and its promise of a cup of tea. There was an unnatural stillness in the air. No guns were firing, no transport moving. A thin column of smoke was rising slowly, twisting and swaying idly in the thin light. The whole world seemed to have slackened its pace to the merest saunter through the sky, with no perceptible disturbance of the morning air, without song of bird or step of man. A vague unreality had taken the place of the visible and audible environment, concealing all the muddle and horrors of the day before, revealing nothing but a sleeping shape stretching out over the chalky downs, blackening the light greenish-grey of the landscape.

As the light grew stronger, this straggling trail of black hardened into its distinguishable components; waggons, dumps of ammunition and stores, battery after battery of guns, big and small. A little below the dug-out, in the dip between it and the ground rising up towards Mametz, a string of guns squatted in a row, and from underneath a bivouac a gunner crept out, stretched himself and walked through the line of guns to a stake in the ground. From this he removed a lamp. Other men followed him, appearing mysteriously from nowhere, and soon there was a bustle of life in this tiny village of nomads.

Far away to the south a shell burst in the empty air. Somewhere behind our hill a big gun fired, another followed it, and suddenly the battery below blasted a stuttering sentence of noises. The Devil had taken his seat at the keyboard to play the opening bars of his morning hymn; another day beginning, the last day for so many, a fine sunny day to devote to killing and bruising. Was it my last day? With a wise obstinacy, the mind refused to dwell on such a thought, and the signalman in my brain shunted such futile traffic into some siding, giving the right of way to the greater utility of a desire for a cup of tea. I found some biscuit and a tin of jam, and sat on an ammunition box near the fire, eating and drinking in silence. When I had finished I went down into the dug-out for my shaving tackle, and as I descended the steps into a crescendo of foul stuffiness I wondered how I had dared to sleep in such a cesspool of smells, and hurried back to the trench to shave.

When I came back to the fire I found Taylor,[4] the Brigade Signalling Officer, seated on a box and drinking his cup of tea. He was a man of forty, quietly carrying about him a reserved air of authority and competence, unhurried in movement and in speech. The technical nature of his work preserved him from interference, and he ruled over his kingdom of men with a certainty of control denied to an infantry officer. No Brigadier could dispute with him concerning the wisdom or unwisdom of his dispositions of men or material. His duty was to give others a means of speech, and as he never failed in his task, his competency was obvious to all.

This morning his face was as grey as his hair, and his eyes were dull and tired. I greeted him and sat down by his side.

'When did you finish your job?' I asked him.

'I've just come from there now, and I'm going back with some more men as soon as they have had a bite of food. It's a long tramp from here to Pommiers Redoubt, and I lost my way coming back ... Lost two men on the job already!'

'Killed?' I asked.

'No, both wounded – shrapnel in the leg. I had a terrible job to get them away. We were out on a line across country and I couldn't find a battalion or anybody likely to have stretcher-bearers. I tied them up as well as I could and went out on a search. I left my torch with them in case I couldn't find my way back in the dark. Just as I was giving it up and going back to them, a gun went off near me, a blaze of light and a hell of a noise. I was down on my face before you could say 'knife', and I crept along till I got a bit nearer, and then I shouted. A gunner came out and yelled to me to come in quickly before they fired again. So I got some stretcher-bearers and got my lads away. Two good men, just when I most wanted them. Still, they are well out of it, poor devils, with a day like this in front of them.'

'What's it like at Pommiers Redoubt?' I asked.

'Just like any other hole in the ground. There's some heavy artillery headquarters there, and we may be glad of their lines before the day is out ... There's a lot of our fellows out there not buried yet ... You know old Evans the padre?'[5]

'Yes, I know him.'

'I met him this morning, half an hour ago, just as it was getting light. He was going to do a bit of burying. I thought he looked queer ... he was talking to himself, praying, may be, when I walked along with him. It was in North Wales Welsh, and I couldn't make much of it. I got talking to him, and I asked him why he was up so early. He said he hadn't been to bed. He went towards Fricourt yesterday evening looking for a grave. Someone you knew, said I ... Yes, my own boy's grave, said he.'

'Good God, I knew young Evans well – he was in the ranks with me,' I answered.

'Well, Evans, poor chap, had heard yesterday evening that his boy was killed near Fricourt the day before, so he went off at once to try to find his grave. He walked about for hours, but couldn't find any one who knew where it was, nor could he find the padre who buried him. He walked till he could walk no more, got a cup of tea from some gunners, and had a rest, and then walked back here. And now he's out again. Going to bury other people's boys, he said, since he couldn't find his own boy's grave to pray over ... What could you say? I left him to turn up to this place ... my Welsh isn't very good, as you know, but I managed to say to him, 'I'm not a soldier now, padre; I'm taking off my hat to you.' And so I did, I took off my tin helmet ... You couldn't talk English to a man who had lost his boy ...'

'No ... not to a Welshman,' I replied.

'But there's a man for you, Gruff ... off to bury other men's boys at five in the morning, and maybe his own son not buried yet, a couple of miles away. There was some shrapnel overhead, but I saw him going up the slope as if he were alone in the world. If I come through this bloody business, I'd like to go to that man's church. The only thing he said that I could make out was that bit of a Welsh hymn – you'll know it, the one they sing at funerals to that tune that curdles your blood worse than the Dead March[6] ... Well, this is no time to be talking of funerals, I'm going back to Pommiers Redoubt – are you coming with me?'

'I might as well,' I replied, 'I'm doing nothing here, but I'd better ask the Brigade Major first, in case he wants me.

The Brigade Major, after some years in the east, was not at his best in the early morning, and in the minimum of words, told me that I could go. Taylor was stuffing some biscuits into his haversack when I came back to him.

'You'd better do the same,' he said. 'You never know where you might land up today.'

'Cheer up, Taylor,' I answered. 'There are so many of us about today that you and I might well be booked for a through trip.'

I cut off a hunk of cheese and put it in my haversack with some biscuits, and filled my water-bottle: pipe, tobacco, matches, maps, notebook, orders – I made sure that these were on or about me.

We set off up the hill, passing the grey and red ruins of Mametz village on our left as we walked up towards Pommiers Redoubt. The guns were firing, and an occasional shell-burst crashed through the air with a venomous answer. Transport was crawling about in the distance, small groups of men were moving, dark against the

Llewelyn Wyn Griffith. (*RWF Trustees*)    Llewelyn Wyn Griffith. (*Martin Wyn Griffith*)

newspaper cutting of 15th RWF in its earliest days at Grey's Inn.

A contingent of the London Welsh Battalions drilling in Gray's Inn Gardens on Monday.

Captain W.A. Howells 15th RWF – see p. 14. (*RWF Trustees*)

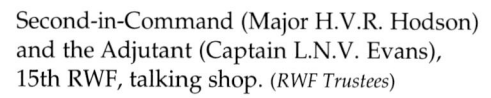

Major John Edwards, 15th RWF. (*RWF Trustees*)

Second-in-Command (Major H.V.R. Hodson) and the Adjutant (Captain L.N.V. Evans), 15th RWF, talking shop. (*RWF Trustees*)

2nd Lieutenant Noel Osbourne Jones, D Company 15th RWF. Killed in a raid near Laventie in May 1916 – see pp. 61–9. (*RWF Trustees*)

WG and his company in tents. WG himself is facing the camera. *(Family of John Bradshaw)*

Soldiers of 15th RWF filling sandbags in the line – see p. 27. *(IWM Q8372)*

Troops being fed hot rations in the line from dixies – see p. 24. (*IWM Q4843*)

A field kitchen in a dugout, being enjoyed by 'old soldiers' – see p. 25. (*IWM E1219*)

ritish trenches on the Western Front. (*RWF Trustees*)

;erman trenches on the Western Front. (*RWF Trustees*)

A communication trench in the Laventie sector, probably during Spring 1915 – see p. 48. *(IWM Q17410)*

A working party carrying stores along duckboards from the support line to the front line – see p. 62. (*WM Q5092*)

Men of 15 RWF resting before the attack on Mametz Wood, July 1916. (*RWF Trustees*)

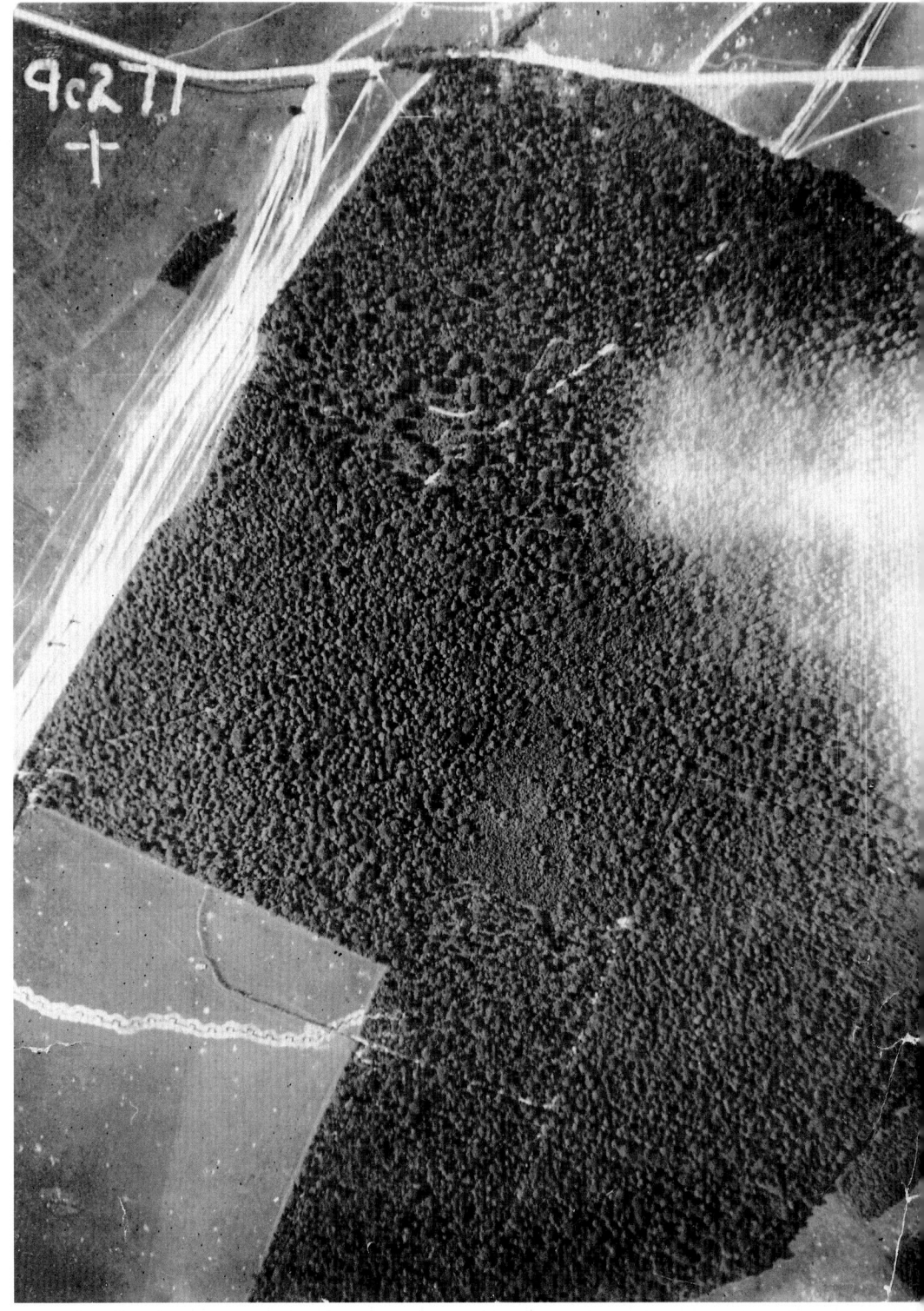

An aerial photograph of Mametz Wood, taken shortly before the July 1916 attack. (*RWF Trustees*)

A German trench on the edge of a wood, such as that faced by 15th RWF during the assault on Mametz Wood.
(*James Payne collections*)

Brigadier Horatio Evans, Major Charles Veal and an unknown officer in Mametz Wood.
(*IWM Q868*)

G.O.C. VIII Corps and staff. From left: not identified, not identified, Brigadier-General Ellington, Lieutenant-General Hunter-Weston, not identified, Major Monk(?) – see p. 131. *(IWM Q736)*

Winifred Wyn Griffith (Wyn) in 1916. *(Martin Wyn Griffith)*

Dugouts along the Yser Canal – see p. 140. (*IWM Q5947*)

Infantry crossing a bridge on the Yser Canal – see p. 139. (*IWM Q2681*)

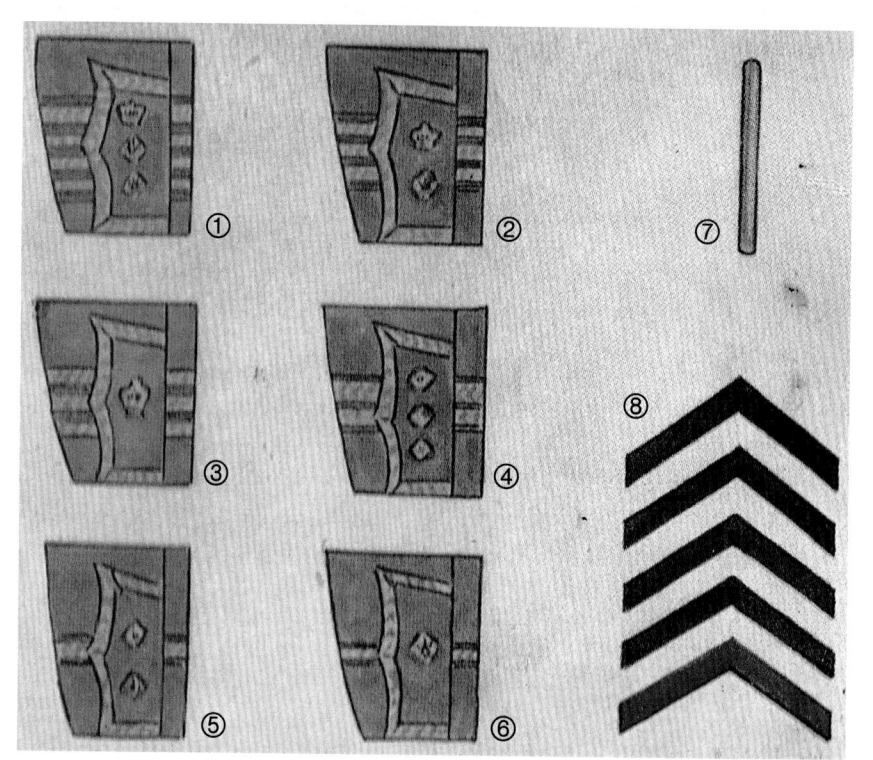

Officers' rank badges as worn during the Great War: ① Colonel; ② Lieutenant Colonel; ③ Major; ④ Captain; ⑤ Lieutenant; ⑥ 2nd Lieutenant; ⑦ Wound stripes (one of these was worn for every wound); ⑧ Service chevrons (red denoted service overseas in 1914; blue, service in 1915, '16, '17, '18). Note ⑦ and ⑧ were worn by all ranks, not only by officers.

Arm bands of commissioned officers: ① Adjutant-General's Branch at War Office; ② Command Headquarters, Ordnance Service; ③ Command Headquarters, Administration Officer; ④ London District Headquarters, A.D.C.; ⑤ Brigade Headquarters, Brigade Major; ⑥ Garrison Headquarters, Garrison Adjutant; ⑦ Signal Service; ⑧ Officer Engaged on Movement of Troops.

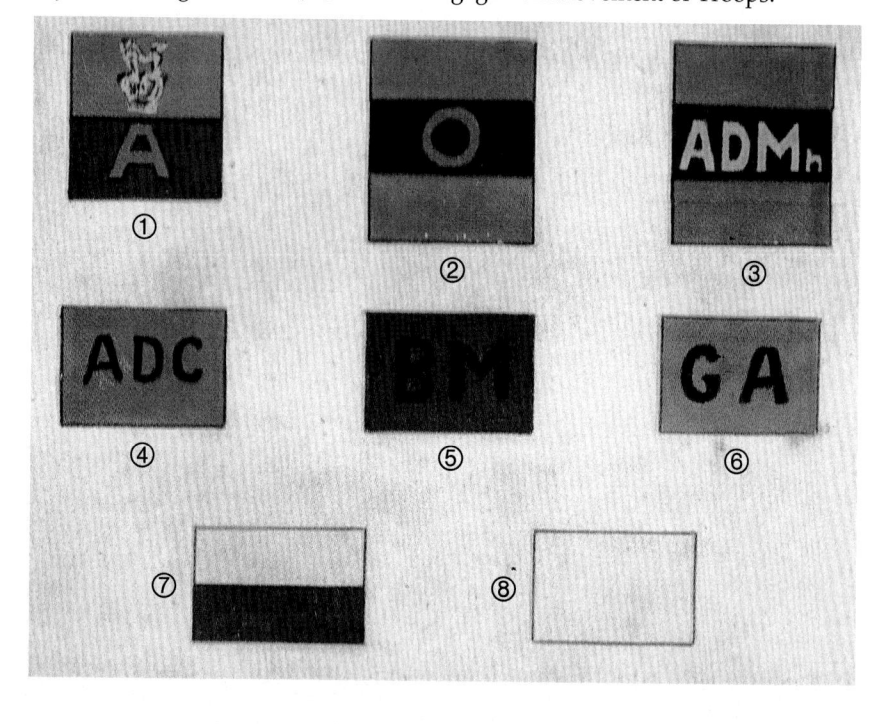

A command dugout in the Ypres sector, probably brigade HQ such as that in which Wyn Griffith would have worked – see p. 140. (*IWM E690*)

Mess, Headquarters XXII Corps. Wyn Griffith mentions few names, and none of the four New Zealanders in this photograph – see p. 150. (*IWM Q6938*)

Australian troops during the Third Battle of Ypres, October 1917 – see pp. 157–8. (*IWM E (Aus) 842*)

King George V visiting Australian troops. To the King's right is Sir Alexander Godley, the Corps Commander; behind is General Sir Herbert Plumer, the Army Commander – see p. 153. (*IWM Q954*)

The Battlefield near Soissons, 1918. By Western Front standards the terrain is relatively unscarred – see p. 176. (*IWM Q57533*)

GOC XXII Corps bids farewell to General Berthelot, 1918. Godley and XXII Corps staff surround Berthelot; Wyn Griffith is among the group to the rear – see p. 178. (*IWM Q9149*)

Wyn Griffith, David Liddle and Major F.A. Pile at Mons, 1918. (*Martin Wyn Griffith*)

The Memorial to the 38th (Welsh) Division at Mametz Wood by David Peterson, unveiled 11 July 1987. (*RWF Trustees*)

A German trench on the edge of a wood, such as that faced by 15th RWF during the assault on Mametz Wood.
(*James Payne collections*)

Brigadier Horatio Evans, Major Charles Veal and an unknown officer in Mametz Wood.
(*IWM Q868*)

G.O.C. VIII Corps and staff. From left: not identified, not identified, Brigadier-General Ellington, Lieutenant-General Hunter-Weston, not identified, Major Monk(?) – see p. 131. (*IWM Q736*)

Winifred Wyn Griffith (Wyn) in 1916. (*Martin Wyn Griffith*)

Dugouts along the Yser Canal – see p. 140. (*IWM Q5947*)

Infantry crossing a bridge on the Yser Canal – see p. 139. (*IWM Q2681*)

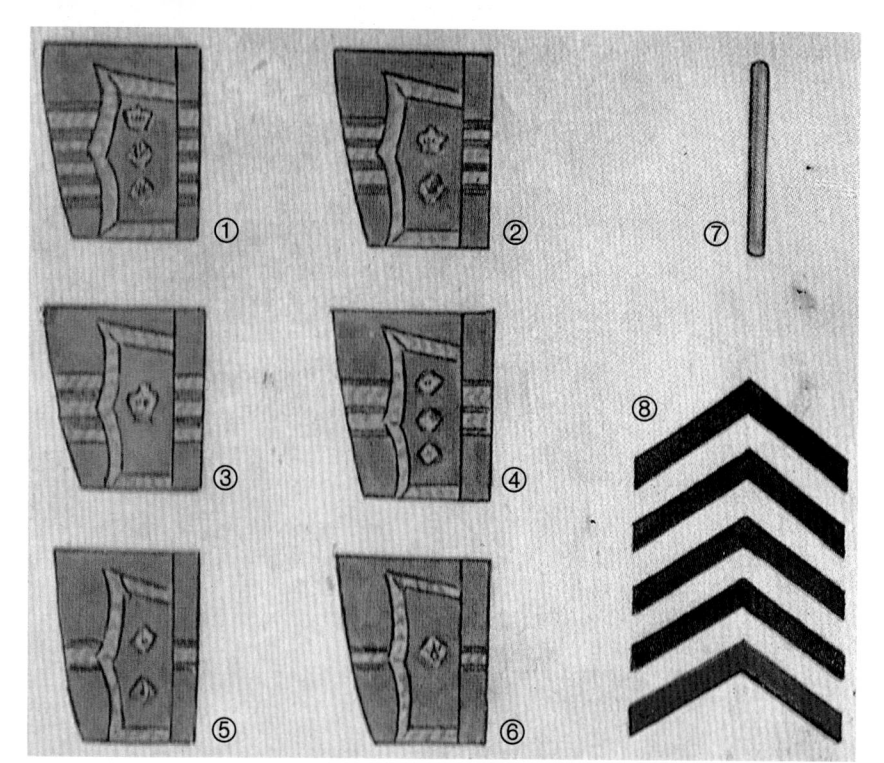

Officers' rank badges as worn during the Great War: ① Colonel; ② Lieutenant Colonel; ③ Major; ④ Captain; ⑤ Lieutenant; ⑥ 2nd Lieutenant; ⑦ Wound stripes (one of these was worn for every wound); ⑧ Service chevrons (red denoted service overseas in 1914; blue, service in 1915, '16, '17, '18). Note ⑦ and ⑧ were worn by all ranks, not only by officers.

Arm bands of commissioned officers: ① Adjutant-General's Branch at War Office; ② Command Headquarters, Ordnance Service; ③ Command Headquarters, Administration Officer; ④ London District Headquarters, A.D.C.; ⑤ Brigade Headquarters, Brigade Major; ⑥ Garrison Headquarters, Garrison Adjutant; ⑦ Signal Service; ⑧ Officer Engaged on Movement of Troops.

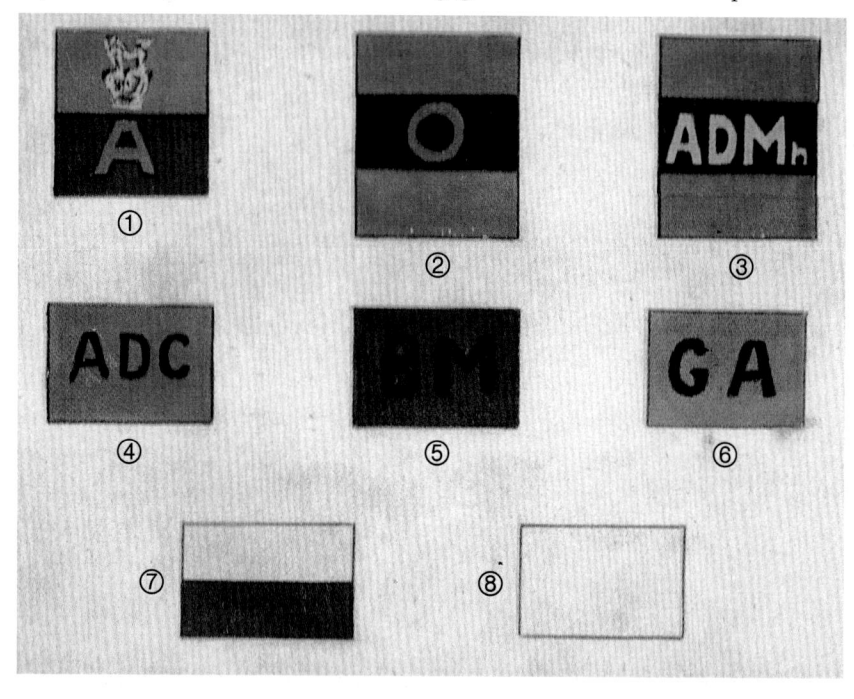

A command dugout in the Ypres sector, probably brigade HQ such as that in which Wyn Griffith would have worked – see p. 140. (*IWM E690*)

I Mess, Headquarters XXII Corps. Wyn Griffith mentions few names, and none of the four New Zealanders in this photograph – see p. 150. (*IWM Q6938*)

Australian troops during the Third Battle of Ypres, October 1917 – see pp. 157–8.
(*IWM E (Aus) 842*)

King George V visiting Australian troops. To the King's right is Sir Alexander Godley, the Corps Commander; behind is General Sir Herbert Plumer, the Army Commander – see p. 153. (*IWM Q954*)

The Battlefield near Soissons, 1918. By Western Front standards the terrain is relatively unscarred – see p. 176. (*IWM Q57533*)

GOC XXII Corps bids farewell to General Berthelot, 1918. Godley and XXII Corps staff surround Berthelot; Wyn Griffith is among the group to the rear – see p. 178. (*IWM Q9149*)

Wyn Griffith, David Liddle and Major F.A. Pile at Mons, 1918. *(Martin Wyn Griffith)*

The Memorial to the 38th (Welsh) Division at Mametz Wood by David Peterson, unveiled 11 July 1987. *(RWF Trustees)*

Mametz Wood

white gashes in the chalk. Scattered equipment lying about underfoot, tangles of wire, small dumps of forgotten stores, all left behind in the advance. Other things were left behind in the advance, part of the purchase price of this downland, grim disfigured corpses rotting in the sun, so horrible in their discolour that it called for an act of faith to believe that these were once men, young men, sent to this degradation by their fellow men. One thought ran in and out of the mind like a shuttle in a loom; any one of the thousands of seconds in this July day might reduce Taylor or myself into a like travesty of living man, useless lumber best thrown away near some such heap of rubble as Mametz, 'where Ruin calls his brother Death'.[7] There was some comfort in the thought that my wife did not know that this day held for me any fuller measure of danger than any other day of war, that for her there was no greater straining of the tense string that ran from hope to fear. And if I were killed, I would turn from man to memory in her heart without leaving a mutilated shell of flesh to haunt her eyes.

'I haven't seen anything of my young brother for some days,' I said to Taylor. 'I wonder what he is doing. He's such a kid, for all his uniform. He ought to be still in school, not in this bloody shambles.'

'He's all right,' replied Taylor. 'I saw him last night. The brigade called for two runners from each battalion, and he came as one of them – he's somewhere near that old German dug-out we came from.'

'I wish I'd known. It was his birthday two days ago, and I've got a little present for him in my valise. I wonder if he'll ever see another birthday ... I don't know how I could face my mother if anything happened to him and I got through.'

'Well, he's got a chance, Gruff – he might be in the line. What do you think of our job today?'

'The General was cursing last night at his orders. He said that only a madman could have issued them. He called the Divisional Staff a lot of plumbers, herring-gutted at that. He argued at the time, and asked for some control over the artillery that is going to cover us, but he got nothing out of them. We are not allowed to attack at dawn; we must wait for the show at Contalmaison, well away on our left.'[8]

'We'll get a good view of that show from Pommiers Redoubt.'

'I dare say, but don't you think that it is a funny thing to keep us waiting in the lobby? We are going to attack Mametz Wood from one side, and Contalmaison is on the other side of the Wood – why shouldn't both attacks be made at the same time? It would spread out the German fire.'

'I suppose it would spread out ours too,' said Taylor, 'but if you are going to start asking "Why" about orders you'll soon be off the Staff or off your head. You might as well say, "Why attack the Wood at all?"'

'But I do say that, Taylor. Look at it now – it's a forest. What damage can our guns do to that place? If you had a good dug-out near the edge of that wood, and a machine gun, how many men would you allow to cross that slope leading up to the Wood? You'd mow them down as soon as they stood up.'[9]

We had reached the high ground at Pommiers Redoubt, and, standing in a trench, scanning the Wood with our glasses, it seemed as thick as a virgin forest. There was no sign of life in it, no one could say whether it concealed ten thousand men or ten machine guns. Its edges were clean cut, as far as the eye could see, and the ground between us and the Wood was bare of any cover. Our men were assembled in trenches above a dip in the ground, and from these they were to advance, descend into the hollow, and cross the bare slope in the teeth of the machine-gunners in the Wood. On their right, as they advanced across the bullet-swept zone, they would be exposed to enfilade fire, for the direction of their advance was nearly parallel to the German trenches towards Bazentin, and it would be folly to suppose that the German machine guns were not sited to sweep that slope leading to the Wood.

'I'm not surprised that the General cursed when he got his orders,' said Taylor. 'The truth about the Brigadier is that he's got too much sense. He was soldiering when some of the fellows above him were still playing marbles. I'm going to see my signallers … I'll see you later.'

A little further along the trench a group of officers were engaged in a discussion over a map spread out on a box. I went up to speak to them, and found that this was the headquarters of a group of heavy artillery[10] concerned in the bombardment of Contalmaison, and about to wipe it off the map, as I gathered.

Taylor came up out of a dug-out. 'We're through to the old Brigade Headquarters, the Division, and to the battalions. How long we'll be through to the battalions is another story,' he said.

Mametz Wood

The General arrived with the Brigade Major and the Staff Captain, looked around him quickly, and turned to me.

'Have you found a good place for us?'

'Yes sir, there's room in the signallers' dugout, but this is a good place for seeing.'

'It's close on seven o'clock. Are we through to everybody, and have the battalions reported that they are in position?' he asked.

'Yes sir.'

'Then send out the report that Brigade Headquarters has opened here. You stay with me, and be ready to take down any orders or messages when the time comes.'

With this he went to consult with the Brigade Major. I stood on a step in the side of the trench, studying the country to the east and identifying the various features from the map. Our guns were quiet, and, although everybody within sight was moving, there was a weird stillness in the air, a brooding menace. Why was I standing here when men I knew were lined up in readiness to expose their bodies to a driving sleet of lead? The thought of the days' torment, doomed, as I thought, from its beginning, to bring no recompense, weighed like a burden of iron. The sound of a heavy bombardment, some distance away to our left, broke in upon the silence and grew to a storm of noise and smoke. Contalmaison was the target, prominent upon a hill until the smoke obscured the hill-top, turning it into a dark cloud hung between a blue sky and brown-pitted earth. Out of this cloud, at intervals of some minutes, an orange sheet of flame made an effort to escape, only to be conquered and smudged out by the all-pervading smoke. It did not seem possible that there could be guns enough in France to create such a fury as this, and my mind went back to the artillery fire of 1915 and early 1916. Our trench bombardments were things of no importance when contrasted with this, and I felt half ashamed to remember that they had frightened me.

At eight o'clock the artillery began its bombardment of the edge of Mametz Wood. A thousand yards away from where I stood, our two battalions were waiting.[11] I read the orders again. The attack was to be carried out in three stages, beginning at half-past eight, reaching in succession three positions inside the Wood, under the protection of an artillery barrage. Smoke screens were to be formed here and there. Everything sounded so simple and easy.

A few minutes after eight, all our telephone wires to the battalions were cut by the enemy's reply to our fire. There was no smoke screen, for some reason never explained – perhaps someone forgot about it. This was the first departure from the simplicity of the printed word. Messages came through, a steady trickle of runners bringing evil news; our fire had not masked the German machine guns in Mametz Wood, nor in the wood near Bazentin. The elaborate timetable suddenly became a thing of no meaning, as unrelated to our condition as one of Napoleon's orders; our artillery barrage was advancing in mockery of our failure, for we were two hundred yards away from the Wood.

A message arrived from the Division. In twenty minutes' time, the artillery would begin another bombardment of the edge of the Wood, and under cover of this we were to renew the attack – in twenty minutes. We were a thousand yards away from the battalions, with no telephone communication; there were maps at Divisional Headquarters, they knew where we were, they knew where the battalions were, and they knew that our lines were cut. A simple sum in arithmetic... Our operation was isolated; no one was attacking on either flank of our Brigade, so that there was complete freedom of choice as to time. With all the hours of the clock to choose from, some mastermind must needs select the only hour to be avoided. He did not ask himself whether the order could reach its ultimate destination in time... the answer to that sum in arithmetic.

Every attempt to move near the Wood was met by a burst of frontal and enfilade machine-gun fire. Shells were falling, taking a steady toll of lives. Later, another order came from Divisional Headquarters. We were to attack again, to make a third effort to penetrate this wall of lead. The General gave some orders to his Brigade-Major, called me to accompany him, and we set out for Caterpillar Wood and to reach the battalions. Although the day was fine, the heavy rains of the preceding days had turned the chalky soil into a stiff glue. The hurry in our minds accentuated the slowness of our progress, and I felt as if some physical force was dragging me back. Haste meant a fall into a shell hole, for we had abandoned the attempt to move along the trench. Shrapnel was bursting overhead, and a patter of machine-gun bullets spat through the air. We passed through Caterpillar Wood, and in a disused trench on our left I saw an artillery officer. I turned off to ask him whether his telephone was working, and learned that he was in communication with a Heavy Artillery Group somewhere beyond Pommiers Redoubt. I ran down the trench to rejoin the General, and we dropped down the bank into the nullah[12] between Caterpillar Wood and Mametz Wood, passing a stream of 'walking wounded' making their way out. There was a dug-out in the bank, with scores of stretchers down on the ground in front, each stretcher occupied by a fellow creature, maimed and in pain. This was the Advance Dressing Station; twenty rounds of shrapnel would have made stretchers unnecessary. Along the bare ridge rising up to Mametz Wood our men were burrowing into the ground with their entrenching tools, seeking whatever cover they might make. A few shells were falling, surprisingly few. Wounded men were crawling back from the ridge, men were crawling forward with ammunition. No attack could succeed over such ground as this, swept from front and side by machine guns at short range. Down in the nullah we were out of sight of the enemy, but fifteen minutes of shrapnel would have reduced the brigade to a battalion, and every minute that passed seemed to bring nearer the hour of our inevitable annihilation. We were caught in a trap, unable to advance, unable to withdraw without being observed. It must ever remain one of the many mysteries of the War why the enemy did not pound us with shell fire, for this was so obviously the only place of assembly.

The time was drawing near for the renewal of the attack, for another useless slaughter. Casualties in officers had been extremely heavy, and the battalions were somewhat disorganized.

'This is sheer lunacy,' said the General. 'I've tried all day to stop it. We could creep up to the edge of the Wood by night and rush it in the morning, but they won't listen to me ... It breaks my heart to see all this.'

'If I could get you through on the telephone, would you talk to them again?' I asked.

'Of course I would, but all the wires are cut, and there is no time to go back.'

'I know of a telephone to an Artillery Group, and they might get you through to the Division,' I answered.

'Find out at once whether I can get through,' he replied.

I hurried up to the trench where I had seen the artillery officer and found that his wires were still uncut, and as I ran back to the General I prayed in my heart that they would hold; the lives of some hundreds of men depended upon it. It did not occur to me that words sent along that wire might fail in their object, that someone sitting far away would look at a map and say, 'No, you must reach that wood at all costs.' Seen in its stark reality, our position was so hopeless that a dispassionate account of it must convince any one, even at a distance of six miles, that to remain where we were would be no less calamitous than to try to advance. The enemy had shown no desire to hold that exposed ridge with men, for his bullets were defence enough, and in a short space of time his artillery must realize that there was a magnificent target in that hollow between the ridge and the bank.

When I came back to the hollow, I could not find the General. I ran from one group of men to another, working my way up the ridge, until I found him organizing the defence of the position against any possible counter-attack. Shells did not seem to matter; my whole existence, up to that very minute, had been of no importance to the world, but my original conversation with that artillery officer, so obviously prompted by what men call Destiny, could lead to the saving of hundreds of lives, and must not fail to do so. I knew that I had been 'chosen' for this. Ten minutes later I sat in the trench while the General spoke on the telephone, tersely describing the utter folly of any course of action other than a gradual withdrawal under cover of outposts, and quoting figures of our casualties. He was arguing with determination. There was opposition, but he won. As I jumped up to start on our way back to the ridge, he stopped me.

'Wait a minute. They are shelling this bank, and this message must get through. Give me a sheet of paper,' said he. He wrote down his order for the withdrawal and gave it to me. 'You go one way, and I'll go another way. Join me in the hollow. Go as fast as you can.' With this he went down the trench, and I ran and stumbled down the bank, still feeling perfectly safe in the hands of Destiny.

Two hours later the General and I were dragging our way from the nullah and back towards Pommiers Redoubt. We sat down in a trench to let a file of men pass by, and I suddenly noticed that his face was grey and drawn.

'Have you eaten anything since this morning?' I asked him.

'No ... have you?' he replied. 'I feel whacked.'

'Will you wait here a few minutes – I'll be back soon,' I said.

I had seen a dug-out, and I went inside it. Some signallers were lighting a fire to boil a mess-tin full of water; they lent me an enamel cup, and in it I put a tablet of compressed tea. The brew was strong and the water was not boiling, but it was a warm drink, and I took it back to the General. It revived him, and we munched our biscuits as we walked along.

Back again to Pommiers Redoubt, but with a difference, in the flat greyness of approaching dusk. The noise of the guns had died down to a sullen scale-practice, with an occasional and almost accidental chord, so different from the crashes of the day. Stretcher-bearers, bowed forward under their straps, were carrying their burdens of suffering across the ploughed and pitted slopes.

'How did you come to find that telephone?' asked the General.

'I happened to notice the artillery officer on my way down, and I went to ask him if his line back was working. Don't you remember my leaving you?'

'No, I don't remember ... Well, it saved the lives of some hundreds of men, but it has put an end to me.'

'Why do you say that?'

'I spoke my mind about the whole business ... you heard me. They wanted us to press on at all costs, talked about determination, and suggested that I didn't realize the importance of the operation. As good as told me that I was tired and didn't want to tackle the job. Difficult to judge on the spot, they said! As if the whole trouble hadn't arisen because someone found it so easy to judge when he was six miles away and had never seen the country, and couldn't read a map. You mark my words, they'll send me home for this: they want butchers, not brigadiers. They'll remember now that I told them, before we began, that the attack could not succeed unless the machine guns were masked. I shall be in England in a month.'

He had saved the Brigade from annihilation. That the rescue, in terms of men, was no more than a respite of days was no fault of his, for there is no saving of life in war until the eleventh hour of the last day is drawing to an end. It was nearly midnight when we heard that the last of our men had withdrawn from that ridge and valley, leaving the ground empty, save for the bodies of those who had to fall to prove to our command that machine guns can defend a bare slope. Six weeks later the General went home.

The next day brought no time for crying over spilt milk. The Staff Captain had become a casualty, and had been evacuated as a shell-shock case, so that it fell to my lot to do his work, poorly equipped as I was for the task. For the first time I realized that, battle or no battle, reports must be made, returns prepared, and administrative work must continue as if we were all in barracks. I did my best, but if there are lacunæ in the statistics, memoranda 'lost' and unanswered, mine must be the blame. The General and the Brigade Major were so concerned with matters of war that I could not in very shame intrude upon their consultations to ask advice on questions that appeared to me to lack fundamental importance. On paper, I promised where I did not perform, and, over the telephone, parried all demands from the Division.

The two remaining brigades of the Division were to attack Mametz Wood in the afternoon of the following day, and we were to be in reserve, ready to take over the defence of the wood if the attack succeeded. This venture was differently staged. A narrower front gave promise of greater support from the artillery, and the approach, bad as it was, did not make success impossible. Until we were called upon to fight, the brigade was to spend its time carrying and working for the others, in spite of our exhaustion in numbers and in strength. At the last moment, the attack was postponed for twelve hours, and it was not until dawn on the 10th July that the flower of young Wales stood up to the machine guns, with a success that astonished all who knew the ground.[13] Two of our battalions had become involved in the fighting in the Wood,[14] and at five o'clock in the afternoon, our brigade was ordered to relieve the attacking brigades and to take over the responsibility for the defence of the sector against any counter-attacks. It was five o'clock in the morning before this relief was completed.

A little before dawn, the General and the Brigade Major went up to the Wood, leaving me to follow them at midday. At seven in the morning, as I was wrestling with some papers that I did not understand, a runner came in with a message from the General. The Brigade Major had been wounded, and I was to go up at once to join the General in the Wood. This, at any rate, was a man's job, and I left the papers in their disarray. A month ago, my military horizon was bounded by the limits of a company of infantry; now I was to be both Brigade Major and Staff Captain to a Brigadier-General in the middle of a battle. I consoled myself with the thought that if I could originate nothing, I could do what I was told to do.

I passed through two barrages before I reached the Wood, one aimed at the body, and the other at the mind. The enemy was shelling the approach from the south with some determination, but I was fortunate enough to escape injury and to pass on to an ordeal ever greater. Men of my old battalion were lying dead on the ground in great profusion. They wore a yellow badge on their sleeves, and without this distinguishing mark, it would have been impossible to recognize the remains of many of them. I felt that I had run away.

Before the Division had attempted to capture Mametz Wood, it was known that the undergrowth in it was so dense that it was all but impossible to move through it. Through the middle of the Wood a narrow ride ran to a communication trench leading to the German main second line of defence in front of Bazentin, a strong trench system permitting of a quick reinforcement of the garrison of the Wood. With equal facility, the Wood could be evacuated by the enemy and shelled, as it was not part of the trench system.

My first acquaintance with the stubborn nature of the undergrowth came when I attempted to leave the main ride to escape a heavy shelling. I could not push a way through it, and I had to return to the ride. Years of neglect had turned the Wood into a formidable barrier, a mile deep. Heavy shelling of the southern end had beaten down some of the young growth, but it had also thrown trees and large branches into a barricade. Equipment, ammunition, rolls of barbed wire, tins of food, gas helmets and rifles were lying about everywhere. There were more corpses than men, but there were worse sights than corpses. Limbs and mutilated trunks, here and there a detached head, forming splashes of red against the green leaves, and, as in advertisement of the horror of our way of life and death, and of our crucifixion of youth, one tree held in its branches a leg, with its torn flesh hanging down over a spray of leaf.

Each bursting shell reverberated in a roll of thunder echoing through the Wood, and the acid fumes lingered between the trees. The sun was shining strongly overhead, unseen by us, but felt in its effort to pierce through the curtain of leaves. After passing through that charnel house at the southern end, with its sickly air of corruption, the smell of fresh earth and of crushed bark grew into complete domination, as clean to the senses as the other was foul. So tenacious in these matters is memory that I can never encounter the smell of cut green timber without resurrecting the vision of the tree that flaunted a human limb. A message was now on its way to some quiet village in Wales, to a grey farmhouse on the slope of a hill running down to Cardigan Bay, or to a miner's cottage in a South Wales valley, a word of death, incapable, in this late century of the Christian Era, of association with this manner of killing. That the sun could shine on this mad cruelty and on the quiet peace of an upland tarn near Snowdon, at what we call the same instant of time, threw a doubt upon all meaning in words. Death was warped from a thing of sadness into a screaming horror, not content with stealing life from its shell, but trampling in lunatic fury upon the rifled cabinet we call a corpse.

There are times when fear drops below the threshold of the mind; never beyond recall, but far enough from the instant to become a background. Moments of great exaltation, of tremendous physical exertion, when activity can dominate over all rivals in the mind, the times of exhaustion that follow these great moments; these are, as I knew from the teachings of the months gone by, occasions of release from the governance of fear. As I hurried along the ride in this nightmare wood, stepping round the bodies clustered about the shell holes, here and there helping a wounded man to clamber over a fallen tree trunk, falling flat on my face when the whistle of an approaching shell grew into a shrieking 'YOU', aimed at my ear, to paralyse before it killed, then stumbling on again through a cloud of bitter smoke, I learned that there was another way of making fear a thing of small account.

It was life rather than death that faded away into the distance, as I grew into a state of not-thinking, not-feeling, not-seeing. I moved past trees, past other things; men passed by me, carrying other men, some crying, some cursing, some silent. They were all shadows, and I was no greater than they. Living or dead, all were unreal. Balanced uneasily on the knife-edge between utter oblivion and this temporary not-knowing, it seemed a little matter whether I were destined to go forward to death or to come back to life. Past and future were equidistant and unattainable, throwing no bridge of desire across the gap that separated me both from my remembered self and from all that I had hoped to grasp. I walked as on a mountain in a mist, seeing neither sky above nor valley beneath, lost to all sense of far or near, up or down, either in time or space. I saw no precipice, and so I feared none.

Thus it was that the passing seconds dealt a sequence of hammer-blows, at first so poignantly sharp that the mind recoiled in unbelief, but in their deadly repetition dulling the power of response and reaction into a blind acceptance of this tragedy, and in the merciful end, pounding all sensibility into an atrophy that refused to link sight to thought. A swirl of mist within me had thrown a curtain to conceal the chasm of fear, and I walked on unheeding and unexpectant.

Mametz Wood

I reached a cross-ride in the Wood where four lanes broadened into a confused patch of destruction. Fallen trees, shell holes, a hurriedly dug trench beginning and ending in an uncertain manner, abandoned rifles, broken branches with their sagging leaves, an unopened box of ammunition, sandbags half-filled with bombs, a derelict machine gun propping up the head of an immobile figure in uniform, with a belt of ammunition drooping from the breech into a pile of red-stained earth – this is the livery of War. Shells were falling, over and short, near and wide, to show that somewhere over the hill a gunner was playing the part of blind fate for all who walked past this well-marked spot. Here, in the struggle between bursting iron and growing timber, iron had triumphed and trampled over an uneven circle some forty yards in diameter. Against the surrounding wall of thick greenery, the earth showed red and fresh, lit by the clean sunlight, and the splintered tree-trunks shone with a damp whiteness, but the green curtains beyond could conceal nothing of greater horror than the disorder revealed in this clearing.

Even now, after all these years, this round ring of man-made hell bursts into my vision, elbowing into an infinity of distance the wall of my room, dwarfing into nothingness objects we call real. Blue sky above, a band of green trees, and a ploughed graveyard in which living men moved worm-like in and out of sight; three men digging a trench, thigh-deep in the red soil, digging their own graves, as it chanced, for a bursting shell turned their shelter into a tomb; two signallers crouched in a large shell hole, waiting for a summons to move, but bearing in their patient and tired inactivity the look of dead men ready to rise at the trump of a Last Judgment.

Other memories steal upon the screen of vision, growing imperceptibly from a dim remembrance of a part into a firmly-built unity of composition as the eye gains control over its focussing, but this image of war in its brutality flashes in an instant, sharp and clear in its uttermost detail. Then, at its first seeing, it was unreal, unrelated to my past, for the mist was within me, but now and for ever it must rise with every closing of my eyes into a stabbing reality that governs the future. So many things are seen more clearly now that the passing years have allowed the mud of action to settle at the bottom of the pool of life.

Near the edge of this ring I saw a group of officers. The Brigadier was talking to one of his battalion commanders, and Taylor, the Signals Officer, was arguing with the Intelligence Officer about the position on the map of two German machine guns. The map itself was a sign of the shrinking of our world into a small compass: a sheet of foolscap paper bearing nothing but a large scale plan of Mametz Wood, with capital letters to identify its many corners, was chart enough for our adventure this day.

'What has happened to the Brigadier?' I asked Taylor. 'Why is his arm in a sling?'

'Shrapnel,' he answered. 'He got hit as he was coming up to the Wood, but he got the doctor to dress it for him. He says it doesn't hurt him, but I expect it will before the day is over.'

'Did you see the Brigade Major ... was he badly hit?'

'Shrapnel in the leg – his gammy leg. The stretcher-bearers took him away, cursing everybody and damning his luck. Seems to me he doesn't know luck when he sees it. You'll have to get down to it now.'

'Yes. Tell me what has happened so far.'

'You never saw such a mess. Nobody knows where anybody is, the other brigades are still here – what's left of them – all mixed up.'

'Are your lines holding? Are you through to anybody?'

'Devil a soul,' answered Taylor. 'As soon as I mend a line the Boche breaks it. You can't keep a line up with that barrage across the bottom of the Wood. There's an artillery F.O.O.[15] just behind you, in that shell hole; I don't know what the devil he's doing up here – he can't see twenty yards in front of him, and all his lines are gone. He might as well be in Cardiff.'

As soon as the battalion commander had gone I joined the Brigadier.

'Is this the Brigade Headquarters?' I asked. 'It is,' he replied. 'It's an unhealthy place, but we've got to be somewhere where we can be found by night as well as by day. Get your notebook and take down the position of affairs at the moment. We have been sent here to take over the line and to make secure against counterattacks. There are four battalions of our brigade, and what is left of four other battalions. We are holding an irregular line about three hundred yards from the end of the Wood, bending back towards the west. The units are very mixed up, and I've just come back from trying to give them their boundaries. They are all straightening themselves out and digging in, but the undergrowth is so dense that it will be some hours before they are in their proper places.'

'Are we supposed to attack and clear the Wood?'

'No. Our orders last night were to take over the line. I've told the battalion commanders to reconnoitre and to push out where they can. We don't know whether the enemy is holding the far end in any great strength.'

'If we have to attack later on, how do you propose to do it?'

'By surprise,' answered the General. 'With the bayonet only. That's the only way to get through the Wood. If our artillery will keep quiet, we can do it. Here's my map – make a summary of what I've told you. It took me hours to get round our line.'

Runners came from the battalions giving news of progress in consolidation, and reporting that the enemy was in considerable strength on the northern edge, with plenty of machine guns. I sat down on a fallen tree-trunk and made a report of the situation, read it over to the General, and went in search of a runner to take it to the Division. Taylor was standing by a large shell hole, talking to his signallers.

'How can I get this to the Division?' I asked.

'Give it to me: that's my job. I've got a telephone down at Queen's Nullah, and if a runner can get out of the Wood and through the barrage, the message gets through.'

'Are the runners getting through?'

'Some don't, and some of those that do don't get back ... Don't give me any messages that are not absolutely essential and urgent. I'm getting short of men – seven down already this morning. I don't know what it will be like when the Boche wakes up. He's got us taped here. Look at those cross-rides – did you ever see such a butcher's shop?'

At this moment a signaller orderly came up to deliver a message. I opened it, glanced through it, and took it to the General. His face hardened as he read it. The Divisional Commander informed us that the enemy's trenches in front of Bazentin were being shelled, and that it was quite impossible that he had any strong force in Mametz Wood. The brigade was to attack and occupy the northern and western edges of the Wood at the earliest possible moment. Indeed, the Corps Commander strongly impressed the importance of clearing the Wood without delay.

While we were digesting this order, and drafting new orders to the battalions, a staff officer came up to join us. His red and black armband showed that he came from Army Headquarters,[16] and he spoke with all the prestige native to a traveller from distant lands who had penetrated to within a few hundred yards of the enemy. He brought orders that we were to carry out an attack upon the two edges of the Wood. The Brigadier listened to him with the patience of an older man coldly assessing the enthusiasm of youth. When the Staff Officer had finished, the General spoke.

'I've just had orders from the Division to attack and clear the rest of the Wood, and to do it at once. The defence is incomplete, the units are disorganized, and I did not propose to attack until we were in a better position. My patrols report that the northern edge is strongly held. I haven't a fresh battalion, and no one can say what is the strength of any unit.'

'What do you propose to do,' asked the Staff Officer.

'My intention is to take the remainder of the Wood by surprise, with the bayonet if possible; no artillery bombardment to tell him that we are coming. I want a bombardment of the main German second line when we have taken our objective, to break up any counter-attack. Do you know anything about the artillery programme?'

'No, I do not. Are you in communication with the Division or with any of the artillery groups?'

'No, except by runner, and that takes a long time. I'm issuing orders to the battalions to get ready to advance quietly at three o'clock, and I'm sending a copy of the order to the Division; if you are going back will you get in touch with them as soon as possible and tell them that I don't want a barrage?'

The Staff Officer left us, and we worked at the orders for the battalions. The enemy was shelling the Wood, searching it, as the gunners say, and there were intermittent bursts of machine-gun fire, with an occasional uneven and untidy rush of rifle fire. On our right a few bombs burst in a flat, cracking thud. At a quarter to three, while we were waiting for the hour, a sudden storm of shells passed over our heads, bursting in the Wood some two hundred yards ahead of us.

'Good God,' said the General. 'That's our artillery putting a barrage right on top of our battalions! How can we stop this? Send a runner down at once ... send two or three by different routes ... write the message down.'

Three men went off with the message, each by a different way, with orders to get to Queen's Nullah somehow or other. Our barrage had roused the enemy, and from every direction shells were falling in the Wood; behind us a devilish storm of noise showed that a heavy price must be paid for every attempt to leave the Wood.

The Brigadier sat on a tree-trunk, head on hand, to all appearances neither seeing nor hearing the shells.

'This is the end of everything ... sheer stupidity. I wonder if there is an order that never reached me ... but that staff officer ought to have known the artillery programme for the day. And if there is another order, they ought not to have put down that barrage until they got my acknowledgement. How can we attack after our own barrage has ploughed its way through us? What good can a barrage do in a wood like this?'

At twenty past three our own artillery was still pouring shells into the wood. None of the runners had returned. Taylor sent three more to try to rescue us from this double fire, but ten minutes later we were left with no worse burden than the enemy's shelling. Reports came through from the battalions that we had suffered severely. As the afternoon drew out into the evening, we nibbled away here and there with fluctuating fortune, but at the approach of night the enemy reinforced his line and kept us from the edge while he pounded away with his artillery.[17]

It was nearing dusk when Taylor came up to me.

'I want to have a word with you,' he said, drawing me away. 'I've got bad news for you ...'

'What's happened to my young brother ... is he hit?'

'You know the last message you sent out to try to stop the barrage ... well, he was one of the runners that took it. He hasn't come back. He got his message through all right, and on his way back through the barrage he was hit. His mate was wounded by the shell that killed your brother ... he told another runner to tell us.'

'My God ... he's lying out there now, Taylor!'

'No, old man ... he's gone.'

'Yes ... yes, he's gone.'

'I'm sorry ... I had to send him, you know.'

'Yes, of course ... you had to. I can't leave this place ... I suppose there's no doubt about his being killed?'

'None – he's out of it all now.'

So I had sent him to his death, bearing a message from my own hand, in an endeavour to save other men's brothers; three thoughts that followed one another in unending sequence, a wheel revolving within my brain, expanding until it touched the boundaries of knowing and feeling. They did not gain in truth from repetition, nor did they reach the understanding. The swirl of mist refused to move.

Within the unclouded portion of my being a host of small things took their place on the stage, drawing their share of attention, and passing on. More orders to draft, situation reports to send out, demands for more bombs, enemy trench-mortars to be shelled into silence, machine guns wanted by everybody. The General put his hand on my shoulder. It began to grow dark. An order came from the Division to say that we would be relieved that night by a brigade from another Division,[18] and that on completion of the relief we were to return to our bivouacs. More orders to the battalions. The wheel was still revolving, while the procession of mere events moved without a break.

I walked towards the large shell hole that served as a shelter for the signallers, carrying in my hand a sheaf of messages for delivery. From the background of bursting shells came a whistle, deepening into a menace, and I flung myself on my face. I remembered a momentary flash of regret that I was still two yards from the protection of that shell hole. A black noise covered everything. When my eyes opened I was lying on my back, further away from the hole. I got up on my hands and knees and crawled to the signallers, still clutching the crumpled messages, and spoke to them. There was no answer. The rim of another large shell hole nearly touched their shelter, and the three signallers were huddled together, dead, killed by the concussion, for there was no mark of a wound.

The wheel came to rest, and I do not remember much of what happened afterwards. The night came, within and without. I have a clear memory of walking up the ride towards the battalions, of tripping over a branch, and of a flash of anger because I hurt my shoulder when I fell. The General went forward to one battalion to make sure that the line was securely held to cover the relief, and I went to another battalion on the same errand. The night seemed to pass in a black film, broken only by the flashes of bursting shells. I am told that I found the battalion.

Some time later, a heavy storm of shell fire drove me into a little trench where I crouched with some men to shelter. We talked in Welsh, for they were Anglesey folk; one was a young boy, and after a thunderous crash in our ears he began to cry out for his mother, in a thin boyish voice, 'mam, mam ...' I woke up and pushed my way to him, fumbling in my pockets for my torch, and pulled him down to the bottom of the trench. He said that his arm was hurt. A corporal came to my assistance and we pulled off his tunic to examine his arm. He had not been hit, but he was frightened, still crying quietly. Suddenly he started again, screaming for his mother, with a wail that seemed older than the world, in the darkness of that night. The men began to mutter uneasily. We shook him, cursed at him, threatening even to kill him if he did not stop. He did not understand our words, but the shaking brought him back. He demanded his rifle and his steel helmet, and sat in the bottom of the trench to wait for the relief, talking rationally but slowly. English voices came out of the dark, enquiring for another battalion of our brigade; more men stumbled by in search of the posts they were to relieve. Our time was drawing to an end.

Dawn was breaking when I reached the clearing. The General had been waiting for me; another wave had passed over our brigade, and all the men of our battalions who were destined to leave the Wood were now on their way down to the bivouacs. He looked at me and asked me if I would like to sit down to rest, but I wanted to go on. We picked our way over the fallen timber and round the corpses, some sprawling stiffly, some huddled against the splintered tree-trunks, until we were clear of the Wood. I was afraid to look closely at them, lest I should recognize one of them.

Below the Wood, the enemy was still maintaining a barrage, but we were too tired to hurry. Our field guns were pushing up towards the slopes, some were in position and were firing to support the attack on the German second line. With them was another brother of mine, a bombardier, but I did not know it. We walked in silence, until the General asked me if I had any food. I found some biscuits in my haversack, and realized that I had not eaten for twenty-four hours.

It was eight o'clock when we reached the old German dug-out and drank a cup of tea. As we were finishing, a staff officer from the Division arrived to tell us that we were to get ready to move at short notice. Protest was useless; the battalions must be clear of the bivouacking ground by five o'clock the next morning, and we must march a distance of fourteen miles to another sector of the front.[19]

The day passed in getting ready for the march, and in trying to write a letter to my father and mother to tell them what had happened. When at last I succeeded, I felt in some queer way that an episode was ended, that all feeling had been crushed out of existence

A forward dug-out' by David Jones. [RWF Trustees]

within me. Night came, but I could not sleep. At two in the morning we set out to join the battalions, and as dawn was breaking over Bazentin, I turned towards the green shape of Mametz Wood and shuddered in a farewell to one, and to many. I had not even buried him, nor was his grave ever found.

Notes

1. 38th (Welsh) Division, having completed two weeks' training in trench-to-trench attacks, was ordered further south on 28 June to the area of Rubempre where it joined II Corps, then commanded by Lieutenant-General Sir Claude Jacob KCB DSO. Here it was to be prepared to follow the Cavalry Corps in the event of a breakthrough and take over Bapaume from them. However the failure of the British attack on the left and in the centre of the Somme battlefield on 1 July altered these plans. 38th Division marched first northwards towards Acheux and then south to Treux where it eventually joined XIV Corps under Lieutenant-General Sir Henry Horne KCB. The Division was to relieve the 7th Infantry Division in and around the village of Mametz on 5 July and prepare to capture the major feature of Mametz Wood. Reconnaissance and probes of the German positions went on from 6 to 9 July.
2. In the British and Imperial armies at this time, the division was the highest military organisation in permanent existence in peacetime: corps were formed in war, or, as Field Service Regulations put it, 'for purposes of command and local administration'. Thus the division was the lowest level at which all arms and services, and their functions, were found represented on the divisional staff and in the division's order of battle. Its staff was large enough to plan and conduct operations simultaneously. In general, a division could take up to five brigades under command for simultaneous or sequenced operations and thus could continue the battle round the clock; its fire support and engineer support were organic; and the division could administer and support itself logistically. All that said, an infantry division in 1917 had very limited capabilities when compared with its modern equivalent: in firepower it equated only to a 2002 mechanised infantry brigade. Moreover a 1917 infantry division had radio communications only upwards to corps; and only minimal ability to observe the battlefield – 38th Division did not even have a divisional cavalry regiment – and it had no organic ability to engage any enemy beyond the range of the contact battle, even supposing such an enemy could be observed.
3. See the explanation on the exercise of command in the introduction. It is probable that the new headquarters location would be prepared by a small activation party with the correct maps and current information which would move in advance of the time for the change of command. Once established the brigade commander would move there and take command leaving the rest of the staff and the baggage to follow. This process is still essentially the same as modern practice.
4. The Brigade Signal Officer was Lieutenant J.A. (John) Taylor RE. Emlyn Davies, who had joined 17 RWF on the same day and in the same village as

Wyn Griffith's brother Watcyn, also served as a signaller. He wrote *Taffy Went to War*. Davies described the instruments we had in a trench dugout equipped with wireless: 'Wireless was used to send messages backwards to Divisional HQ, not forward, when telephone lines were cut by shellfire. The sets were light and simple, primitive even, crystal type and with a Morse key – in those days, no voice messages were possible. Later a one-valve set was introduced; later still to include two valves: a considerable improvement but still inferior to those used by the Germans. Our signals were difficult, sometimes impossible to read and reception was complicated by the vast number of transmissions heard simultaneously. Our operators had to concentrate on their allotted station, picking up its individual tune in competition with other stations of greater strength. To wear headphones for a four-hour stretch imposed considerable strain. Reception was made more difficult still by the loud and persistent German transmissions from their station at Bruges and consequently, much jamming resulted, often rendering communications devoid of sense. Aerials were often cut and brought down by shellfire and the immediate erection of a replacement was essential. The first requirement was at least one but usually two trees fifty to a hundred feet apart. The signallers attached a guy rope to the aerial. This guy had to be long enough to clear the tree and land where it could be secured to the trunk. The guy was fastened to the stem of a defused rifle grenade which was then pushed into the rifle muzzle. The rifle was firmly held with its butt resting lightly on the ground, leaning at about forty-five degrees, and the grenade was fired. With good luck and much practice the contraption sailed over and beyond the trees.' (Emlyn Davies *Taffy Went to War* (Knutsford, 1976)).

5. The Padre was later identified by Mrs Patricia Evans as the Reverend Peter Jones Roberts, a Welsh Methodist minister from Barmouth who had joined up as a chaplain aged 51, beyond the usual age limits. He had four sons, all of whom were commissioned into the R.W. Fusiliers. The second son was captured in late 1916; the third badly wounded in 1918. The youngest got into the war in 1918 and survived. The boy whom Roberts was looking for was his eldest, Glyn, who had been commissioned in 1915 and was serving in the 9th Battalion, which was not in the 38th Division but was close by. He had been killed on 3 July and Roberts had spent a week searching for him.

6. This is probably *Crug y Bar*, by Thomas Charles (1762–1834) who founded the Welsh Sunday School movement and who wrote many fine hymns. The village of Crug y Bar lies in Carmarthenshire between Llandovery and Lampeter and is reputed to be the site of an ancient battle, hence its name. The Non-Conformist chapel there dates back to the last quarter of the 18th Century.

7. This line is from Percy Bysshe Shelley's poem *Alastor: or, the Spirit of Solitude* composed in 1815.

8. This was the attack by the 17th Division. 115 Brigade had been ordered to make a small attack on the eastern edge of the wood, beginning at 8.00 a.m.

9. The original orders issued by GHQ for the attack on 1 July had left out Mametz Wood as it was felt to be too hard a task; the attacking formations were to move east and west of it. Not only was the wood huge and dense,

MAMETZ WOOD

but the German second line was only 300 yards from its northern edge and therefore the positions in the wood could be easily reinforced.

10. This could well have been an Army level Royal Garrison Artillery brigade, employing 6-inch, 8-inch, 9.2-inch or 12-inch siege guns or howitzers; or even railway howitzers of 9.2, 12, 15 or 18 inch calibres. Such brigades could be allocated to the corps for a specific period by the Army Commander, General Sir Herbert Plumer. The normal calibre of the corps-level artillery brigades was a 60-pounder. At the beginning of the war, the Germans held a huge advantage in artillery with their large calibre *Krupp* guns, capable of long range, indirect fire, observed and corrected by telephone, telegraph or aircraft. In the British and French armies, artillery was generally still used to fire in the direct mode (i.e. with the target visible to the gunners) in support of troops in combat, and was of smaller calibre – 75mm for the French, 13 and 18-pounder for the British.
11. 16th (Cardiff City) Battalion the Welch Regiment and the 10th South Wales Borderers (1st Gwents).
12. A Hindustani word for a small river valley, in common use by regular soldiers who, like Wyn Griffith's brigade major, had served in India.
13. At 3.30 a.m. a heavy concentration of fire was put down on the southern edge of the wood with a smoke-screen laid on the eastern and south-western flanks. The assault went in at 4.15 a.m. with 114 Brigade in the east and 113 Brigade in the west. By 1.00 p.m. both brigades had secured the German's wood support trench at the cost of heavy casualties including two Commanding Officers of RWF battalions, Lieutenant-Colonels R.J.W. Carden and O.S. Flower. Ronald James Walter Carden had transferred to command 16 RWF from the 17th Lancers in November 1915. He is described as '... a gifted leader with a touch of fanaticism. He addressed his battalion before going into action: "Make your peace with God. We are going to take that position, and some of us won't come back – but we are going to take it." And tying a coloured handkerchief to his walking stick he said, "This will show you where I am." Carden, stick aloft, was a conspicuous figure. He was shot, fell, rose again and went on to the edge of the wood where he was killed.' (*Regimental Records*, Volume III). Oswald Swift Flower (1871–1916) was a pre-war regular officer who had joined the regiment in 1892 from the Militia and served in Crete, Malta, China (including Peking and Tientsin), Burma and India. He retired on grounds of health in 1912 but was recalled to duty in 1914, acting as Brigade-Major during the raising of the service battalions. He took command of 13 RWF in July 1915.
14. 17 RWF and 10 SWB had been sent to reinforce 114 Brigade.
15. Forward Observation Officer. This officer controlled the fire of the guns by telephone or runner, adjusting targets as required. Although differently equipped, all armies still use this system.
16. At that time, all staff officers wore red gorget patches on the lapels of their Service Dress tunics, and a red band round the cap. Armbands denoting the appropriate staff branch were also worn. These marks were viewed with some disdain by the infantry, which had a poor view of the staff generally, whether or not this was deserved. Because of the divisive effect this had, the wearing of

staff insignia was restricted after the war to officers of the rank of Colonel and above, which remains the case today. Armbands were discontinued, except for staff college exercise appointments.
17. The Divisional History, however, records that 'On the 11th July at 3.15 p.m. the 115th Brigade advanced and cleared out the Germans on the northern edge of the wood.' Robert Graves was in Mametz Wood with the 1st Battalion of the Royal Welch Fusiliers shortly afterwards and wrote thus of what he saw in his autobiography *Goodbye To All That*: 'Mametz Wood was full of the dead of the Prussian Guards reserve, big men, and the Royal Welch and South Wales Borderers of the new-army battalions, little men. There was not a single tree unbroken... There had been bayonet fighting in the wood. There was a man of the South Wales Borderers and one of the Lehr Regiment who had succeeded in bayoneting each other simultaneously. A survivor of the fighting told me later that he had seen a young soldier of the Fourteenth Royal Welch bayoneting a German in parade-ground style, automatically exclaiming as he had been taught: "in, out, on guard..."'
18. This was the 21st Division.
19. This was to Coigneux in order to relieve the 48th Division, taking over the line just south of Hébuterne and Gommecourt, opposite the notorious German strongpoint in the village of Serre.

Chapter 8

The Gleaning

15th RWF Memorial at Gray's Inn

It was early in the morning of a fine day in July. The clear air and fresh sunlight, the green fields, the white road and the pale blue sky all combined together to make a fit setting for a pageant of youth in bright colours. There was a quality in the hour and the place, a harmony in the open countryside, indescribable save in terms of serenity. Nature stood still, poised securely in a major key, unrelated to the life of man and unconcerned with his discords. Against this background of freshness and purity a slow-moving worm of dingy yellow twisted itself round the corner made by a jutting shoulder of the downland. The battalions of the brigade were marching in column of fours along the road, and from a little distance it was clear that there was a lack of spine in the column. No ring of feet, no swing of shoulder, no sway of company; slack knees and frequent hitching of packs, a doddering rise and fall of heads, and much leaning forward. Fatigue and exhaustion in a body of men attain an intensity greater than the simple sum of all the individual burdens of its members warrant. This loss of quality in a unit marching away from the Somme battlefield was made more evident by the rising memory of the sturdy column that swung its way down the hedge-bound lanes in the early mornings of the end of June, a bare fortnight past, singing and laughing in the happiness of relief from the fetters of the trenches in Flanders. Today the silence was unbroken, save by the shuffling of feet and the clanking of equipment.

The intensity with which we had striven to attune the mind to a soldier's way of thinking, to the cultivation of a quick and semi-instinctive assessing of military worth, showed itself in this first impact. Here was a weapon, all but shattered on so rough usage, fallen in quality from a spear-head into a ploughshare, fit only to turn the soil and to revert to a quiet preoccupation with the tenancy of a sector where war played at husbandry. Back to the digging of trenches, to the daily struggle against the fall of earth, to the assiduous draining of water; no other verdict was possible. It did not seem necessary to give exact shape to thought, to translate into words the inner meaning of this decay; to look at the column, to turn away and to look again, was exercise enough to leave an abiding sense of pain.

Gradually, and almost imperceptibly, the mind ceased to dwell upon this impression of decline. The habit of being a soldier was but newly acquired, and the power of concentrating upon the narrower military importance of the phenomenon had not completely overlaid the older endowments of life and upbringing. Our future use became a thing of less moment than our present helplessness. The weight of tired limbs and a dragging pack, the burning blows of a hard road upon swollen feet, the inescapable burden of a rifle, the pull of an ammunition pouch upon a sore shoulder, the reiterated blows of a water-bottle – these, and a thousand other pains, sounded clearly through the air, drowning the note of serenity rising from the green countryside.

A walk along the column brought a new aspect of our condition into view. A captain was leading a battalion, subalterns and company sergeant-majors were marching at the heads of companies, corporals in front of platoons. Men were marching abreast who had never before stood together in the same file. There are no gaps in a battalion on the march, though many have fallen, but the closing-up that follows losses tells its own tale. The faces of many silent and hard-eyed men showed that they were but half-aware of their new neighbours, newcomers who jostled the ghosts of old companions, usurpers who were themselves struggling against the same griefs and longings, marching forward with minds that looked backwards into time and space.

The long-stretched agony of the week had scoured something out of every man in the column. Experience had added nothing to our inheritance, for the days were spent in an endeavour to hold something of what we possessed, in a stern defence of the outposts of the soul. Man had fought against the tiger, no less than with his fellow man, against the overwhelming terror of sudden fear as implacably as he fought against danger. There had been no victory, no triumph. Eyes were dull and slow-moving, coated with a film that turned their opacity into a revelation of all the anguish that lay behind them. Who has not met the dumb protest in the stare of such eyes, lingering even into the days of peace?

Suddenly a turn of the mind brought to light another measure of our state. The four battalions marching up from the Somme made a column but little longer than the span of one battalion on the way down: we had left behind us nearly two thousand men of our brigade. The measure of our condition was the measure of the price paid for Mametz Wood; the largest of the woods in the Somme battlefield had reduced a strong division to a shadow. In the capture of this obstacle to our advancing line we had discharged our immediate task, only to be ourselves flung aside as of little worth.

We did not ask whether the reward were equal to the sacrifice; it may be that there is no equality in such matters, that war is the very negation of all value. Confined as we were in a world governed by a force operating ruthlessly in one direction, there was a wall on either side of our path. All that could happen to us was, at the whim of this force, a quicker or slower progress along our narrow alley, lacking knowledge of our destination, impotent to control our motion. We could not know whether our destination would prove to be our destiny, nor was it given to us to glance over the walls at other ways of climbing the hill. This is not to say that our attitude was one of fatalism; when one may not look to the right and left, there still remains another dimension. If resistance were of no avail, non-acceptance sprang up within us all as a natural reaction against the method of our employment. It was not so much that we admitted our inability to gauge the need for such a task; we did not even doubt that the capture of Mametz Wood was an indispensable operation, we imagined no evil fate choosing us as a weapon.

It would be untrue to suggest that our discontent rose up against the existence of a Battle of the Somme, or that we rebelled inwardly at the likelihood of another experience of this nature. There was no discussion about the relative merits of rival methods of attack or of alternative fronts. Although our lives were the letters that went to its spelling, the word strategy was never on our lips. We held no opinion on such high matters, but the generosity with which we disclaimed knowledge of so large a territory of the world of soldiering heightened the confidence, amounting almost to arrogance, of our condemnation of certain practices then in high favour with our superiors.

To every one of us it was bitterly clear that wars could not be won by piling up corpses in front of machine guns. Shellfire was inevitable, and its dangers were fair risks of war, but when one line of men had failed to satiate the hunger of machine guns, there was nothing inevitable in sending forth another wave to destruction. The argument was not vitiated by isolated instances of success here and there, at a price never quoted. Nor indeed was there anything of the inevitable in a constant failure to link up the loose threads of intention scattered over the battlefield, an omission that was made catastrophically evident to us in the gap that divorced artillery support from infantry action.

These were the thoughts that built up a weight of dissatisfaction, dragging at our heels day and night, clogging all power to eliminate the needless tortures of battle. All war was bad, but the thinking of our masters made it worse: wrong was in the saddle, all the world over. If we had devoted our lives to the study of war, this inward revolt against the method of our governance in the field might have risen clear of vagueness into a definite plea for another way of war-thinking, but we were neither civilians nor soldiers. We had lost the layman's power of judging between the rival theories of experts, without capturing the acquiescent confidence of a soldier. All the counsel we could give amounted to little more than a cry of 'Not thus ... not thus.'

Added to the burden of fatigue and grief we were governed by a dark feeling of personal failure. Mametz Wood was taken, but not by us, it seemed; we were the rejected of destiny, men whose services were not required. The dead were the chosen, and fate had forgotten us in its eager clutching at the men who fell; they were the richer prize. They captured Mametz Wood, and in it they lie.

Part Two

Beyond Mametz

Chapter 9

Salient

The badge of VIII Corps

Writing now,[1] on the last day of 1957, I cannot hope to be able to recreate on paper the life I led during the rest of the war. So far as emotion goes I wrote the war out of my system in *Up To Mametz*, and it gave me great relief: I have now grown old and too far removed from it to be able to repeat the effect of that book. Another war has intervened, and a greater loss.[2] But it is a great pity that after finishing it I did not at once write the book I had inside me: the war and the regular soldier and the staff as seen through the eyes of a temporary soldier forced into daily contact with it all, joking and critical, undoubtedly somewhat conceited, willing to learn and given to argument even with my betters, desperately anxious to do well – if only to avoid being sent back to the trenches! Now I can only try to do full justice to a much-maligned profession, and especially to commands or staffs that were the target for all the many published war books. I saw both sides of the war, and I was anxious to be fair to top and bottom of the army, when I learnt their different tasks.

I was in the Army for four and a half years, three of them on active service as an infantry officer, a company commander, and finally as a general staff officer on what was called 'Operations' (to distinguish it from Intelligence!), so that I had to undergo a series

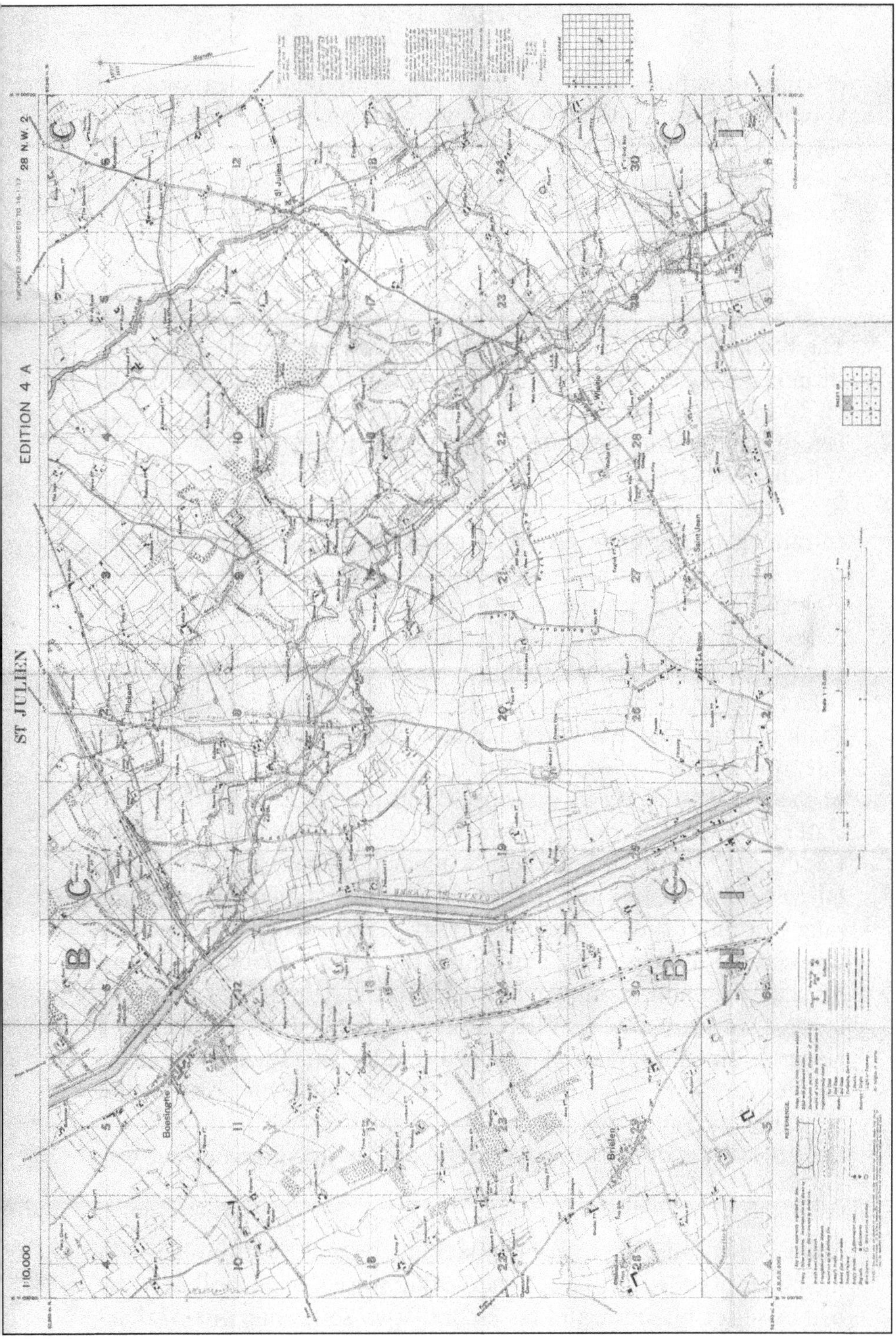

Map 5: The Trenches in the Yser Canal Sector.

of transformations of body and mind. This involved a series of apprenticeships, and now, forty years later, I can recognize a succession of events that remain in my memory and bring with them a resurgence of emotions associated with learning the various trades.[3]

* * *

The 38th (Welsh) Division, withdrawn after the Somme and much shrunken in size,[4] was transferred northwards. We began our move on 30 July, at 4 a.m., having been up two hours before that. It was beautiful country, just like Winchester. At 11 a.m. we bivouacked for a couple of hours in a field near Beauval, and reached the rail-head at 2 p.m. I began entraining the brigade group at once. At 5 p.m. on 1 August I entered the last train, and we reached our destination at 11 p.m. that night. We started off marching early on 3 August. We reached the pretty village of B–[5] about 7 a.m. in time for breakfast. I found a good billet in the chemist's shop – the best I had had so far.

July 1916

Here, we were to hold the trenches near Serre[6] and Hébuterne,[7] in chalk country where the trenches and dugouts were deep, dry and safe. Brigade headquarters operated from one of these. I was acting as a "learner" on the staff of 115 Brigade, doing the work of both Brigade Major and Staff Captain, for they had both been wounded.[8] We were assembled in billets behind the line and re-forming ourselves, when the telephone rang – or buzzed, to be accurate, to say that the Corps Commander was coming to inspect us, and would the Brigade Commander and his staff meet him, mounted, at a certain field – then take him to the troops. We were now in VIII Corps, commanded, so I heard, by a General something Weston. I replied that the Brigadier had gone to hospital, and that I was all that was left of the staff, but that I would appear at the right spot and find one of the Colonels to do duty for the Brigadier – one of them was temporarily in command but was not living at Brigade HQ.

August 1916

I could not find my horse, and walked to the spot to wait. Then came a cavalcade: the Corps Commander on a glorious hunter with his name branded in big letters on the horse's flank, followed by five or six of his staff, and his escort – two sergeants, one of them carrying a flag. I saluted: he saw I had no tabs on me, and asked who I was. I said Captain Griffith and tried to explain. He looked at me sternly and said 'You should say Captain Griffith, 15th Royal Welsh Fusiliers, acting as Brigade Major and Staff Captain. Remember that!' 'Yes sir,' I said. 'Now my boy, do you know who I am?' 'Yes, sir, you are the Corps Commander.' 'Ah yes, but do you know who I *am*?' 'Yes sir, General Weston', I replied. 'Yes, Aylmer you know, General Aylmer Hunter-Weston, commanding VIII Corps.[9] Take me to the field. Why aren't you mounted?' 'Our horses haven't come up yet sir,' said I. 'Take a horse from my escort and ride by my side and tell me all about everything, my boy, you shall be my guide, philosopher, and friend.'

I walked towards his escort and took a horse from one of the Corporals, and rode up to him as gracefully as I could on a strange and somewhat surprised horse. He led off on his superb mount, a pedigree horse. But my horse would not walk alongside his and he turned angrily and said, 'I told you to ride with me, not behind me.' 'I'm sorry, sir,' I said, 'but this horse has been trained to walk behind yours.' 'You are quite right. I'll hold mine back. Never be afraid to give a good reason.' He inspected the Brigade and made a speech and then went away. This was my first, but not my last, encounter with Hunter-Weston – Hunter-Bunter as he was called behind his back.[10] He had commanded the 29th Division in Gallipoli, the VIII Corps from its formation, and after the war became an MP. There are multitudes of stories about him, some apocryphal, but most of them true: brilliant, exhibitionist, ambitious and erratic. He was never popular with his inferiors, equals or superiors, and was generally held to be a bit mad.

General Evans had not come back to us and he was sent back to England. After a spell, two officers came to us: first of all Captain J.H. Davies as Staff Captain.[11] Jim Davies had been at Camberley with me[12]: in civil life he was a curate who flouted his Bishop and enlisted as a private soldier, and a good soldier he was too. Later on he was badly wounded and the last I heard of him was that he was a vicar in a parish in Bristol – I have not seen him since. I thought to myself that if he could be promoted to a staff captaincy there were hopes for me. But they were to be long delayed!

Our new Brigade Major was Major Arthur Derry,[13] a regular soldier invalided home from Gallipoli, a man of about forty, I suppose, and a fine specimen of his profession. He taught me how to be a staff officer – at least he began the long process. Accurate, conscientious, loyal and much too modest about his own powers. Our new Brigadier was a strange specimen named Hickie,[14] a regular soldier, and brother to a better known Hickie who was a Major-General commanding the Ulster Division.[15] A stupid man, far and away the most stupid soldier I ever met: lazy, greedy, a bore in the mess. Fortnum and Mason sent parcels and food which he had ordered regularly, delicacies which he put by his side on the table and never offered to anybody. It took all of Derry's tact and polite naturedness to keep the mess in tolerable shape: Derry of course ran the brigade.

The second most stupid soldier I met was Brigadier Price-Davies,[16] who commanded 113 Brigade in which I began my career as an officer. He won the Victoria Cross and Distinguished Service Order in South Africa as he was too dull to be frightened – he was always called 'Jane' by his fellow regulars (I disguised this in *Up to Mametz* because he was then still living). And when, one day, Hickie said to me, 'Don't you think he's a bit slow?' I didn't know what to say except 'yes' without a smile on my face.

After a quiet time around Serre, during which I managed a week's leave,[17] we moved to the Ypres salient where we spent a long time, mostly on the left flank next to the Belgians and on the canal.[18] We were still in VIII Corps. Part of the time, Brigade HQ was in a dugout on the canal bank, wet, slimy, rat ridden, and under continuous shellfire or mortar fire. It was just the plain routine of war, going up to the front line to inspect and report, trying to drain the water-logged trenches, moving out on relief into a château at Elverdinge in the woods.[19] I know enough of trench life to be mighty thankful that I was living in the comparative comfort and safety of Brigade HQ, even though the battalion HQs were only yards away from us. The Army must have found my name somewhere, for I was suddenly told to go to join a field artillery brigade, and then to a field company of Royal Engineers, as part of my staff training.[20]

October 1916

The gunners were covering us, and I enjoyed my visit there, for I found that the battery commander was Major J.O. Williams,[21] an Anglesey man and a good Welshman – strangely enough, he became an Inspector of Taxes on my staff in St George's Hanover Square in 1940. I spent several mornings on the OP (observation post) with the Major, firing the guns – great sport – and visiting

'Elverdinghe, North-West of Ypres', by David Jones 15th RWF. [RWF Museum]

the 4.5-inch howitzer batteries and the wagon lines. In the afternoons we fraternized with our Belgian neighbours, looking at their German guns and their French 75s. I remember having tea with them in Poperinghe, and also dining with them, beginning with port *before* dinner, and ending with rum brulé, and staggering home to find ourselves in the middle of an SOS barrage.[22] After leaving the battery I went to the artillery group headquarters for a while, and saw a shoot directed from an aeroplane. That afternoon I went for a walk across the fields and watched a Bosche plane trying to bring down one of our balloons: the observer jumped clear and the Bosche missed the balloon. The Engineers were in reserve, in a canal bank a long way back, and all I remember of that, except for some pleasant rides on horseback, is that the sappers dynamited the canal for fish. This was somewhere near St Omer, but I have forgotten the name of the village.[23] All was peace and comfort; that, I remember, was enough.

The only bright spots were occasional leaves home and they were few. The army had forgotten all about me, as I thought. But I was content and I wrote to Wyn every day. I also wrote some poems, some of which were privately printed by Gerald Hayes under the untranslatable title of '*Hiraeth*' – longing, homesickness, or nostalgia, or what you will.[24] There is no English equivalent. Wyn, at home, was working as a draughtsman at Cammell Laird's shipbuilding works in Birkenhead, and living with her mother in Liverpool. She was the first woman ever allowed into the design office of Cammell Laird, and here she did drawings of submarines and battleships, and copied parts of machinery. The war seemed, in the winter of 1916/17, as if it would never end.

AUTUMN 1916

Like some faint-coloured robe
My mistress weaves around her waist,
The truant mists of night so many-faced
With starry eyes, cling sadly to the trees.
She in the joy of morn will don
The bright and happy garments of delight,
In winding pools will drown the memory of night.
The wak'ning leaves move slowly in the dance of dawn,

Lo, silently the grey mists creep away,
And leave the colours of the conquering day
Their victory to flaunt.

Camp D
1 October 1916[25]

* * *

Back again with the Brigade in the salient, with the normal alarms and excursions, except that I found to my surprise and pleasure that I had been mentioned in despatches for what I did on the Somme. I knew that I had been recommended for the Military Cross, but I did not expect to get that. Then out of the blue there came an order telling me to report to the General Staff of VIII Corps[26] at Lovie Château[27] for more training in staff work, and I was very glad that I was to be on the operational side, not on Q, which dealt with supplies etc.[28] And so I found myself once more in contact with Hunter-Weston, but at a distance. My immediate chief was Brigadier General Ellington,[29] a very quick, able and short-tempered soldier who afterwards became Marshal of the Royal Air Force – I sometimes see him, hobbling on two sticks, at the United Services Club when the Athenaeum is closed, but I have never spoken to him. He had nothing but contempt for his corps commander, and was obviously eager to get away. I cannot remember the names of the GSO IIs, with whom I shared a room, except one was Major Monk, an Indian Army regular.[30] There was also a GSO III, a regular soldier whose name and personality are dim.

2 February 1917

It was not a happy office, and it could not be, with a *prima donna* for a General and a disgruntled chief of staff. Everybody was jumpy, for the corps commander sacked people right and left as the fancy took him. In the back of the château there was a collection of maps of the whole front, kept up to date by the Intelligence staff, and after dinner, Hunter-Weston came out into the back with his guests: they were invited to 'come and visit the fronts with me'. Guests every night nearly – he cultivated the Belgians, and if he wanted to sack a battalion commander he would invite him to dinner, tell him he looked tired, and a spell at home was what was wanted, and he would arrange it. He liked to show off. We always tried to get into the G office before he had finished dinner, for we had to go through the hall, but one night he caught me. 'Tell me,' he said, 'what is the exact state of our wire, and the German wire, here?' (He pointed to a map of the salient). I had been up to the line a few days before, and told him. 'Excellent,' he said, while his guest tried to look impressed. 'Go up there now and report to me tomorrow how it stands.'

I went back to the office and told Ellington. He said tersely, 'Get on with your work – he will have forgotten by tomorrow.' He had a system of bells on his table – I mean the corps commander had – and one day he rang for the senior staff officer present. As I was alone, I went into his room armed with pencils, black, red, and blue, a notebook and a map: had I gone without them, he would have sent me back. Hunter-Weston was leaning over a map of the salient showing the disposition of the troops. 'IX Corps has given way, the Belgians driven back: the only available reserves are the corps mounted troops. They will parade at 8.30 a.m. tomorrow here and I will inspect them. Issue the orders.'[31]

March 1917

I went back to my table and began drafting the operation orders when Ellington came in and asked me what I was doing. I told him: I said I hoped it was not true. He smiled, and said, 'He's going to sack the officer commanding the mounted troops, that's all.' 'Will he get up to inspect them?' I asked. 'Of course he will,' said Ellington, 'that's the way he does it.'

To go round the trenches with Hunter-Weston was an ordeal, for he walked so fast and asked questions all the time, criticized everything and everybody, turned tired officers out of their dugouts to answer his questions. He was full of vigour and unexpended physical energy. No one respected him, everybody feared him, and the better soldiers despised him for his showmanship. His tours around the trenches were more like an MP, visiting his constituency than a General inspecting the position. He had great ability, but it ran riot. I recall him addressing the London Welsh at great length: '... and, my men, if you keep on working in that splendid fashion of which I know you are capable, if you say to yourself as you take up each shovelful of earth "this is for the Empire", I know that you will contribute your share to the defeat of the monstrous enemy, and we shall soon be top BOG on the DOSCHE.'

SALIENT

One day he visited the line in the Salient, taking General Hickie and Major Derry with him. He excelled himself that day. Coming up to the headquarters dugout of the Cardiff City Battalion, he found a pair of 'gum boots, high,' and an empty tin outside. 'What refuse heap is this?' 'This is the battalion headquarters, sir,' says Colonel Smith.[32] Then he went into mess kitchen and saw a refuse pail. 'Now Colonel, what's wrong with this?' Colonel Smith looked at it and after some hesitation said 'it ought to be empty.' 'No, no, that's exactly where you are wrong. Refuse pail empty – shows it isn't being used. It must have a lid. Why ought it to have a lid?' 'To keep off the flies.' 'Exactly. To keep off the flies.' After this he said, 'Where is your refuse heap?' They took him round, and there he delivered an oration ending up with '... and why do I come here? Why does the GOC-in-C come to inspect a refuse heap? Because people will say, 'if the GOC-in-C can inspect a refuse heap, so can I, and everybody will then go there.'

He went up to the front line, and into one of the saps. There he found a lance-corporal, a typical silent and suspicious Welshman. 'Corporal, shake hands with me.' Lance-corporal does so, meekly wondering if this is friendliness or lunacy. 'Corporal, I am proud to shake hands with you. You are one of the outposts of the British Empire. This is a proud day for you, Corporal: you will be able to write home and say 'this day the GOC-in-C, General Aylmer Hunter-Weston, shook me by the hand, Good day, Corporal.'

On the way down the communication trench he met a party of pioneers working under an officer. 'I have seen some of your poor dear little men working there. They are only playing with the mud. Now this is the way you drain a trench. Do you know what a boring rod is?' 'Oh yes, sir, I am an engineer, and I know something about drainage.' This had no effect, and he started on a ten minute lecture on drainage, the officer looking very bored indeed. On his way again, he came to a sergeant at the end of the pioneer party, working on some trench boards. 'Now sergeant, is this the way to put down trench boards? Do you think they are right?' The sergeant, an Anglesey man, very deliberate and very Welsh, replied 'no sir – that is why we are here, to put them right.' The Corps Commander turned about in silence. He questioned and bullied a young machine-gun officer practically into tears.

One of my jobs was to keep the corps war diary, full of confidential information about the war, and I was horrified when

I was told to prepare an extra copy for him. When I asked what he did with it, I was told that he sent it home to his wife, with a long covering letter – typed and signed Aylmer Hunter-Weston – describing everything he had done and all the people he had seen and entertained. This in spite of the censorship, and quite openly, for I saw and read his letters regularly.

It was a bitterly cold winter, and we suffered much from having to sleep in cold huts, but compared to the troops in the line, we were very comfortable, and I had no illusions about my good luck: each time I went up to the line I came back and thanked my stars, wishing only that I could get a staff job, a real one. But nothing came my way, and there was nothing I could do but wait and hope. Spring came and went, and then, in April 1917, I was told that I must go back to my battalion.

17 April 1917

This was a great shock, and the end of my hopes of promotion. I packed up my kit and gear and set off despondently: the 15th RWF was in billets in some village behind the line,[33] and there were not many that I knew left to greet me. I took over C Company from Cundall,[34] and tried to take up the routine of company work; but I

'Brielen', by David Jones. [RWF Trustees]

found it very small beer after what I had been doing, and my heart was not in it.[35]

The battalion was in the Ypres Canal sector, which was first held by the 38th (Welsh) Division on two brigade fronts: 114 Infantry Brigade was usually on the right, just clear of the north side of the town of Ypres and holding two battalion frontages – one in the sector called Irish Farm, and the other in the Turco Farm sector – and with two battalions in support on the canal bank. The next brigade, usually 113 Infantry Brigade, also had two battalions in the front line, holding the Lancashire Farm and the Zwanhof Farm sectors, again with two battalions in support on the canal bank. When the division first came into the area, the French were to our left, but we took over their ground and this sector, called the Boesinghe sector, was usually held by 115 Infantry Brigade.

In this part of the line, only the width of the Yser Canal separated the combatants. The canal itself was shallow and less water than slimy filth, strewn with empty bully beef and jam tins; it was no longer a canal but a drain in which rats alone thrived. The stream running parallel to the canal, called the Yperlee, flowed muddy and strong especially in times of flood. It was incredible that any man could drink its water and live, but many did. The canal bank was a very important place, and if the salient was to be held, it was vital that the Germans should not get across the canal. As well as the infantry battalions, there were many other units: brigade headquarters, engineer field companies, tunnelling companies, gun batteries, dressing stations and the rest. It had its church, its hospitals, and its shops – which did a roaring trade, earning profits which would make any profiteering grocer at home go green with envy.

The various bridges in the sector became infamous. These were wooden structures, some well built and able to carry heavy traffic, but there were a number of much less substantial foot bridges. Bridge 4 was the biggest, best known, and at night, the most crowded with men and vehicles. Bridge 6 was almost as busy, as the main Royal Engineer stores and ration depot were at the western end. Bridge 6D, which served the northern part of the Zwanhof sector, was called the 'Blighty' Bridge – so-called because those who were hit crossing it did so from close range and so rarely got home to Blighty. The death rate was heavy and minor casualties frequent.

The many cemeteries were an ever-present reminder of an active enemy.

The accommodation in trenches was very poor at first: the shallow dugouts and raised trenches provided little comfort and less safety. But the constant badgering of the brigade commander caused us to improve it rapidly. The best dug-outs were occupied by brigade headquarters. Next came the dugouts of the Royal Engineers and some of the battalion headquarters, the most famous of which was Fusilier House in the Zwanhof sector. There was then a wide gap between these desirable residences and the company dugouts.

At night, mules, horses, wagons, trucks, ration parties, loud-voiced sergeants, profane and angry men, all turned into indescribable uproar. There was the constant coming and going of men in single file, troops relieving, troops being relieved, men coming to and fro from wiring parties, men going to hospital, men going on leave, men going to baths. Still, all the rations, stores, and much else, did as a rule reach their destination each night.

Each battalion took its turn in the line every three to six days – there was no exact regularity lest we should set a pattern that the watching Germans would pick up and punish. The route up to the line was a long one, past La Brique and La Belle Alliance; then up Huddersfield trench, or Headingly, or in and out of Skipton.[36] Before a great deal of hard work solidified the line, it consisted more or less of isolated posts held by parties of six or eight men under an NCO, on a flat desolation of shell holes, mud and a few splintered trees, ruined farmhouses and stagnant pools. There were strong points, such as Hill Top, Turco, and Fargate with its old French dugouts: it narrowly escaped destruction when one of our 'flying pig' trench mortars fell short.[37] Skipton was where our line ran almost into the point of the German salient, called by us Caesar's Nose. Colne Valley was no place to stay, with its broken dugouts and water collecting in the trench. Nothing remained standing from Zwanhof Farm, but its bricks made excellent dugouts for us in Welsh Harp.

In Lancashire farm trench, the pleasant smell of a soup kitchen fought against the stench of the old farm pond, the blue clay dug out by the tunnelling companies, and that universal, unforgettable, trench smell of charcoal braziers, wet sandbags, chloride of lime, creosote, latrines and fried bacon.

Wyn Wheldon spoke thus of it[38] in a long article just after the War:

> There was a strong social life on the canal bank. No one could walk along the trench boards on the old tow-path, or behind the western bank, without meeting friends and acquaintances, both among the officers and men. Visits to neighbouring dug-outs were frequent, and many a happy meal was shared in those surroundings. Welsh was heard everywhere in greeting, denunciation, and warning – and in snatches of Welsh hymns.

The Royal Welch Fusiliers consisted mostly of Welsh-speaking Welshmen whose background was similar to my own. In Welsh, we could all talk freely, officers and men alike and with each other, without impinging in any way on matters of military protocol that seemed to belong exclusively to the world of English.[39] This created a bond of unity, that sense of being an enclave within a community.

This was the Regiment in which Robert Graves, Siegfried Sassoon, David Jones, Vivian Pinto and Frank Richards all served, authors of the best of the war books. But they did not speak Welsh, and so there was a world into which they could not enter. This does not detract from the value of their books, but it impoverished them at the time. The men I knew were of my own kin because we spoke the same language, the one we had inherited, not the one we used as we learned our trade of soldiering.

Let me give an instance of what I mean. The scene is the canal bank near Ypres: some desultory shelling, an occasional rattle of machine-gun fire, a Very light shooting up into the blackness and falling to make it even darker. A company waiting to go up into the trenches on relief, waiting, 'always bloody well waiting', for the order to move up the communication trenches to the front line. They start singing, in harmony, being Welsh, a fine old Welsh hymn tune in a minor key. The Brigadier General asks me, 'Why do they always sing these mournful hymns? Most depressing – bad for morale. Why can't they sing something cheerful, like other battalions?' I try to explain to him that what they are singing now is what they sang as children, as I did, in chapel, in the world to which they really belong. They are being themselves, not men in uniform. They are back at home with their families, in their villages. But he does not understand. Nor can he, with his background.

Every day, and sometimes more than once a day, the Colonel[40] would inspect his battalion front, no one knew the hour of his coming. Nothing escaped his keen eye – bad duckboard here, there a weakening of the wall, fire-step to be repaired in one bay, two men had dirty rifles, one man did not know where company headquarters stood, three men did not know where to find the ammunition boxes, and one lance-corporal seemed doubtful where the gas alarm was situated. He would enter our dug-out, take out his notebook, and begin his chronicle of shortcomings. The law of average must hold, and there must have been occasions when he asked a man of normal intelligence where the bombs were stored, and heard the simple truth told without hesitation, but I was never made aware of such strokes of good fortune. I knew only too well that if the Colonel must ask a searching question, it would be hurled at the most stupid man in the company.

He was a good officer, and a kindly man, who concealed his feelings in spurts of sharp and sudden sentences.[41]

'Get that parapet higher, d'ye see?'

'Yes, sir.'

'No good tinkering at the bay, see? Rebuild it.'

'Yes, sir.'

'Don't like that bomb-store, d'ye see?'

'Yes, Colonel.'

'Dam' dirty rifle one fellow had: jump on his sergeant, see?'

'I will, sir.'

'Well, I must be going on ... No, thanks, I won't have a drink ... Good morning.'

In the nature of things, there can be little cordiality between a Colonel and his junior officers in war time, but we respected him and liked him, and felt that his brusque ways were not the whole of the man. There was an underlying sympathy with a young man bearing a heavy burden of responsibility, though it was well concealed on a morning parade when we were out of the line. He was considerate in small things; once only did I know him to accept an offer of whisky and water in a company dugout in the trenches, on a day of sweltering heat, and then he looked at the bottle to see how much we had before he accepted. He declined our hospitality on many occasions when he was obviously tired, from an unselfish disinclination to impoverish us. If on his visit he found the company commander asleep, he would not let him be disturbed: greater men than he were not so considerate.

The Brigade commander, General Price-Davies, whom I mentioned earlier, was a daily plague to his brigade. He was slight, athletic in build, and good-looking: his mind was slow in working, but tenacious to the point of obstinacy. He spoke slowly, in a prim way. It would be a misuse of words to call him brave, but he was certainly fearless. I have heard an uncharitable company commander, labouring under a grievance, say that he was too stupid to be frightened of anything but reason. He took a delight in exposing himself to fire, quite forgetting that the infantry officer who was his unwilling companion was being forced into a foolhardy challenge of the powers that troubled him day and night, when the Brigadier was far away from the line. He had little sense of humour, but I once saw him laugh at an incident that might have brought trouble upon my head.

It was a cold and wet night, and I was following him along my sector, listening to an interminable catalogue of minor faults. We came to a Lewis Gun post, and as we approached it the gunner fired a drum of ammunition. He did not recognize the General, who asked him:

'Was that you firing then?'

'Yes.'

'What were you firing at?'

'Don't know.'

'Then why did you fire?'

'Just to bloody well amuse myself,' said the stubborn Welsh collier, in his close-clipped South Wales speech. The General turned away and laughed, to my great relief. The same General was going round the trenches near the same place at night some time later. Just before coming to a dead end, he jumped over the parapet to inspect the wire. He came back into the trench near the sentry, who shouted at him:

'Halt! What the bloody hell d'you mean by jumping over by there without saying nothing?'

'It's alright, I am your General.'

'I don't care who the bloody hell you are, I was going to stick you anyhow.'

The Brigadier wore a mackintosh jacket over his uniform, a pair of mackintosh trousers over his breeches, and a steel helmet that tended to slide over his left ear. There was no visible mark of rank at first, but later he fixed on his helmet the crossed sword and baton. His real badge of office was a wooden staff exactly four feet six inches long, and with this he tested the height of the top layer of sandbags on the parapet over the fire-step. It was decreed that this height of four feet six inches must never be exceeded – there was little danger of any shortage, but a tall man standing on the fire-step felt acutely conscious of his upper eighteen inches. This mackintoshed figure, with boyish face and pouting expression, conscientiously measuring his staff against the trench wall, and finding a quiet satisfaction in the rare tallying of the two heights, commanded a force of three thousand men. In the stagnant condition of our war-making, it might be said that though he was the titular head of this body, to which he issued orders, he commanded no one. He elaborated for our benefit orders he had received from above, but he was no prime mover. He led no one, nor did he ever taste the thrill of throwing mass against mass. We were tenants of an estate of mud, and he was high bailiff, holding us to a careful tenancy, meticulous even in his overseeing of our domestic economy. He was zealous in his administration, sparing not himself, nor others, struggling manfully with a burden that appeared to us to be a little too large for his capacity, and concealing this by an untiring expenditure of physical energy.[42]

Luckily for me, this period with the battalion did not last long, for orders came for me to report to the General Staff of II ANZAC Corps at Bailleul.[43] Off I went as fast as I could, and that was the last I saw of my battalion.[44]

2 June 1917

Notes

1. This chapter and all that follows is based on the draft of Wyn Griffith's intended sequel to *Up To Mametz*.
2. Wyn Griffith is no doubt referring to the death of his son John, killed on active service with the RAF in 1942.
3. This theme is developed in Wyn Griffith's later essay 'The Pattern of One Man's Remembering'.
4. The casualty figures for the Royal Welch Fusiliers are given in Regimental Records thus: 13th Battalion, CO and 3 officers killed, five wounded, no figures for ORs. 14th Battalion, 6 officers and 67 men killed, CO, 9 officers and 233 men wounded. 15th Battalion, 12 officers and 250 men killed and wounded. 16th Battalion, CO, 2 officers and 43 men killed, 5 officers and 186 men wounded, 64 men missing. 17th Battalion, 6 officers and 30 men killed,

CO, 14 officers and 197 men wounded, 37 men missing. The casualties in Wyn Griffith's brigade, 115, are given in the War Diary as 17 Officers killed, 44 wounded, 9 wounded and on duty; 167 men killed, 709 wounded, 162 missing [TNA WO 95/2560 115 Inf Bde War Diary].
5. Not identified.
6. About 20km (12 miles) south of Arras.
7. A fortified village behind the old British front line from which the 56th (London) Division had attacked Gommecourt on 1st July 1916.
8. *Up To Mametz*, pp. 228–230, although no names are given. The 38th Division history gives Captain C.L. Veal as the Brigade Major.
9. Lieutenant-General Sir Aylmer Gould Hunter-Weston KCB DSO GStJ (1864–1940) was commissioned into the Royal Engineers in 1884 and served in Waziristan, Dongola, and South Africa. He commanded VIII Corps in the Dardanelles and on the Western Front form 1915 to 1918. He retired in 1919. He was Unionist MP for Buteshire and North Ayreshire 1916–1935. He died as a result of a mysterious fall from a turret at his family house.
10. This nickname pre-dates the Billy Bunter stories, so cannot be an allusion to Hunter-Weston's girth, and Wyn Griffith gives no clues. The *Oxford English Dictionary* and Chambers *Dictionary of Etymology* suggest that 'to bunt' is to head-butt, perhaps an allusion to Hunter-Weston's lack of finesse; the older Dictionary by Dr Johnson gives the following meaning for bunter: 'A cant word for a woman who picks up rags about the street; and used, by way of contempt, for any low vulgar woman.'
11. James Henry Davies MC was commissioned on 8 April 1915, was promoted Captain on 16 July 1916. By the end of the war he was a Major, at which point he relinquished his temporary commission and returned to civil life. Nothing more is known of him.
12. i.e. they went through officer training together.
13. According to the 38th Division History Major Arthur Derry DSO arrived in July, 1916. Wyn Griffith's diary confirms this, giving the date as 18 July. In 1914, Derry had been DAA & QMG of the Welsh Division (TF) He was still a Major at the end of the war.
14. Brigadier-General Carlos Joseph Hickie CMG (1873–1959) was commissioned into the Glosters in 1893, transferred to the KOYLI in 1902, and again to the Royal Fusiliers in 1912. In 1914 he was Brigade Major of the East Lancashire Infantry Brigade (TF). He was appointed to command 115 Infantry Brigade in August 1916 and according to Wyn Griffith's diary he arrived on 30 August. He also commanded 224 and 7 Infantry Brigades.
15. Major-General Sir William Bernard Hickie KCB (1865–1950) actually commanded 16th (Irish) Division, and was later elected to the Senate of the Irish Free State in 1925 until its dissolution in 1936.
16. Brigadier-General Llewellyn Alberic Emilius Price-Davies VC CMG DSO (1875–1965) had been commissioned into the KRRC and won the VC at the Blood River in South Africa in September 1901. A substantive Major, temporary Brigadier-General, he commanded 113 Brigade from November 1915 to November 1917. He was the brother-in-law of Field Marshal Sir Henry Wilson who was at this time commanding IV Corps. In fact, Wyn Griffith's first

brigade commander would have been Brigadier-General Owen Thomas, MP. Thomas raised and trained the brigade but, because of his age, he was denied the chance to command in France. Three of his four sons were commissioned into The Royal Welch Fusiliers; all three were killed.

17. According to Wyn Griffith's diary, this was 17–25 August 1916.
18. This was the extreme left, or northward, flank of the British Expeditionary Force in Flanders (Belgium), and on the inter-Army Group boundary with the Belgian Army which held the line from the Ypres canal to the sea. It was one of the most heavily fought-over areas on the Western Front, and had seen the first use of poison gas in 1915.
19. The château lies 4 kilometres (2 miles) north-west of Ypres. The village was the centre of many camps, training areas, stores, hospitals and facilities for rest for troops in the salient. It was almost entirely destroyed by artillery fire being a known British centre and road junction. A light railway ran to Poperinghe for the carriage of casualties and supplies. The château was used continuously as a headquarters and was also badly damaged. At one point it was accidentally set on fire when a cook let some fat catch fire. It was rebuilt later.
20. Generally, an infantry brigade would expect to be assigned a brigade of three batteries from the Royal Field Artillery, and a field company of Royal Engineers, to support the fighting battalions. These units were detached from the divisional troops under the command of the CRA (Commander, Royal Artillery – a Brigadier-General) and the CRE (Commander, Royal Engineers – a Colonel), respectively.
21. J.O. Williams MC held a temporary commission in the RFA, and according to the Army List, he was a Captain in May 1917.
22. i.e. artillery fire called down by telephone in an emergency on a pre-registered target, using all guns in range and not otherwise committed: in case of a surprise attack, or to cover the withdrawal of a fighting patrol for example.
23. Possibly St Momelin, just north of the town on the canal.
24. Subsequently, Griffith also wrote and published *The Barren Tree And Other Poems*. (Penmark Press: Cardiff, nd [1947]), a small volume of fifteen powerful poems which are not all about Griffith's War experiences but *The Song is Theirs* follows the progress of the Great War ending at Mametz Wood.
25. The draft of this poem is in Wyn Griffith's Army Book 136, now in his personal papers at the National Library of Wales. It was later printed with some minor variations in *Hiraeth*.
26. The corps level of command did not exist in peacetime in the British Army of the period. This may explain why, although it was very rare for brigades to change division, divisions were constantly moved between corps at the orders of Army HQs – two levels of command higher up – or even GHQ. Hence, perhaps, Wyn Griffith's earlier comment that 'we were still in VIII Corps'. This meant that there was little chance for mutual trust and understanding to grow between division and corps commanders. The exceptions were the ANZAC and Canadian Corps. VIII Corps had been formed in Gallipoli, and subsequently moved to the Western Front. It had the highest casualties of any corps on 1 July 1916, and accomplished the least. At this time it had command of the 4th, 29th, 31st and 38th (Welsh) Divisions, as well its corps troops.

27. La Lovie Château is in the village of Proven, about 4km (2 miles north-west of Poperinghe and about 12km (7.5 miles) north-west of Ypres. It was a British HQ from May 1915 onwards. VI Corps was here until February 1916, followed by XIV Corps, then VIII Corps in July 1916. Fifth Army took over the house in November 1916 and remained there until November 1917. King George V used the house during one of his visits to the front in July 1917.
28. Because of the priorities laid down in *Field Service Regulations,* the General Staff, or G, branch, responsible for intelligence, orders and instructions, liaison, signals, mapping, codes, ciphers and security, held primacy; the Brigadier General, General Staff (BGGS) was responsible for policy, the coordination and general supervision of all work, and training. The A and Q branches under the AA & QMG were responsible for administrative staff work and orders, all matters relating to logistics, discipline, welfare, honours and awards, and was subordinate to G.
29. Later Marshal of the Royal Air Force Sir Leonard Ellington GCB CMG CBE (1877–1967). He was Chief of the Air Staff 1933–1937, and Inspector General of the RAF 1937–1940.
30. There is no Major Monk listed in the Indian Army or on the General Staff at this time. It is probable that Wyn Griffith disguised the name, as he does elsewhere, for reasons of his own – perhaps because at the time of writing the individual was still alive.
31. It would be unusual at this stage of the war for a corps in the line to be allocated mounted troops, other than its organic horse transport or supply units. Cavalry and Yeomanry regiments on the Western Front were concentrated into the Cavalry Corps, which was GHQ's arm of exploitation for any breakthrough made by offensive action. This reference seems to be to a combat unit, however, and therefore it must be assumed from the use of the term 'officer commanding', that this was a regiment of cavalry attached to the corps troops.
32. Lieutenant Colonel F.W. Smith commanded the 16th (Cardiff City) Battalion of the Welsh Regiment from May 1916 to the end of the war.
33. This village could well be Brielen, described at much the same period by David Jones in *In Parenthesis.*
34. Captain H.J. Cundall was commissioned from a London Regiment Territorial Force battalion and joined 15th RWF in January 1916. Having handed over C Company to Wyn Griffith, he commanded A Company until the battalion was broken up; thereafter no more is known.
35. According to the War Diary, the battalion had a quiet time in the salient, and usually did trench duty on the Yser Canal. It was, though, 'a long and weary period of trench warfare... Numerous raids were organised and a mass if muddy trenches were gradually tuned [by grading] into dry and comfortable ones'.
36. It was the usual practice to name trenches, often after the home towns of the units that had first dug them – in this case, the Duke of Wellington's Regiment (West Riding).
37. The 'flying pig' was a Canadian mortar of 9.45-inch calibre, throwing a shell weighing 91 kilograms (200lbs). It had a range of only 400 yards and was generally very unreliable.

38. Wheldon, W.P. 'The Canal Bank at Ypres' in *The Welsh Outlook*, Volume VI, March 1919. Wyn Wheldon was the father of Sir Huw Wheldon, the Controller of the BBC, who served in the Royal Welch Fusiliers during the Second World War.
39. While there was undoubtedly a good deal of Welsh spoken in the trenches and the bonding value of this shared culture must have been immense, Wyn Griffith is seeing things, after the lapse of forty years, through deeply rose-tinted spectacles. It is not possible to determine the nationality of all those who served in The Royal Welch Fusiliers during the War, because of the destruction by German bombing during the Second World War of the personal files of many (not all) of those who had served in the Great War. However, most entries in the records *Officers Died in the Great War*, and *Soldiers Died in the Great War*, give the place of birth. From this, it is possible to obtain a good indication of the Welshness of the Regiment. During the War, the Regiment raised forty battalions, of which twenty-two served abroad. Of these, fifteen sustained over 200 casualties. In these fifteen battalions, an average of forty-seven per cent gave Wales or Monmouthshire as their place of birth. The figure was highest in the Territorial battalions at around sixty per cent, and generally lowest in the regular battalions which had, in peacetime, recruited strongly in London and Birmingham. The service battalions in 38th (Welsh) Division average just over forty per cent: in Wyn Griffith's own battalion, the 15th (1st London Welsh), this figure is a mere twenty-seven per cent. The idea that the Regiment spoke only Welsh during the war is therefore not sound, and in danger of creating yet another myth of the Great War. Nor does it do service to the many patriotic men who gave their lives, and who spoke no Welsh, but considered themselves no less Welsh for it. For a fuller analysis, see P.A. Crocker 'Some Thoughts on The Royal Welch Fusiliers in the Great War' in *Y Ddraig Goch*, September 2002, pp. 135–140.
40. 15 RWF was now commanded by Lieutenant-Colonel (later Brigadier) Compton Cardew Norman CBE CMG DSO (1877–1955), or 'Crump' as he was known. A regular officer, he had served in South Africa and with the Royal West African Frontier Force. He was wounded three times during the war, and commanded no less than four battalions. He later commanded 2 RWF 1920–1924, 158 (Royal Welch) Infantry Brigade 1927–1929, and was Inspector General of the RWAFF and the KAR 1930–1936.
41. This description, which appears in Wyn Griffith's 1917 diary and evidently describes Norman, was transcribed by him into the original edition of *Up To Mametz*, where he used it to describe the then Commanding Officer, Lieutenant-Colonel R.C. Bell. I have restored it here to its original owner.
42. Wyn Griffith's remarks on the Commanding Officer and Brigade Commander are repeated in his article in *Wales on the Western Front*.
43. 16 kilometres (10 miles) south-east of Ypres.
44. 15 RWF was one of the battalions selected for disbandment in February 1918, when shortages of manpower became acute in the BEF, and it was necessary to reduce each infantry brigade from four battalions to three in order to keep the rest up to strength. This led to a reduction in the number of units per mile of front and was a contributory factor to the success of the German Offensive in

Salient

March 1918 (see below). The BEF routinely lost about 10,000 men per month (outside major offensives) – killed wounded, gassed, sick or injured, captured, discharged or absent without leave. This was roughly one division's strength each month and lack or replacements quickly became apparent. In 1918, there was a political agenda in denying Haig reinforcements, in order to prevent further costly offensives, although there was no shortage of men. There were around one million trained men in Britain at the time, and about the same deployed in other theatres of war or elsewhere overseas.

Chapter 10

ANZAC[1]

The badge of II ANZAC Corps

Bailleul was a pleasant little town, battle scarred by the war, and I reported to Brigadier General George Grogan,[2] the Brigadier General, General Staff (BGGS), and found that I was to be a learner under him, and that everything was set for the Battle of Messines. The G office was in the Town Hall facing the square and I joined a small mess. In those days, the operations staff of a corps consisted of a BGGS, two GSO IIs, who were majors, and a GSO III, a captain. Few men were less impressive at first sight than Grogan: he was short, lithe, keen-faced, but a most hesitant talker, all 'ers', preoccupied and at times remote, but essentially likeable. The corps commander, Sir Alexander Godley[3] (afterwards Governor of Gibraltar) was his exact opposite: six feet five in height, and his two ADCs were six feet seven and six feet four. Thin, handsome, very definite in speech and manner, a fine soldier and well thought of by his colleagues. He was in command of all the New Zealand forces, and our corps consisted of two Australian divisions and the New Zealand Division,[4] all first class fighting troops. My immediate chief, GSO II Operations, was Major Sydney Buxton Pope,[5] an Indian Army man, very quiet and able, who kept Samuel Butler's *Notebooks* on his table. There were three

3 June 1917

150

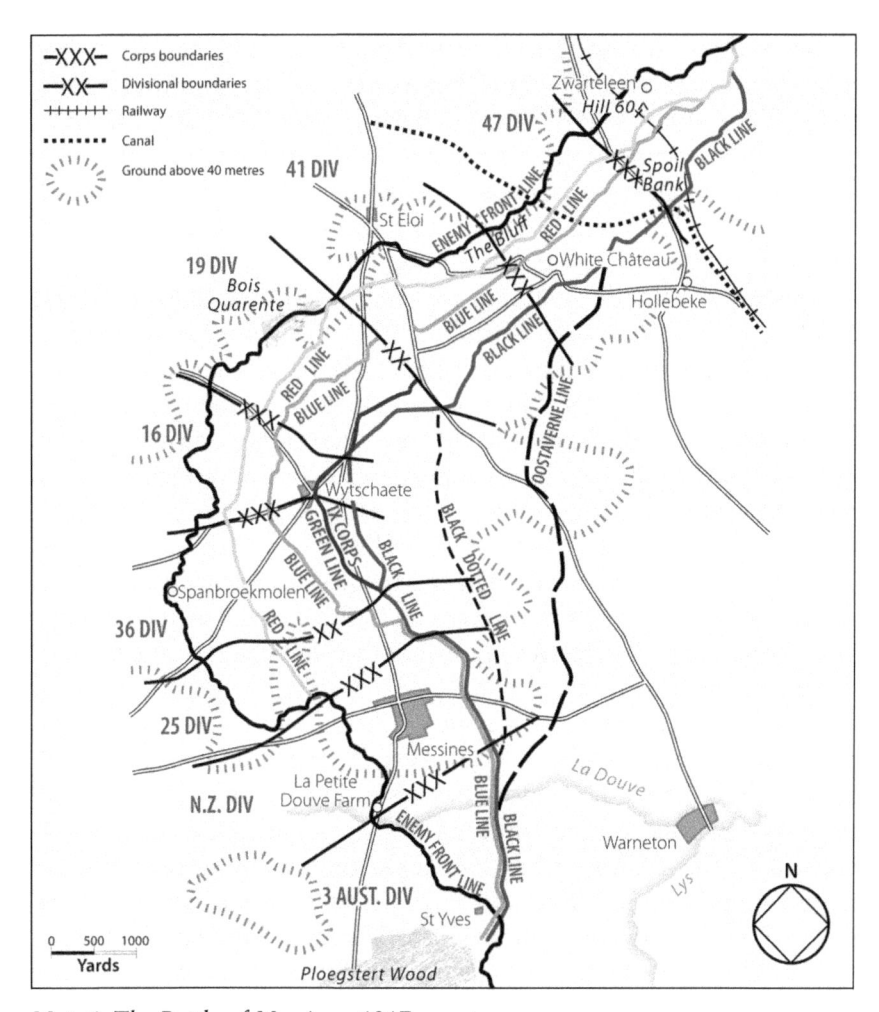

Map 6: The Battle of Messines, 1917.

other brigadiers on the staff: Panet of the Royal Engineers,[6] Martin Powell of the Artillery,[7] and Delaforce of Q,[8] with another whose name I have forgotten, and who commanded the heavy artillery.[9]

The Battle of Messines was about to begin, and we were all set.[10] One of the first things I did was to go to IX Corps headquarters and get a pass for Mount Kemmel. We got shelled on the way, I remember, but it was a magnificent view of the battle area. The main attack opened early on 7 June, and everything went well – like clockwork in fact for the Bosche were fairly overwhelmed by the violence of our barrage and counter-battery fire as well as the steady advance of the creeping barrage and the infantry advance. Messines Ridge was soon ours. The new 3rd Australian Division was on the right of our attack and did extraordinarily well. They were heavily gassed while assembling in Ploegsteert Wood, so much so that out of five platoons who were supposed to cross the Douve were reduced to fifty effectives. These fifty with their gas masks on did what had been expected of more than two hundred.

The New Zealanders were in the centre and took Messines very quickly; their methods for clearing out the village were something to see. The commander of the first brigade of the division, a miner from the west coast and before the war captain of a volunteer company, was killed leading his brigade at the top of the ridge. The new 4 New Zealand Infantry Brigade arrived just in time but were kept on road mending and carrying party duty until a week or so into the battle, when they were allowed into the line. The British 25th Division was on the left of the attack and had the furthest to advance but it too did very well. We took Oosttaverne as well, but apparently we were driven out again. There were no other serious counter-attacks that day or the next.

A squadron of the corps cavalry – Australians – was following the infantry closely and General Godley launched them over the hill as soon as we had the ridge. They rode down a sniper's post and took nine prisoners, then captured two guns and pushed on, much cheered by the infantry. They sent back some useful information to the headquarters too. We picked up prisoners every day as well as thirty-three Bosche guns, some of which were hidden in odd places.

Then the next day, 9 June, the GSO III was wounded and went home, and to my delight I was told that I was to succeed him and that I could put on my red tabs and get my red band for my cap straight away without waiting for the Gazette.[11]

The tide had turned for me at last, and I felt proud and important in red. Besides, I would be drawing pay at the rate of £400 a year, a tremendous jump up for me. I could hardly believe my good fortune: me, a temporary soldier, a mere assistant Surveyor of Taxes, a full-blown staff officer, and on a corps staff at that. Looking back now, I must have been more competent than I thought, for I had no influence of any kind. General Grogan (brother of Stephen Grogan the author[12]) must have made up his mind quickly to give me a chance like this, during a big battle.

The corps chief of staff[13] sent for me and said I was to go up to establish an advanced information centre just behind the front, with H.C. Bradshaw (a Liverpool architect who later became secretary of the Fine Arts Commission).[14] This was a new idea; aeroplane messages of enemy troop movements were to be dropped near us, and we had a battery of six-inch guns under our direct command. Our job was to correlate information and send it back to Second Army Headquarters, to General Plumer. Off I went, feeling very flattered at being chosen, and the scheme worked well – the only reference I have seen to it in war histories is in Liddell Hart's book.[15] I stayed there until 15 June, making frequent visits to the divisions whenever possible. I remember about that time seeing the captured German guns and machine guns in the square at Cassel; also I remember that the King and the Prince of Wales visited the headquarters on 14 June. The King shook hands with all the senior members of the corps and divisional staffs.

As Bailleul was now getting very heavily shelled, we packed up the HQ there and moved to Flêtre.[16] We found a good HQ building,

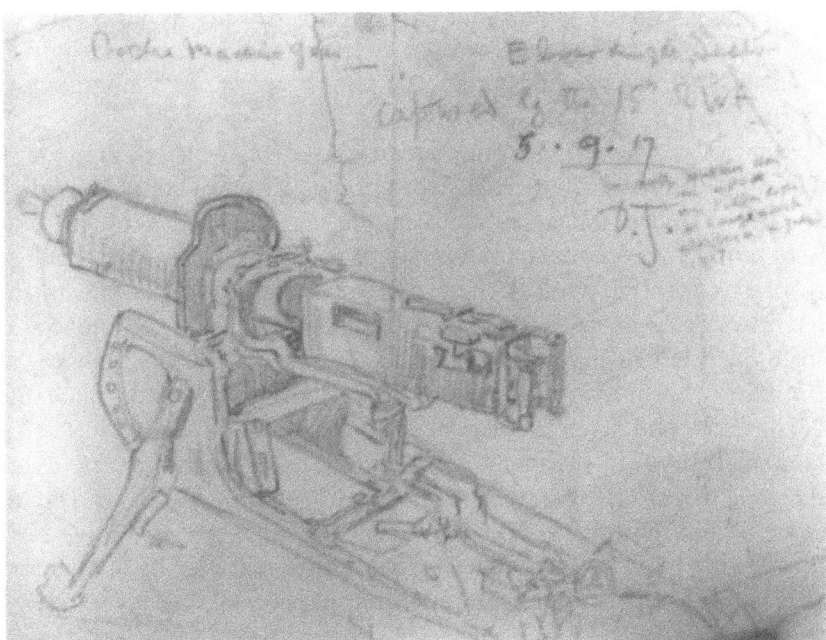

Captured German machine gun, by David Jones. [RWF Trustees]

and I found a nice billet. The G office was in a round tower where D'Artagnan is supposed to have slept. One of the privileges of being a staff officer was that your chances of going home on leave were good, and I was able to go home for a week on 23 July. Wyn and I went to Rhiw[17] for the first time, in lovely summer weather – we got a great welcome there and we stayed in the cottage, Ty Uchaf, which my father and mother rented. I was now where all my father's family sprang from, and I linked up into the clan and enjoyed myself. Rhiw worked its magic on us both.

Major Percy Hansen VC MC joined us as GSO II Operations,[18] a Major William Platt DSO as GSO II Training.[19] Foss was another VC on the staff,[20] and Percy Hansen later on collected a DSO as an immediate award for gallantry (foolishness, really, for he was reprimanded at the same time). We were a happy and efficient team. Platt is now General Sir William Platt, of Keren [East Africa] fame, and I met him at the Athenaeum. I have repaid some of his kindness to me by putting him, to his delight, on the drama panel of the Arts Council, for drama is his great passion. Percy Hansen was a six-footer, blond and handsome, a godson of Queen Alexandra, and the most lovable of men. He was godfather to our John. He knew everybody in high society, at home, in France, and in the United States, and he was known as Piccadilly Percy. He won his VC and MC at Gallipoli. We became the firmest of friends, two men utterly unlike each other in every way, and this I regard as one of the strangest happenings of my life.

Our mess was interesting: Stranack, a bent-nosed gunner,[21] Mason[22] of the Ordnance, delicate and sensitive, David Liddell – a son of Princess Christian's Equerry[23], very musical, who carried with him some records that always bring the war back to me: Bach's Concerto for two violins (first two movements only – the third has always come as a surprise to me ever since), the solo cello from the Bach Suite in C minor; the orchestral version of Debussy's *En Bâteau, Capriccio Viennese*. It was an unexpected touch of civilization. As I listen to the concerto nowadays, I am back in 1917, in a small town in Flanders, with lorries and guns thundering over the *pavé* toward the opening stages of the Battle of Messines. David came to stay with us in North Wales after the war, but I have lost touch with him now and do not even know whether he is alive or not. He went to Paris to paint, but what happened after is unknown to me.

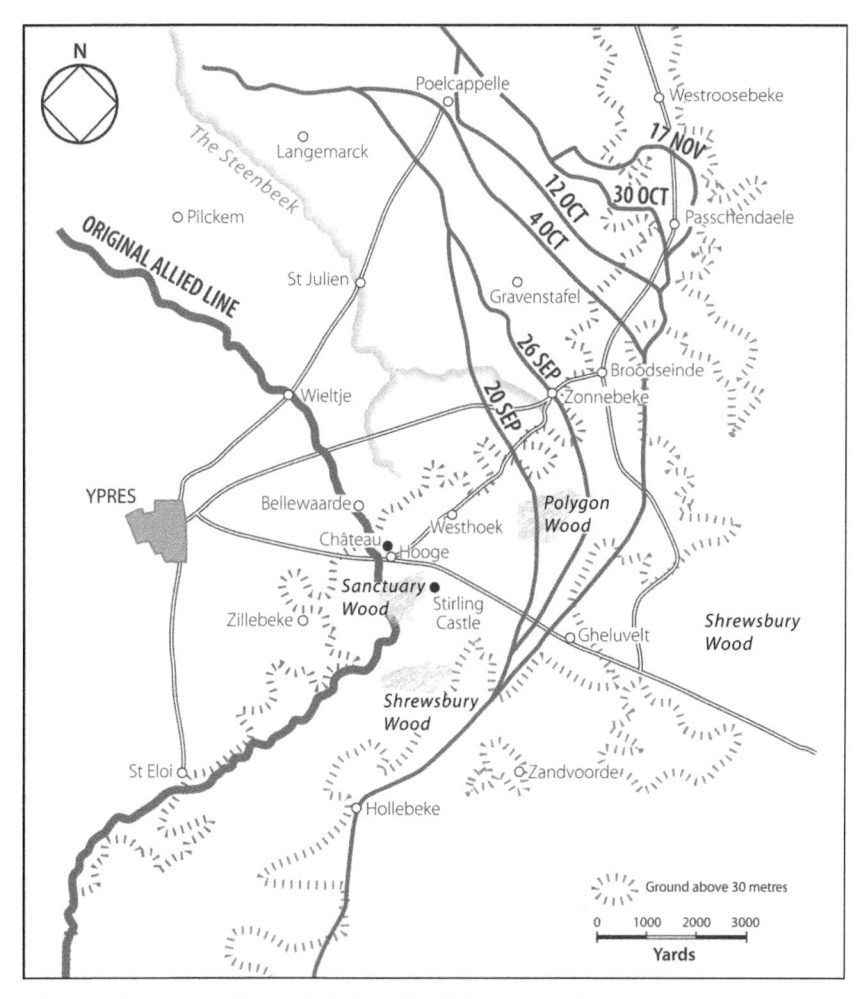

Map 7: The Battle of Broodseinde (Third Ypres), 1917.

One result of the Battle of Messines, so far as we were concerned, was that our reputation as a corps staff grew very high, and from that time on, we became a kind of flying column. Whenever there was trouble any- **August 1917** where, Godley and his staff were sent to deal with it. I had only just got back from leave when the flag went down on the big show up north.[24] Our part in it was confined to counter-battery work and a barrage. Things went well on the left, quite well on the right, and not too well in the centre. We also used gas when the wind was blowing in the right direction. I recall one incident on 29th Division's front at the end of August. 200 gas cylinders were brought up but about forty were damaged in transit. The rest were installed ready for a discharge from several different points. In the event, the wind was not entirely favourable so only a portion were discharged. According to the battalion in the line at that point, the Germans detected the gas almost at once, probably from the hissing, as the trenches were quite close together. They put up flares, followed by a red rocket bursting into white balls, then opened up a heavy rifle and machine-gun fire as they obviously expected an attack to follow. Soon afterwards this fire was followed by trench mortars and artillery. Our artillery then joined in, firing for about half an hour, until the enemy's fire dwindled away. Patrols then went across, some of which penetrated the German line and found that in some places, the gas had reached the Germans before they knew anything about it. There was still a strong smell of gas on the ground.

For a month or so, I was lent to Second Army HQ, to General Sir Herbert Plumer[25] and Major-General Charles Harington,[26] and with Anthony Eden[27] we kept Plumer in touch with what was happening in the front.

September 1917

I did not like Eden, and few things have surprised me more than his subsequent career. The Army HQ was in the fine old hill-top town of Cassel in Flanders,[28] and it was a privilege to work with General Harington. One day he asked me into his room and showed me Plumer's original plan of attack out of the Ypres salient, and Gough's plan – the one that was put into operation. They showed clearly that what had happened, in spite of Gough's ambitious plans, was exactly what Plumer had foreseen. 'Don't talk about this, but remember it,' he said.[29] I remember a very successful day on 20 September, when we captured all our objectives. Our casualties were slight and our men took 400 prisoners: I recall seeing a lot of them in the cages. We were kept pretty busy, even though there were minimal counter-attacks and those there were, were smashed by our guns.

Martin Powell, our general commanding the artillery, much deserves a book to himself. Tall, thin, forward-leaning, given to mumbling to himself or to his dog, he looked like an Irish farmer. A great fox-hunting man – master of the Meath Hunt.[30] Charles Bentinck[31] was another MFH on our staff, and our corps badge was a fox-hound. David Liddell was Martin Powell's staff officer, and the two were like father and son. His casual, nonchalant, unfussed way concealed Powell's brilliance and it was characteristic of him that when he had to prepare a complex artillery operation order, the first thing he did was to sit down, clear his table, get out two packs of patience cards and play a game of 'Miss Milligan'. While he did so, he sang to himself two lines over and over again of what must have been a music hall song:

> Worthington, Worthington
> I'd rather have a bottle of Worthington

Then he got up and dictated his operation order to a shorthand typist.

There came a time when he nearly ruined the *Entente Cordiale*, but that was somewhat later, and I must not forget to relate the incident.

Army Orders provided that if you had been out in France for two years (I think) on end, you could have a month's leave if you could be spared. I was one of the lucky ones and got away, and Wyn and I spent a week of it in the Gogarth Abbey Hotel in Llandudno, and a wonderful month it was. I think it was then – or possibly a little earlier, in 1917, that I turned down an offer of a job in London. The Cabinet Secretariat was just being formed at 12 Downing Street, and I was told that they could do with me there. But I did not want to leave the Army. Had I gone there, I might now have been somewhere much higher up than I am! Or lower down!

After Messines[32] we were always in some mêlée or other, and we were sent to Passchendaele in the October to try to push things round.[33] Our attack started on 4 October: 11 a.m., 3rd Australian Division and the

October 1917

New Zealanders told us that they had made over 2,000 yards and their men were digging in and lunching on the Blue Line. Everything was going well and we had taken about 1,600 unwounded prisoners plus another 400 wounded. Our next attack went in on 9 October. This was the 49th and 66th British Divisions. It was an appalling night for the approach march and the men were dead beat before they started the attack. Despite this, and the terrible state of the ground, our men gained the first objectives – only about 300 yards – and took only about 300 prisoners: an indication that there was hard fighting. We had much less information than usual coming through. The flag fell at 5.25 a.m. on 12 October for our next attack.

The weather continued to be bad and again the approach march was extremely difficult. On the morning of the attack it was not raining, but overcast and very cold. It was again the turn of the New Zealanders and 3rd Australian Division. Information was coming in all at once, especially from Monash.[34] Early on things went well but in the afternoon it began to pour with rain, thus putting a stop to our advances which made only about 500 yards; the New Zealanders were held up by a very strong defence on the Bellvue Spur and were never really able to close up to the enemy. We took about 500 prisoners. Thus in eight days, the corps had moved forward 3,000 yards and taken about one prisoner per yard gained. Our own casualties were not unduly heavy: 3rd Australian Division lost 4,700 killed, wounded and missing; the New Zealanders 4,400; 49th Division 2,000 and 66th Division the same.

We were all disappointed at not having taken Passchendaele itself: there is no doubt that some of the Australians did get into the village and others established themselves on Crest Farm, only 1,000 yards from the centre of the village, but they were blown out by Bosche field guns firing at them over open sights at point-blank range from Passchendaele station and the château to the east of the village; and by machine-gun fire from the other flank. The courage and tenacity of these men was beyond description; we felt that no other troops in the world – even Welshmen – could have attacked under such conditions and made the progress they did. Even dead tired, their morale was still high.

On 15 October we were relieved by the Canadian Corps and I was able to go on leave on 22 October. When I got back, the headquarters was at Hazebrouck[35] but General Gwynn sent me to relieve Heywood[36] as liaison officer at the Second Army Centre for a few days. I was there on 10 November when the Canadians and II Corps attacked in pouring rain and a gale of wind, early in the morning. There was much fighting and very heavy shelling, and the rain kept up all day. Even so some aeroplanes went out. The enemy counter-attacked on 13 October but our guns squashed it: I never heard such gun fire.

Notes

1. At this point there were two ANZAC (Australia and New Zealand Army Corps) formations, I and II ANZAC Corps. I Corps contained the 1st, 2nd and 5th Australian Divisions, II Corps the 3rd and 4th Australian and the New

ANZAC

Zealand Division. In late 1917, all five Australian divisions were concentrated into I Corps, which became the ANZAC Corps, and II Corps was re-designated as a British Corps. This concentration was made necessary by the Australians' refusal to break up formations after heavy casualties, in order to keep others up to strength. The ANZAC Corps with five divisions was in numbers, therefore, equivalent to a British Corps of three divisions. However, the Australians were all volunteers and although this slowed reinforcements, it maintained their superb fighting qualities. The ANZACs viewed themselves as a *corps d'elite*, and were often used as such. Indeed, the formation of national corps for Australia and Canada during the war can be viewed as a significant factor in building these new nations. Although their fighting qualities were legendary, so was their indiscipline out of the line.
2. Brigadier-General George William St George Grogan VC CB CMG DSO? (1875–1962). He was commissioned into the Worcesters and served in West Africa before the war. He commanded 23 Infantry Brigade during the war, and, in 1919, the 1st Brigade Russian Relief Force.
3. Later General Sir Alexander John Godley KCB KCMG (1862–1957). He commanded the New Zealand Expeditionary Force throughout the war, the New Zealand and Australian Division at Gallipoli, I ANZAC Corps February 1916–March 1916, II ANZAC Corps until it became XXII Corps in 1917. He was Governor of Gibraltar 1928–1932.
4. The VIII Corps order of battle for Messines was in fact the 25th (British), 3rd and 4th Australian, and the New Zealand Divisions.
5. Later Major-General Sydney Buxton Pope CB DSO (1879–1955). He had served on the North-West Frontier before the war, and in the 1920s he commanded the brigades at Razmak and Bannu, and subsequently the notorious Waziristan District 1931–1934.
6. Brigadier-General Alphonse Eugène Panet CB CMG DSO (1867–1950). Panet was a French-Canadian, born in Quebec and educated at the RMC, Kingston. He had then been commissioned into the Royal Engineers and before the war had served in South Africa and Burma.
7. Brigadier-General Edward Weyland Martin Powell CB CMG DSO Ld'H (1869–1954) was commissioned into the Royal Field Artillery in 1889 and had served in the South African War.
8. Brigadier-General Edwin Francis Delaforce CB CMG Ld'H CdeG late Royal Artillery (1870–1954).
9. This was most likely an Army level Royal Garrison Artillery brigade. By 1917, the British Army had begun to receive large numbers of heavy calibre guns, with improved ammunition – especially fuses – and to master the techniques required. Arguably, by 1918, the Royal Artillery was better at gunnery than its allies and opponents.
10. Messines has been described as the best-prepared battle of the Great War, based on Plumer's principles, described by Harington, Plumer's chief of staff, as 'Trust, Training and Thoroughness'. Between half and one-third of the artillery available to the First, Third and Fifth Armies was moved north to support Second Army's offensive, a total of 2,266 guns and howitzers, 428 heavy mortars, and 700 heavy machine guns. This was a gun to every seven

yards of front, and at least 1,000 rounds of ammunition per gun were available. These had been moved up on the 115 miles of broad gauge and 85 miles of narrow gauge railway laid for the operation. In addition, 300 aircraft – twice those available to the Germans – were available. Twenty-one large mines had been dug under the German position. Plumer's staff had issued four new manuals to the Army, one each for infantry, artillery, engineers and signals. These captured the lessons of the Somme and directed the training for the next battle. The troops were carefully briefed, trained and rehearsed for the operation.

The attack opened at 3.10 a.m. on 7 June with the explosion of nineteen of the mines (two failed to detonate), followed by the barrage. The shock was felt in London. The objectives of the operation were limited: to capture the German position from St Yves to Observatory Ridge; to capture as many as possible of the German guns in the vicinity of Oosttaverne and north-east of Messines; and to consolidate a position to secure the possession of the Messines–Wytschaete ridge and then establish a series of positions in advance of that line.

II ANZAC Corps was to attack on the right (south) of the Army, and capture the eastern shoulder of the ridge, including the buttress formed by Messines village. It was faced by one German regiment of three battalions, in three echelons, backed by reserve counter-attack troops.

The operation was stunningly successful and, despite difficulties in the final phase, forced the Germans to withdraw on 11 June. The operation cost both sides about 25,000 casualties.

11. *The London Gazette,* in which official notification of all appointments and promotions was given.
12. Ewart Stephen Grogan DSO (1876–1976) was the author of, among other woks, *From Cape to Cairo: the First Traverse of Africa from North to South.*
13. Brigadier (later Major) General Sir Charles William Gwynn KCB CMG DSO C*de*G L*d'*H (1870–1963). Gwynn was commissioned into the RE and served in West Africa, the Sudan, and Abyssinia. When the R.M.C. Duntroon was established in Australia in 1911 he was appointed as an instructor. He was GSO I of 1st Australian Division at Gallipoli and was appointed chief of staff to Godley on 16 February 1916.
14. Harold Charles Bradshaw CBE was later Secretary of the Royal Fine Arts Commission, and served on many other official bodies connected with the arts. He had been a Territorial before the war and was commissioned into the Royal Engineers; he received the Italian War Cross for his service during the war.
15. 'Meticulous organization and forethought marked every stage of the preparation, but this was based on personal touch – staff officers continually visiting the units and trenches – not on paper reports and instructions. Another feature was the special intelligence scheme, whereby the information obtained from prisoners, ground and air observation and reconnaissance, photography, wireless interception, and sound ranging, was swiftly conveyed to an Army centre, established for a fortnight at Locre Château, and then shifted and disseminated by summaries and maps.' Liddell Hart's *History of the First World War,* p. 420.
16. 6 kilometre (4 miles) north-west of Bailleul, towards Cassel.

ANZAC

17. Rhiw is on the extreme south coast of the Llyn Peninsula in North Wales, about half-way between Abersoch and Aberdaron.
18. Later Brigadier Percy Howard Hansen VC DSO MC CdeG (1890–1951). He was Danish by birth, and won his VC at Gallipoli with the 6th Lincolns. He later served in Palestine and throughout the Second World War.
19. Later General Sir William Platt GBE KCB DSO (1885–1975). He was GOC-in-C East Africa during the Second World War, and was responsible for the conduct of operations in Eritrea and Somaliland against the Italians, and Madagascar against the Vichy French.
20. Later Brigadier Charles Calvely Foss VC CB DSO (1885–1953). He won his VC at Neuve Chapelle in 1915.
21. Major C.E. Stranock DSO was a pre-war regular officer of the Royal Engineers. No further details of him are known.
22. Not identified.
23. David E. Liddell MC held a temporary commission in the Royal Artillery and was Gazetted as a Captain on 12 February 1917.
24. The Third Battle of Ypres, which began on 16 August. See the next chapter for II ANZAC Corps role in the later stages.
25. General Sir Herbert Plumer, later Viscount Plumer of Messines (1857–1932), known as 'old Plum-and-Apple' by the troops, later Governor of Malta, and High Commissioner in Palestine. Arguably the most consistently successful British general of the war, he prepared meticulously for every operation and despite his blimpish appearance, he had the genuine respect and affection of the troops.
26. Later General Sir Charles ('Tim') Harington KCB (1872–1940). He was DCIGS in 1918 and C-in-C Army of the Black Sea in 1920.
27. Later the Rt Hon Sir Anthony Eden, 1st Viscount Avon KG MC PC (1897–1977) Foreign Secretary three times between 1935 and 1955, and Prime Minister of Great Britain 1955–1957. He is best remembered for the abortive Suez expedition. Wyn Griffith's acquaintance with Eden can only have been short, for according to his biographer, Eden joined the staff of Second Army after the battle of Messines and left in the spring of 1918 to be Brigade Major of 198 Infantry Brigade.
28. Cassel lies about half-way between Ypres and St Omer and is situated on the summit of the 156 metre (500 foot) Mont Cassel – a significant feature in low-lying Flanders. Major road junctions converge from several directions. Plumer's headquarters was in the Castel Yvonne overlooking the plateau with Ypres and Messines Ridge in the distance.
29. See above. Gough's plan, approved by Haig, was highly ambitious. It required the capture of 6,000 yards of ground on the first day, including the neutralisation of the German main position, pivoting on the French rather than on the Gheluveldt plateau which should have been secured in a preliminary operation; their counter-attack divisions; and most of their artillery. It was alleged in Gough's later autobiography that Plumer had acceded to the plan, and even encouraged Gough to go 'all-out'. This passage seems to give the lie to that. At the end of the war, Plumer had his papers destroyed, and this appreciation may well have perished at that time.

30. Wyn Griffith's MS says the Westmeath, however Bailey's Hunting Directory lists Brigadier-General E.W.M. Powell as Master of the Meath Hunt from 1919 to 1922.
31. Brevet Major Lord Charles Cavendish Bentinck DSO (1868–1956) was half-brother to the 6th Duke of Portland.
32. After Messines, the conduct of operations passed to Gough's Fifth Army, and Second Army was relegated to a supporting, diversionary role. At one point, Plumer had to instruct Godley to cease harassing the Germans with quite so much enthusiasm, as he was incurring unnecessary casualties. In August, 4th Australian Division was transferred to I ANZAC Corps for Third Ypres; II ANZAC Corps was moved into Second Army reserve and given command of the 41st Division and the 66th (2nd East Lancashire) Division; 3rd Australian Division, and the New Zealand Division.
33. By September, the Allied attack at Ypres by Gough's Fifth Army (see below) had ground to a halt. Under pressure from London, Haig switched the main effort to Plumer's Second Army. Plumer devised three phases of operations, using novel tactics and intensive training and preparations. The first was the battle of the Menin Road on 20 September. This was completely successful, prompting Ludendorff to say that 'the power of the attack lay in the artillery'. In fact, the power of the attack lay in the use of combined arms: massive artillery yes, but also gas, tanks, aircraft, mechanized transport, careful logistic stockpiling: all the ingredients of modern war except real-time communications. The second phase was the attack on Polygon Wood on 26 September; and the third, planned for 10 October but launched on 9, was the capture of the Gheluveldt Plateau and the village of Broodseinde by twelve divisions on only 14,000 yards of front. This is the operation to which Wyn Griffith refers, for II ANZAC Corps was brought up from reserve and took over part of Fifth Army's front, extending Second Army northwards. This was the third of Plumer's 'hammer blows' that all but broke the German Army. Had it done so, however, Plumer would still have faced the enduring problem of the Western Front until 1918: that an attack could break in to an enemy position, but not break through: the ability to exploit, and support the exploitation with firepower and supplies, was just not there.

After the success of this operation, Haig ordered the final clearance of the Passchendaele ridge, despite the lateness of the season and the now-severe weather. Gough and Plumer both protested, but the operation went ahead anyway. I and II ANZAC Corps were to lead the attack, and almost everywhere these failed. II ANZAC Corps tried again on 12 October, relieving 41st and 66th Divisions with 3rd Australian and the New Zealanders, but in appalling weather, the attacks again failed. The corps lost 6,000 casualties in one day, and questions have to be asked about Godley's judgment in pushing the second attack.
34. Later General Sir John Monash KCMG KB VD (1865–1931). He was a pre-war Militia officer who became Australia's best known soldier during the Great War. He commanded a brigade at Gallipoli, and at the time of this account was commanding 3rd Australian Division. In May 1918 he took command of the ANZAC Corps.

35. From the beginning of the war, this was a place well known to thousands of British soldiers who passed through the town en route for Ypres or the Somme. It was a key road and rail junction, half way between St Omer and Bailleul, and had at various times housed the headquarters of the Cavalry Corps, I Corps, First and Second Armies.
36. Captain Marcus B. Heywood MVO DSO was a Territorial Officer of the Northumberland Hussars Yeomanry, who was Gazetted to the General Staff on 1 June 1916.

Chapter 11

Kaiserschlacht

The General Staff cap badge

During a leave period in the early spring of 1918, Wyn and I had gone to Ffordd y boedal,[1] a farmhouse at the foot of Cader Idris. No sooner had I got there than a telegram came ordering me to return to France, so back I went straightaway. The incident caused great excitement locally, and everybody thought I must be very important. I returned from leave late on 17 March 1918 and saw General Gwynn, then went to bed. I found the messes altered too: Major Stranack had left and we now had a Colonel Evans, the Labour Commandant,[2] Lieutenant Colonel Man of the Ordnance,[3] Major Alabaster of the Engineers,[4] and Captain Dabell of the Artillery.[5]

March 1918

The Corps had been moved to Mont Noir since my departure and we were in good huts in the thickly wooded grounds of a château,[6] high up on a good hill, from the top of which we could see the coast on a clear day. On 20th, Percy Hansen went on leave, but as soon as the battle broke out down south he was ordered back: [7] he had no more than 24 hours in Paris. In our part of the line the situation was very quiet apart from some gas shelling just prior to the attack down south, and exceptionally heavy shelling of the back areas with high velocity guns, especially on Hazebrouck, Bailleul and the railway

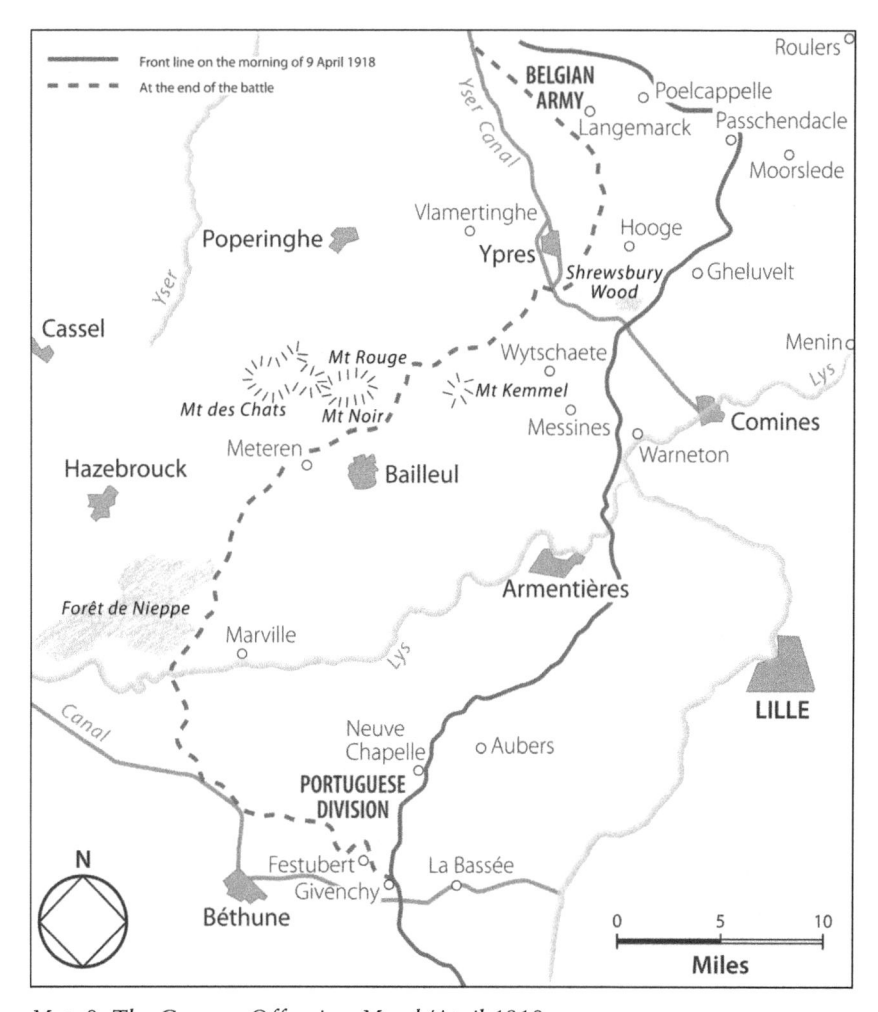

Map 8: The German Offensive, March/April 1918.

lines. It culminated on Saturday 23 March when the Hun knocked down the fine old tower of the *hôtel de ville* in Bailleul.

During the hectic days of fighting down south, our share in the battle was confined to sending troops and guns to help – all this done at high speed, naturally, but it was little enough compared to what the others were doing at the same time on the Somme. And during this time, when telegram after telegram arrived saying that the Hun had captured this place or that, there was no sign of any depression or of anything but complete confidence in our final victory. Everyone was cheerful, delighted at the thought of so many

Bosche being killed. It was extraordinary that Bosche prisoners taken by us were very sceptical about their 'victory' – they said that they had heard that tale too often!

On 28 March the weather turned cloudy. We heard that the New Zealand and 4th Australian Division had done very well on the Somme, as everyone expected. When 3rd Australian Division were told that they were going south, they yelled, cheered and put their hats on their bayonets, and sang – a very fine sight, and one that would have surprised the enemy. This was the day that the King came to watch the troops moving south, and he got a fine reception. Plumer was with him, looking as well and as pleasant as ever. Over the next couple of days the news from the south was much better: we were told that seven German divisions had been scuppered on the Scarpe, each of them carrying six days' rations – good work! Our airmen were having things all their own way, and practically every plane we had took a trip down to that part of the line.

Easter fell on 31 March that year. I remember that day because the New Zealanders suddenly pushed out a six-mile gap in our line, having carried out several successful local attacks and squashed two Bosche attacks, capturing many prisoners and machine guns. They finished up holding ground south of Hébuterne, where I had been with my brigade after the Somme. It was just after this that Foch was appointed to 'coordinate' the allies – some people construed this as 'generalissimo'. Something appeared to be needed, though! That night, the enemy shelled Bailleul with long-range guns.

I woke up on 9 April shortly after 4.00 a.m. to hear a heavy barrage, the high velocity guns all at work.[8] It was a misty morning, which made it almost certain that the Hun would attack. I went in to the office and found that the shelling was falling between La Bassée and Laventie – nearly twenty miles away: it sounded nearer. During the day, the Bosche met with some success and the noise of battle was very plain. We had a great deal to do to secure our position, and keep in touch with the corps on our right (IX), as the Bosche started to exploit the situation on his northern flank in the direction of Armentières and Messines. The next day, the HQ packed up and moved to Steenvoorde[9]. During this critical period, when the Germans nearly reached the Channel Ports, we were put in charge of the Kemmel Hill sector, the last defence, and at one time there were eleven divisions under our command.[10] That shows the high opinion held of Godley, and I suppose of his staff. It was a desperate time, a

KAISERSCHLACHT

whirl of work, six of us in a small office, at it night and day, while the Bosche were fighting to capture Wytschaete and the ridge. I had no time to keep any record of what happened.

On 15 April, to our great joy, we withdrew from the Broodseinde ridge. As soon as there was stability, we moved back to Corps HQ, to find that II French Cavalry Corps[11] was marching up to reinforce us, French troops were already pouring in through the town in large numbers, both cavalry and infantry. The next morning, the Bosche captured Wytschaete. French cavalry were still pouring in, and Godley sent me off with Collard[12] to find the French General and stop him – the roads were thick with transport, and defence in depth had cluttered the countryside. I found General Robillot[13] at Zuytpeene:[14] he was a quaint figure, small and plump with grey moustache and a merry face, and quite tidy in appearance for a French General! His *Chef d'Etat* was a Colonel Broullaire, a very capable man with a queer habit of carrying his tortoiseshell pince-nez hanging over one ear. He wore a Sam Browne belt complete with revolver and all the gadgets! In my best French, I explained that the roads forward were so congested that it would be impossible for him to advance. He bridled and said they were cavalry and did not depend on roads. 'But your artillery and transport do,' I replied. He was forced to agree. I then asked whether it was true that his corps had travelled all these miles in two days that we could not believe it possible, that no one but the French could have done it. The butter did its work, I was asked to lunch, and the French corps stayed where it was.

15 April 1918

For the next couple of days I was back and forward between the two corps as the French consolidated behind us. On 17 April I found the French Corps HQ had moved to Rubrouek[15]. I found them in an estimanet with the Corps Commander and the G staff sitting in the bar, he dictating orders in true Napoleonic fashion. My Corps Commander came in, so I got him to ask General Robillot if I might live at XXII Corps HQ and visit from there. This was arranged, so the next day I met the French who had again moved, this time west to Watten on the canal north of St Omer. We had a long and not very fruitful discussion about boundaries: it was very hard to pin them down to anything definite. Very soon afterwards, XXII Corps moved to Zuytpeene, where the French had been: I had never seen such heavy traffic as there was that day between Cassel and Poperinghe, not

21 April 1918

even in the days of the Ypres battles the previous year. The French did not keep any intervals in their transport, and as there were four streams of traffic it took a long time to get anywhere. I did however manage to get to Hoograaf where I found HQ 9th Division, and close by, 21st Division. 6th Division was very comfortably housed near Brandhoek.

I think I can claim to be one of the few who have seen a General fighting a battle. As a rule, corps headquarters were some distance from the scene of battle, for obvious reasons, the chief of which was the necessity of maintaining communications forward and back, for there was no radio in those days. Godley said, 'I can't fight a battle from here. Find me a signal office as far forward as you can.' Really, I needed to find a dugout or a strongpoint near a signals station, big enough to hold him, Grogan and me, to be the advanced Corps HQ. I found such a place, near Poperinghe, and there the three of us and some signallers went: lines were run directly to five divisional HQs, to the Generals themselves, and to the Army HQ so long as shelling did not cut the lines. There were two telephones, and my job was to listen and keep a record. With maps and orders and reports before him, Godley moved brigades about, closed up reserves, and took full responsibility upon himself for directing the battle to stop the German advance. It might have been the Napoleonic Wars: he moved brigades and battalions and batteries to meet the varying hazards and opportunities as the battle raged on our front. Our men fought magnificently, though tired out after days of fighting against fresh Hun divisions specially trained in open warfare: 9th, 49th, and 21st Divisions did gloriously, but the Hun took Kemmel from the French.

23–25 April 1918

Early the next day, the French and our 25th Division, which was placed under French command, were to counter-attack and recapture Kemmel Hill and the village. No bombardment at all could be heard, and I found out that none had taken place, as the French had not got orders out to their artillery groups. 25th Division however took the village and about 400 prisoners, but the French did not break in, and they had to come back again.

By the accident of being on duty at the time, I was one of the actors in a strange interlude. Percy Hansen had gone to take Winston Churchill round the front:[16] there had been a heavy bombardment on the whole of our front from Zillebeke to Meteren, which had since calmed down, but

29 April 1918

the enemy had attacked both us and the French. I was alone in the G office when the telephone went. It was one of our artillery colonels to say that a French artillery regiment reported that the Germans had captured the last two hills, Mont Rouge and Mont Noir.[17] I said I doubted it, and would he confirm. The situation was fluid, but I did not believe it to be as bad as that, which would put Dunkirk at the enemy's mercy. I went straight to tell General Grogan, and he agreed that I ought to let GHQ know. I did so, and told Gort (afterwards Field Marshal)[18] who nearly had a fit. However, I stoutly maintained that it was not true. Nor was it: the enemy had driven in some of our advanced posts and got as far as Hyde Park Corner, but were soon driven back by a counter-attack led by a French Captain of Dragoons: I mention this because Winston Churchill refers to it in his history of the war.[19] In fact it was a wonderful day for us, as the C-in-C (Haig) came down and sent wires to 9th, 21st, 25th and 49th Divisions congratulating them on their stand, after which he went to II French Corps.

There was a lull then until 4 May, by which time there were general indications of an enemy attack.[20] The French in fact attacked first, and took many prisoners, doubtless meeting and disrupting the German attack. Wireless intercept told us that the Germans were much disorganised by this, and so we doubled our harassing artillery fire. The enemy renewed his attack on 8 May, however, trying to get to Dickebusch, just south of Ypres. He took our front line in places but counter-attacks drove him out in the evening.

On 12 May we handed over command of the sector to II French Corps and moved back to Bollezelle[21] for a rest. Platt went off to Boulogne to prepare a staging area for incoming American divisions, so Dodd[22] of the **June 1918** Intelligence and I went along too, and had an excellent lunch at the Souverain Moulin. This pleasant life continued until 5 June, when we hustled off south in cars to near Amiens, to be under the direct orders of Foch,[23] and to be responsible for maintaining the junction between the French and British Armies: when the German intentions on the Marne began to emerge, Foch withdrew the eight French divisions from Flanders and in addition, he asked for four British divisions[24] to be made available to him and moved south astride the Somme. It was these four divisions that we were to command. In addition, all other troops within a certain area were to be under our command if the Germans attacked the junction, as they were expected to do. This was a pleasant change, for we were not in the line, and all we had to do was to study the country and the communications in case we had to go into action. We were near enough to the sea to be able to dash down in a car for a bathe near Dieppe, or walk in the forest of Arques: it was really a holiday, subject to four hours' notice. Nothing happened for some time.

Notes

1. This is nowhere near Rhiw, but in Snowdonia, between Dolgellau and Harlech.
2. Lieutenant Colonel H.J. Evans CMG DSO became a temporary Brigadier on 30 March 1917, having been recalled from retirement.
3. Brevet Lieutenant Colonel H.W. Man DSO.
4. Brevet Major E.O. Alabaster RE.
5. Lieutenant A.H. Dabell MC RA was Gazetted as a temporary captain on 28 January 1917.
6. Possibly the Abbey on the Mont des Cats, West of Mont Noir.
7. Wyn Griffith is cursory about this great offensive, the *Kaiserschacht*, or Operation *Michael*, which nearly broke the Allies. With the end of operations in the east after the Russian Revolution, the Germans had transferred forty-two divisions to the Western Front. The US Armies had yet to arrive in strength so that by March 1918, 170 Allied divisions faced 192 German divisions. The British had extended their line in the 5th Army sector to take over a stretch of the front from the French; moreover all British divisions were under strength. The administration at home had withheld reinforcements from the BEF to prevent offensive action and the casualties of 1916 and 1917. At the same time, new defensive tactics had been adopted, with the line organised into forward, battle, and rear zones – but in Fifth Army there were insufficient troops to man the line, and the defences were in poor shape. The Germans too used new tactics, with the assault spearheaded by *Sturmbatallionen*, and supported by a hurricane bombardment of gas and high explosive. The attack, although expected, was launched on 21st March and before it was halted in front of Amiens, cost Fifth Army 1,000 guns and 70,000 men. Subsequent attacks were launched in Flanders and in Champagne; however even when penetrations were made, the Germans were as usual unable to exploit, for they had left their three cavalry corps as an observation force on the eastern front. The offensive cost Germany 250,000 casualties according to the British Official History. With such losses, the Germans could no longer go on the offensive and even without the arrival of the Americans, the force ratio had shifted irrevocably to the Allies.
8. This was the start of Operation *George I*. Where German attacks in early 1918 took place in fog or mist, they usually succeeded in penetrating the Allied outpost line, and getting into the main defensive line. When the weather was clear, however, German attacks generally failed, with horrific casualties.
9. About halfway between Cassel and Poperinghe.

KAISERSCHLACHT

10. XXII Corps took an active part in the Battles of Bailleul, 13–15 April 1918 when it commanded 9th, 39th, 62nd (2nd West Riding) and 64th (2nd Highland) Divisions; First Kemmel 17–19 April when it commanded the same four divisions plus brigades of the 24th Division; Second Kemmel 25–26 April when it commanded 9th, 21st, 25th, 39th, and 49th (West Riding) Divisions, and brigades of the 6th and 30th Divisions; and Scherpenberg on 29th April, when it commanded 6th, 21st, 25th, 39th and 49th Divisions and brigades of the 9th and 31st Divisions. If it commanded eleven divisions at one time, this was probably at a period of relief in place of one set of divisions by another.
11. II (French) Cavalry Corps order of battle included the 28th, 39th and 154th Infantry Divisions and the 3rd Cavalry Division, plus corps troops.
12. Major (temporary Lieutenant Colonel) A.M. Collard DSO DCLI.
13. Général Félix Robillot (1865–1918).
14. About 4 kilometres (2.5 miles) west of Cassel, and therefore only eight kilometres (5 miles) behind HQ XXII Corps.
15. A small village about 8 kilometres (5 miles) north-west of Cassel.
16. Churchill was Minister of Munitions at the time.
17. The chain of hills that runs from the Messines–Wytschaete Ridge westward from Mount Kemmel, through Mounts Rouge and Noir, to Cassel, is a prominent feature jutting out into the flat plain of Flanders. Well sited British defences on these features shattered the first German attack in the area in April; by the time of the German's second attack, the area had been handed over to French troops, who lost the position. Even so, and although all the gains of 1917 in the Ypres area had been lost, a decisive penetration was prevented.
18. Later Field Marshal John Standish Surtees Prendergast Vereker, 6th Viscount Gort, VC GCB CBE DSO?? MVO MC (18816–1946). He became Chief of the Imperial General Staff in 1937, jumping directly from Major-General to General, but stepped out of the post to command the BEF in France in 1939, with near-disastrous consequences. He was subsequently Governor of Malta during the great siege, a mission which he conducted with enormous leadership and example. His personal courage was never in doubt, as witness his many decorations and his nine mentions in despatches. On this occasion, Wyn Griffith's memory is playing tricks on him: Gort had been appointed GSO II in General Headquarters on 30 June 1916, but left to command the 4th Grenadiers on 17 April 1917 – a full year before this event.
19. 'At about 10 o'clock on April 29th I was breakfasting with Sir Douglas Haig ... when the following message was put into his hand: "G.O.C. 39th French Division reports that there is no doubt but that the enemy holds Mont Rouge and Mont Vidaigne. Troops on right of Scherpenberg badly cut up ..." Simultaneously there arrived from General Plumer a confirmatory message requesting the Chief of Staff to come at once to the Headquarters of the Second Army ... I motored to the area of Sir Alexander Godley's Corps ... but at the Corps Headquarters faces were beaming. The French Commander had telephoned that it was all a mistake and that nothing of importance was occurring.' *The World Crisis 1916–1918, Part II*, p. 445.
20. This was Operation *George II*.
21. 10 kilometres (4 miles) north-west of Cassel

22. Major A.H.R. Dodd of the 17th Cavalry, Indian Army.
23. Marshal of France Ferdinand Foch OM GCB (1851–1959) became Supreme General of the Allied armies on 26 March 1918 during the German offensive, when Haig offered to put himself under Foch's authority for the first time. Foch only ever had authority to coordinate, however, not to compel his allies to action.
24. These were the 15th (Scottish), 34th, 51st (Highland) and 62nd (2nd West Riding) Divisions.

Chapter 12

Armistice

The badge of XXII Corps

It was on the 13th July 1918 that the telephone went when I was alone again in the G office. It was GHQ. We were to move south immediately with our four divisions,[1] and place ourselves under the orders of General Robillot, now promoted and commanding the French Group of Armies *Maistre*,[2] so-called because of its first commander, General Maistre. I told General Grogan, and early next morning Castello (a London solicitor on our Intelligence staff)[3] and I set out in our Vauxhall car to find Robillot's HQ, and glean what we could so as to make whatever arrangements were necessary. I remember well that there were hardly any Union Jacks to be seen anywhere en route, for the French thought we had let them down.[4]

July 1918

Eventually we landed at Vitry-le-François[5] so late at night that we could do nothing more that day, so we went to bed. We had found out from the French that a German attack by their Seventh Army was imminent south of Rheims, and that we would have to go into action to keep the line if possible. The German intention was later found to have been the capture of Chalons, and subsequently of Rheims. No sooner had we got into bed than the barrage began, some fifteen or so miles away we thought.[6] We got up, but we had to wait until dawn, and then we set off for Chalons-en-Champagne. Going into the staff office there I saw a yellow-bearded French General, with one eye and a wooden leg, stumping up and down and

173

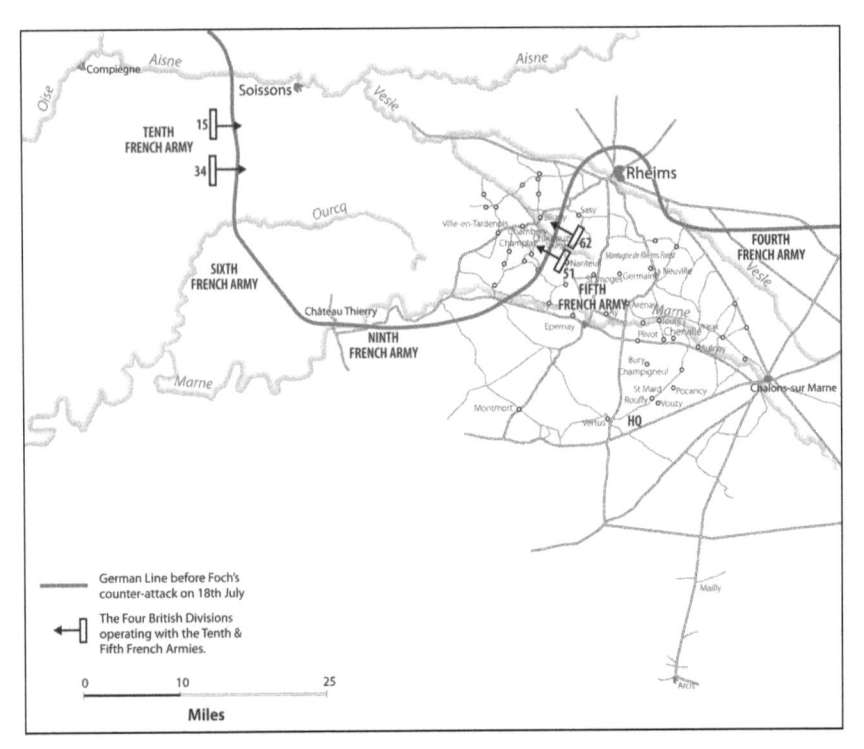

Map 9: The Second Battle of the Marne, 1918 (History of the 62nd (West Riding) Division).

crying 'C'est fini, c'est fini!' I saluted and said 'Qu'est-ce que c'est que c'est fini, mon général?' 'La guerre est fini,' he replied. He was General Gouraud and in one sense, he was right.[7]

I got hold of a telephone and managed to get through to GHQ where I found Godley, and arranged to establish our Corps HQ at Vertus, ten miles south of Épernay on the Marne.[8] Godley and Gouraud, as it turned out, knew one another from Gallipoli which made things a lot easier. Our four divisions came down and we took over the front by the Montagne de Rheims, taking over from an Italian corps, under the command of the Conte d'Abricci, who were supposed to be responsible for guarding the bridges over the Marne and demolishing them if need be.[9] But the Italians could not tell me where the demolition charges were, nor could their staff tell me where exactly their front line was.

Our artillery had to take over the defence, and the SOS barrage lines, on very scanty and inaccurate information. It was that which nearly broke the peace between us and the French. Martin Powell decided that he must go and see the French artillery general at the Army Group HQ: wherever he went, David Liddell went too, and I was sent as well. On our way, Powell said 'I'm going to tell the French "Toot ate on confusion". That's right in French, isn't it?' I pointed out to him that it was hardly a tactful thing to say, true though it was. After much pleading, David and I persuaded him not to say anything in French, but to talk to us in English and we would translate. When we met the French general, David and I explained our difficulty at length and were getting near an agreed solution when Martin Powell burst in with his 'Toot ate on confusion', several times repeated. The French general took umbrage at this and got very heated. However, we assured him that Powell was referring to the British forces generally, and not to the French artillery, and we burst into a paean of praise for everything French, and their gunners in particular. Eventually, the Frenchman thawed and sent out for a bottle of champagne. As we drank success to the French, out came Martin Powell with his phrase, but it had by now become a joke, and we assured them that that was all the French he knew, and that he was always mumbling it to himself all day.

As things turned out, the German attack was held, and we went straight into the planning for our part in Foch's great counter-attack. It had been decided to attack all round the salient at Rheims, so we lost two of our divisions to the French Tenth Army: the 15th went to the XX Corps, and 34th went to XXX Corps. We were left with 51st and 62nd Divisions, and although we de-trained in the Fourth Army area, we were to go into action under the Fifth Army. Just after midnight on 19 July, two of the G staff officers were sent out to the two divisions with orders to concentrate behind the Italians by noon that same day and prepare to take part in a general attack along the whole front on 20 July. General Godley held a conference at noon with the Italian and French Generals at the Italian HQ. The two GSO Is of the divisions then had to come to our HQ for written orders and to tie up all the coordinating details. It was 5.00 p.m. before the orders went to the divisional commanders, and 9.00 p.m. before they could get orders to their brigade commanders. Zero Hour was to be 8.00 a.m. next morning, so there was no time for any reconnaissance and the approach march was chaos. Nor could our artillery get into action. It must have been hell for the troops. By a miracle, the assault

19 July 1918

brigades were able to cross the start line on time, and with a ragged supporting artillery barrage from Italian and French guns on a wide front of 9,000 yards, on a brilliant, sunny morning.

As it turned out, going straight in to the attack was the right thing to do. We were fighting continuously for the next week but we advanced nearly two miles, took more than 1,000 prisoners including two battalion commanders, and 120 machine guns. We also recaptured thirty French artillery pieces. The fighting was very bitter and the Bosche resistance was furious: they had no choice but to hold on as our attack on both sides of the salient threatened their line of retreat and their communications. Things were particularly rough on the western edge of the forest of the Montagne de Reims; the woods were full of thick undergrowth chest high, extremely difficult to get through, and interlaced with wire. Our sappers and pioneers had to blow and cut a way through as if it were a jungle. In the villages of the valley of the Ardre – Ouitron, Marfaux, Espilly, Les Haies and Nappes – the houses all had deep cellars for storing wine and the Germans made good use of these as strongpoints. Our casualties were fairly heavy but the proportion of killed to wounded was lighter than usual, only about one to eight, rather than the usual one to four that we expected.

We got along surprisingly well with the French and at one time we had two French divisions under our command. All the senior French commanders visited the headquarters and were very pleasant and complimentary about what we were doing. Despite his earlier troubles, Martin Powell was able to get the French and Italian gunners to fall in pretty well with our ideas and the artillery support improved greatly as things went on. Their ammunition was chiefly high explosive rather than shrapnel and accordingly our men liked it very well: many said it was the best barrage they had ever had! The supply arrangements and medical cover worked well too, especially given the distance we were from our normal supply depots and hospitals.

At the end of a week, our front was reduced by half so that one brigade from each division could be rested. This allowed us to keep going as the men were very tired, although in remarkable spirits. We still had Australian **27 July 1918** and New Zealand corps cavalry and cyclists, despite having lost our ANZAC divisions. They were very keen to get into the fight but the opportunities for pursuit were small.

ARMISTICE

During the later part of our stay on the Marne, we moved our HQ forward to a château on the hill above Rheims. It belonged to Moet et Chandon,[10] and the cellars were full of champagne. For the next three weeks we had nothing to drink but champagne – we bought it at two francs the bottle – and did not disturb Moet et Chandon's cellars. It is a good drink, taken in sufficient quantity, in a tumbler. Until we got to the château, the Archbishop of Rheims had been living there, and in memory of the Jackdaw, I relieved His Eminence of a small book and some manuscript notes in Latin. The French artillery was all around us, and my batman, Woods, a South Wales miner, came to me to say that there were some nice copper pans in the kitchen which 'them Frenchies was knocking about something cruel, break your heart it would, and carrying them away.' I gave him some money and told him to buy a few for me, which he did. Next time I went home on leave I took them with me, to Wyn's astonishment and delight, though she did say that it would have been better if I had brought some more clothes! If any of the Chandon family visits my daughter-in-law's kitchen, they could claim them.

When the battle was over,[11] our troops were reviewed by General Robillot, and I found myself with a French *Croix de Guerre avec palmes*, and a wonderful citation in their Orders, which said

August 1918

> Captain Llewelyn Wyn Griffith, HQ XXII Corps. A skilful and energetic staff officer during the recent operations, he rendered the greatest possible services to the chief of staff at Corps and carried out his duties on every occasion in perfect style and the greatest possible precision.[12]

I had now been three times mentioned in despatches and given a military OBE.[13] And to crown everything, the French government invited us to spend three days in Paris at their expense: Percy and I stayed at the Regina because the Corps Commander was staying at the Ritz; we lounged about, and I was taken by Percy to a nightclub for the first (and last) time in my life – a dull business, and we did not stay long.

General Berthelot, commanding the Fifth Army,[14] published a Special Order to mark the departure of XXII Corps on 30 July 1918.[15]

> Now that XXII (British) Corps has received orders to leave the Fifth French Army, the Commanding General expresses to all the thanks and admiration which the great deeds that it has accomplished deserve. The very day it arrived, feeling in honour bound to take part in the victorious counter-attack which had just stopped the enemy's furious onslaught on the Marne, and had begun to hurl him back in disorder to the north, the XXII Corps, by forced marches and with minimum opportunity for reconnaissance, threw itself with ardour into the battle... Your French comrades will always remember with emotion your splendid gallantry and your perfect fellowship in the fight.

Godley replied

> That we have been fortunate enough to participate under your command in this, the Second Battle of the Marne, will ever be a source of great pride to us all, and we count ourselves lucky to have been so closely associated with you and our gallant French comrades ... I would like to take this opportunity of asking you to convey to your staff our great appreciation of all the help they have given us. No trouble has been too great for them to take on our behalf and everything possible has been done for us.[16]

We moved up north again, and as the war drew towards its end, we found ourselves near the salient and in familiar country.[17] We liberated Valenciennes;[18] I remember a parade in the square and a reception by

2 November 1918

the municipality in evening dress, with Godley standing tall and still, the Prince of Wales fidgeting by his side,[19] me just behind with the G staff and the two ADCs – Viscount Cranbourne[20] and the Earl of Eltham[21] (now Marquis of Salisbury and Cambridge respectively).

When the end came we were near Mons.[22] During the evening of 10 November we intercepted a German wireless message authorizing their delegates to accept the Armistice conditions, and so we expected to hear at any moment that hostilities were to cease.

No news came through in the night. When I came in to breakfast next morning I heard that hostilities were to cease at 11.00 a.m., the actual order having come through by wire at about 07.00 a.m. This was

11 November 1918

ARMISTICE

repeated at once to our divisions and to the 16th Lancers – the Corps Cavalry – out in front. I went out in the Q car about 10.00 a.m. to see the Lancers and 63rd Division, a very eventful journey as the roads and bridges had been blown up by the retreating Hun. We had to ford a river and go over fields, and although we saw a lot of our men, we found very little excitement anywhere – but everyone was pleased enough. When 11.00 a.m. came and with it the ceasefire, a pioneer working on the road merely said 'Another bloody war over,' and went on digging.

The Belgians were of course jubilant, and we were soon forced to drink a couple of glasses of bad red wine that one farmer said he had hidden from the Germans. It was noticeable how the farms were better stocked in Belgium than in France, whether because the Hun could not get the stock away, or because he wished to treat the Belgians better, I do not know.

We had outrun our supplies in the hurried chase of the Germans, and we would have had bully beef for dinner if Tim Pile,[23] afterwards in command of Anti-Aircraft Command in the Second World War, had not taken out his horse and run down some partridges for us. We had nothing to drink. After dinner we got an order from First Army for the advance to the Rhine. To our intense delight we found that XXII Corps was one of the six British Corps (plus the Australians and Canadians) scheduled to advance and occupy Germany. We were also told that we would form part of the Second Army under General Plumer, which pleased us, as we had served under his command at Messines and Passchendaele in 1917, and at Ypres in 1918, and we knew his staff well. Next day, we heard that our Corps would consist of the 4th, 51st (Highland), 52nd (Lowland), and 56th (London) Divisions. We knew them all except the 52nd. I went out early to go around 11th, 56th and 63rd Divisions to relay the orders; 11th and 63rd were very disappointed.

There was no ceremony about our entry into Mons on the day after the Armistice, though there was a reception at the Town Hall later on. I found Mons crowded with civilians, all making holiday and walking abroad in the streets. I did not stay long but out of curiosity I went to a chemist's shop and asked the price of some ordinary toilet soap – and found it was 10 francs a tablet. I wondered how the Belgians had managed to keep clean! Butter was 25 francs a kilo, but at a little village shop five miles away, it was only 10 francs, so I came to the conclusion that the Belgian shopkeepers were, as usual, making hay while the sun shone.

General Horne, Commanding First Army, was officially welcomed into Mons on 15 November. Flags were flying everywhere and all the inhabitants were out; the bells played most wonderful tunes all the time. A large number of our troops and the Canadians marched past Horne in the *Grande Place*: our men looked magnificent, as did the artillery. I saw a number of our escaped or freed prisoners: some looked well, all looked glad of their freedom. Then we went down to the railway station and nearby, we saw two cars and a crowd of people outside the Café de l'Espérance. Going closer, we saw that the cars were Bosche, and had a big white flag about the size of a blanket tied to them. The sight of this cheered us, and we went into the café to look for Castello. On one side of the room, twenty hale, hearty and clean looking British officers were obviously enjoying their lunch. On the other side, sitting alone and looking miserable, were some German officers who seemed frightened of the crowd – a day I little thought I should live to see!

In Mons, we began to learn what the years of enemy occupation had meant to the ordinary men, women and children of Belgium. I had an excellent billet with a lawyer, his anglophile wife, and a daughter engaged to be married to a Belgian advocate. **December 1918** Our Mess was in a palatial house. Life was something of an anti-climax, for though the administrative people were busy; there was nothing to do on the operations side. The Germans had left a lot of timber in the town, and our sappers built a squash court, so we had exercise in plenty. Christmas came, and Godley called us all together and said we must give the children a Christmas party. We pointed out that there were so many of them that we could not get them all into the Town Hall. 'No matter,' said Godley, 'the party will last three days if necessary, and if some of them come more than once, it doesn't matter. Fill them with food and presents. Send some lorries to Paris to get oranges and apples and toys, if there are any, and plenty of buns. We'll fill them up with biscuits and buns.' And so the canteen funds provided the money, and lorries were sent to Paris to buy food and toys. It was a good party! I do not know how many thousands of children of all ages and sizes came to the party, nor how often they came. Some of the smaller ones had never seen an orange before. They ate their buns at the party – they could not wait – and they took buns home with them. Nobody cried; they all looked starry-eyed in wonder at this profusion. And towering above them all stood General Godley. Six feet six inches in height, as happy as any child at the party.

The lawyer's daughter wanted to get married, and I took her and her mother to Brussels to buy her trousseau, in an Army car of course, and I stood them lunch. They were very kind to me, and I learnt to my astonishment that I was the only man who had ever been alone with the daughter – her courting took the form of sitting by her fiancé looking at an album, while papa and mama and I sat and talked. Papa told me that much as he admired the British, he would be glad to see us go: we were putting ideas into the heads of the women folk and upsetting the relationship between the sexes by being content to be friendly.

In the New Year, Godley decided to entertain the nobility of Belgium by giving a dance in Brussels. There was plenty of money in the canteen funds, and so we were to do them proud – they had not had a square meal during the war, and we must see that they sat down to something solid: no buffet nonsense. Knives and forks, and champagne to drink.

January 1919

So the lorries went off again to buy food and wine. The regimental band of the Grenadier Guards was fetched, and a jazz band from the American Army Air Corps, together with two eightsome reel teams from the 51st (Highland) Division. It really was a party, and the nobility were overwhelmed. When midnight came, the floor was cleared, the spotlights put on, and the Highlanders danced to the pipes. Godley's staff officers were detailed to act as masters of ceremonies, so David Liddell and I were charged to see that no young girls were left without partners, and that the older folk had plenty to eat. We both did so successfully that a few days later he and I went to visit a Baron something-or-other, who ran the Musée du Congo Belge,[24] but we paid more attention to his pretty daughters than to his exhibits. David was in danger of finding himself tied up to one of them; being married, I was of no importance.

To pass the time in Mons, we decided to go in for music. We found that the professionals at the *Conservatoire* were having a hard time, so we persuaded a string quartet to give a concert. We browbeat the staff into attending it. This put heart into the musicians, and the Opera House was opened. We went there in force. I hired a cello and took lessons; David bought a clarinet and did likewise.

But my chief concern was to get demobilized and to get home. I got a telegram from GHQ offering me a better job if I joined the Army of Occupation in Germany,[25] with Godley and Plumer, but I said no. In February 1919 my liberation orders came through. I said goodbye to them all, and went to London to meet Wyn. I had been in France since December 1915, three and a quarter years of war, and had been lucky enough to escape being wounded or sick. I went straight to Cox's Bank[26] to see about my gratuity, which amounted to £400 – a lot of money. And then, in a London hotel, I fell a victim to flu – the very violent form of it which killed more people than did the war.[27] Wyn nursed me, and I came through. I called at Somerset House[28] and found to my surprise that in my absence I had had several promotions, and they very kindly posted me to assist in a tax district in Liverpool, where Wyn and I could live with her mother for the time being. And with this, my Army career came to an end.

February 1919

It would be an understatement to say that I found it difficult to settle down to civilian life. I stayed in uniform until I got new civilian clothes, and they felt light and strange at first. I suppose I was the first ex-staff officer who turned up in a tax office in red tabs and medal ribbons. I missed the freedom, the exercise, the companionship, the sense of responsibility and of being at the centre of important happenings. And it was ten years since I had lived in a house as part of a family. If it had not been for the joy of being with Wyn, I would have been utterly miserable, a man lost and aimless, out of tune with all he met, speaking a different language. I had learned a lot from the Army – it was my university – and I had lived familiarly with people whose station in life was far above my own, men of widely differing attainments and interests. I got on well with them all, without knuckling to any of them, just as I had got on well with the private soldier. I had acquired the habit of taking responsibility upon myself, of quick decisions and instantaneous readiness to act upon my judgment.

In some ways I was fortunate. My chief was a charming Irishman named Heffernan, the staff were agreeable, tired out after heavy work during the war. Another ex-serviceman, Charles Foulsham (afterwards Sir Charles, and chief Inspector of Taxes)[29] came to an adjacent office and was a good friend. The trouble was that I had to settle down and learn new and complicated laws and totally different work – taxation was not what I knew it when I joined the

Army – and this took hours upon hours of study in which I was not fundamentally interested. Nor was office work congenial. It all seemed so unimportant, somehow. However, I was in a good job, getting reasonably well paid, and the prospects were good, and I had much to be grateful for. After all, I was not a back room boy: I was in daily contact with the public.

Wyn's mother lived at 18 Rutland Avenue, Sefton Park, with her unmarried daughter Doll, Wyn and me, and Gertrude's boy, John Shaw, aged five. It was a happy household. But we wanted a house of our own as soon as possible. Houses were scarce and very expensive to buy – to rent impossible, for although there had been little destruction of property, there had been no new building during the war. It was no use going to ask estate agents, and all we could do was to scan the *Liverpool Echo*. We wanted to get out into the country somewhere within reach, for life on the pavements did not satisfy me: we were expecting our first child and could not in fairness go on indefinitely sharing a house, grateful though we were to Wyn's mother for her kindness and forbearance.

John was born on 29 October 1919.[30] We went into rooms in New Brighton for a spell, and then one day I saw a house advertised for sale in Neston, price £800: a big price in those days. I went out and saw it: yellow brick, semi-detached, in the Hinderton Road, with three entertaining rooms, eight bedrooms and a dressing room, on three floors, with a small garden back and front. Wyn came out and saw it and nearly had a fit: it was so enormous and we had very little furniture. Still, we had to have a house, and we bought it on a mortgage. All that remained for me now, at the age of 28, was to settle down with Wyn to build a new life for ourselves together.

> October 1919

The knowledge that the Somme and Passchendaele had more than decimated the youth of Wales, had almost destroyed a generation of my countrymen, may have brought me closer to my own country and helped to make me devote myself to playing a part in some kind of reconstruction of what we regarded as our national culture. But, on the other hand, it may only have been the pull of generations of my forebears. I had much to be thankful for, and I knew it. I escaped physical hurt and financial loss, I emerged capable of dealing with daily life, fortified by the steadfast love of a wife who suffered torments of suspense for four years of war. My reward is that when I think of the war, the elements of fear, of real and imagined danger,

'Rats killed in an old dug-out', by David Jones 15th RWF. [RWF Museum]

of discomfort and of deprivation, of filth and of repulsiveness, of anger and hate, of contempt for the ignorance above which insisted on the continuance of Passchendaele have lost their strength. They have been overlaid by the memory of men who can no longer speak.

Notes

1. These were the 15th (Scottish), 34th, 51st (Highland) and 62nd (2nd West Riding) Divisions.
2. The Army Group consisted of the Fourth, Fifth, Sixth. Ninth and Tenth French Armies, and the Italian II Corps (see below).
3. Not identified.
4. This is a reference to the German penetration of the front along the Fifth Army sector during Operation *Michael*, which had brought them close to Paris.
5. Vitry is about 20 kilometres (15 miles) south-east of Chalons, and therefore Wyn Griffith and Costello would have had to retrace their route the next morning.
6. This was the start of the German *Friedensturm* offensive, the fifth and last of their great attacks in 1918, which began on 15 July. The barrage began at 1.00 a.m. The way in which the French General was right was that this was the Germans' last fling. With its failure, Ludendorff recommended a withdrawal to the Hindenburg Line to shorten the front and therefore make a number

ARMISTICE

of divisions available in reserve, to counter the Allied counter-moves which he knew would come – not least once the US Armies began to arrive in large numbers by the end of the year.

7. This officer appears to have been General Henri Joseph Eugène Gouraud (1867–1946). Wyn Griffith clearly did not appreciate who this was – he was commander of the Fourth French Army, and had lost an arm – not a leg – at Gallipoli. The passage of forty years to the time of writing explains the lapse of memory. Despite Gouraud's pessimism, he received praise for his handling of the German attack. His Official Appeal to the French and American soldiers under his command on 16th July said that: 'We may be attacked from one moment to another. You all feel that a defensive battle was never engaged in under more favourable conditions. We are warned, and we are on our guard. We have received strong reinforcements of infantry and artillery. You will fight on ground which by your assiduous labour you have transformed into a formidable fortress, into a fortress that is invincible if the passages are well guarded ... None will look behind, none will give way. Every man will have but one thought – "Kill them, kill them in abundance, until they have had enough." And therefore your general tells you it will be a glorious day.'
8. 20 kilometres (15 miles) due south of Rheims.
9. II Italian Corps arrived in France on 25 April 1918 in response to the German offensive in March, as a sign of mutual aid following the assistance provided by the British and French governments to Italy the previous year. It was deployed on the inter-Army boundary between Fifth and Tenth French Armies, between Rheims, Soissons, and Château Thierry.
10. This was the former Abbey of Hautvilliers, where Dom Pérignon had perfected the process of making Champagne. It had been confiscated during the Revolution, and was put up for sale in 1816 when it was bought by the Chandon family.
11. XXII Corps took part in the attack on Buzancy (15th Division) and the capture of Beugneux (34th Division) on 28 July, and the Battle of Tardenois 20–31 July.
12. *Extrait de l'Ordre Général* No. 363 dated 17 August 1918. *The London Gazette* entry was in the Supplement No. 31109 dated 3 January 1919. Wyn Griffith actually received the medal by post on 27 May 1919.
13. *The London Gazette* entries for the Mentions in Despatches are November 1916, January 1917 and March 1919. The OBE Gazette is January 1919. Wyn Griffith's medal card is in PRO WO 372/8.
14. Général Henri Mathias Berthelot (1863–1931).
15. *Ordre Général* No. 63 dated 30 July 1918; file ref. 1863/3.
16. The reply was published along with the Order, and dated 31 July 1918.
17. Again, Wyn Griffith is curiously silent about the great offensive, the Hundred Days that began at Amiens in August 1918 and carried the Allies to a victory far sooner than anyone had predicted, and well before the US Army was able to exercise any influence on the result. It was during this phase of the war that the British Army, bearing the brunt of the attack, broke the Hindenburg Line and drove the Germans back without rest. Its casualty figures were as high as the

worst days of 1916 and 1917, but the results justified the losses. It is arguable that the British Army showed during this final period of the war that it learned the hard lessons of previous years, and had become the best battlefield fighting force in the world; it has probably never been better than it was in late 1918.
18. The date given in the Official History is 2nd November 1918, before the Armistice: the Germans had to be driven out of the town by XXII Corps and the Canadians.
19. The Prince of Wales was serving at this time on the staff of the Canadian Corps, which had taken part in the liberation of the city.
20. Robert Arthur James Gascoyne-Cecil, 5th Marquis of Salisbury (1893–1972)
21. Sir George Francis Hugh Eltham GCVO, 2nd Marquis of Cambridge (1895–1981).
22. It is a curious fact that the final operations of the war took place close to the opening battles of the BEF near Mons.
23. Later General Sir Frederick Alfred ('Tim') Pile GCB DSO MC, 2nd Baronet (1884–1976. He was GOC Anti-Aircraft Command in 1939 and remained in this post until 1945. He is mentioned in Alanbrooke's Diaries; Alanbrooke had no opinion of him at all.
24. La Musée Royal du Congo Belge was established at Tervuren in Belgium in 1913. The identity of the baron has not been established.
25. The first British Army of the Rhine was composed of twelve divisions, 273,000 men. By March 1919 this force had largely been disbanded and replaced with Young Soldiers units. The Army originally occupied Cologne, and later Wiesbaden. It gradually reduced until, on its withdrawal in 1929, it consisted of a mere two brigades.
26. Cox's and King's, the Army Agents.
27. The great Spanish flu epidemic lasted from 1918 to 1919. Despite its name, it was first detected at Fort Riley, Kansas, USA on 11 March 1918. It was a truly global epidemic, killing between 50 and 100 million people – probably more than the Black Death and certainly far more, as Wyn Griffith says, than did the war. Its ferocity resulted partly from a high rate of infection – as much as fifty per cent, and partly from the severe symptoms: haemorrhage from the mucous membranes in the nose, stomach and intestine, bleeding from the ears, and massive oedema in the lungs, often resulting in the victim's death by drowning. Many other victims died from secondary bacterial pneumonia caused by the flu. The death rate was up to twenty per cent of those infected; normally flu has a death rate of around 0.1%. Wyn Griffith was, therefore, lucky to live.
28. Somerset House on the Strand was then the headquarters of the Inland Revenue. It later housed the ational records of births, marriages and deaths, and is now home to the Courtauld Institute.
29. Sir Charles Sidney Foulsham Kt (1892–1955) served in the Artists' Rifles and the Suffolks. He was Chief Inspector of Taxes 1943–1952.
30. The Wyn Griffiths had two sons: John Frimston, born in 1919, was killed during a raid on Lubbecke, Germany in 1942; and Hugh Alan, born in 1925, who at the time of writing lives in Florida, USA.

Appendix

The *Second* Christmas Truce, 1915

Much has been written about the Christmas Truce of 1914, which was well covered by the press at the time; however a second truce which occurred in December 1915 and which involved a Welsh battalion was suppressed. Word of it began to surface in the early 1930s but it is only in the last few years, and during 2014 in particular, that a detailed account has emerged.

In December 2014, at Frelinghien on the French-Belgian border, a remarkable commemoration took place. 100 years before, Captain Clifton Stockwell of the 2nd Battalion, Royal Welch Fusiliers, and Captain Friedrich Freiherr von Sinner of the 2nd (Silesian) *Jaeger* Battalion, had met in no-man's land to exchange compliments, beer and Christmas puddings.[1] On the same spot, their grandsons met and made the same exchange watched by soldiers of the British and German armies, local people and visitors from Britain and Germany.[2] By a strange irony, given the prominence I popular mythology of games of football played in No-Man's Land at Christmas 1914, the spot where they met is now a soccer pitch.

That first Christmas truce has become a symbol of reconciliation, a glimmer of the light of common humanity among a mass of darkness. Even at the time, although officially frowned upon, the truce was much covered in the press – including *The Daily News,*[3] *Daily Mirror,*[4] *Manchester Guardian*[5] and the *Illustrated London News*[6] – and there was an understanding, even though anti-German feeling was running high at home, that where chance threw men together in war, even when they were on opposing sides, there was a shared companionship based on experience. The poet Siegfried Sassoon, another Royal Welch Fusilier, commented, as did others, that there was often more comradely feeling between soldiers of the opposing armies, who shared the same dangers and privations, than between soldiers and civilians. Sassoon was in no doubt, for example, that troops would relish the opportunity to take on the pro-war press, or politicians in safe billets, rather than the Germans.[7] Robert Graves like Sassoon, served in the 1st and 2nd Battalions of the Royal Welch Fusiliers and remarked that the men at the front loathed striking munitions workers at home far more than they hated the Germans and would be 'only too glad of a chance to shoot a few.'[8]

Long after the war, in 1962, Graves wrote a short story on the truce.[9] Graves, did not reach France until early 1915 and so had not been present at the first Christmas Truce. He did, however, know the soldier-writer Frank Richards who had been present at the 1914 Truce and helped him write his account of the war in 'Old Soldiers Never Die'. The story portrays a fictional infantry regiment, but the events of December 1914 that he describes are very clearly those at Frelinghien – albeit an amalgam of what 2 R.W. Fus., their neighbours in the line, the Seaforth Highlanders, and indeed the Germans, had experienced. Graves went on in his story to describe a second truce, at Christmas 1915, in which the same two battalions again ended up facing each other in the line and in which the survivors again meet in No-Man's Land.

1915 had been a year of battles which A.J.P. Taylor aptly described as having no meaning other than as names on a war memorial.[10] From the British point of view, it had been a year of bloodshed for no advantage either on the Western Front or at Gallipoli. It was also the year that saw the first use of poison gas, the first *Zeppelin* raids on England, the sinking of the liner *Luisitania*, and the rapid increase of submarine warfare. In France and Flanders in December 1915, a much larger British Army was holding a much longer stretch of the front and it was now under the command not of Sir John French, who had been in command at Christmas 1914, but of Sir Douglas Haig. Haig had only taken command of the B.E.F. a few days before Christmas, on 19 December 1915,[11] but he was determined that there would be no repetition of the events of 1914. Firm instructions were issued right down the chain of command, reminding everyone of the 'unauthorized truce' of the previous year

Appendix: The *Second* Christmas Truce, 1915

and ordering that 'nothing of the kind is to be allowed this year'.[12] Many divisional and brigade commanders issued orders that any German showing himself was to be shot.[13] On the German side, too, there were orders against fraternization, threatening the direst consequences: any visits, agreements not to fire on each other, exchanges of news or whatever were not only strictly forbidden, but would be counted as 'verging on high treason' – in other words, a capital crime.[14]

So is there any truth in Robert Graves's story? At Christmas 1915, both the 1st and 2nd Battalions of the Royal Welch Fusiliers were out of the line, resting.[15] Thus far, Graves is wrong. However there was a Royal Welch Fusilier battalion in the line: the famous 15th Battalion, the 1st London Welsh, in which served many other notable literary figures of the war: Llewelyn Wyn Griffith, author of *Up to Mametz*; Wynn Wheldon, father of Sir Huw, later controller of the BBC; David Jones, whose iconic (but difficult) work *In Parenthesis* is based on his experiences with 15 R.W.F. Then there was Bill Tucker, whose book *The Lousier War* is one of the few accounts we have of life as a P.o.W. in Germany during the Great War; Tucker later worked for many years on *The Times* and helped launch *The Times Atlas of the World*. There was also Harold Gladstone Lewis, who wrote *Crow on a Barbed Wire Fence*. Last, the Welsh shepherd and bard from Trawsfynydd, Ellis Humphrey Evans, or Hedd Wyn, who was killed on Pilckem Ridge in 1917.

15 R.W. Fus. was a war-service battalion and had arrived in France in November 1915.[16] It had seen no serious action thus far and had no reason to feel animosity towards the Germans on a personal level – with the exception of those who had lost friends or brothers in other battalions. Just before Christmas the battalion was in the line at Laventie, just a few miles south of Frelinghien. Here, in the cold and wet of December, the line was described in the diary of an officer of a unit then holding the sector, Captain Carlos 'Pip' Blacker of the 1st Battalion Coldstream Guards:

> It consisted of a line of breastworks through which you could keep watch and shoot. The view through one of these loopholes was not inspiring. Across a stretch of no-man's-land you beheld a conspicuous line of enemy breastworks which looked pale grey in the middle distance ... At the foot of both lines ran narrow belts of rusty wire which looked dark against the grey

sandbags beyond. And between those two belts lay a mostly featureless waste, patched with dead goosefoot and docks and pocked with shell-holes, the deeper ones half-filled with slimy water... A confrontation, winding away into seeming infinity on each side, alive with watchfulness.[17]

15 R.W. Fus was not all together in the line, but each of its companies was under instruction from a different battalion of 2 Guards Brigade, and it was thus spread along a lengthy stretch of the line.[18] This dispersion solves the puzzle of why there are such differing versions of events among the witnesses in 15 R.W. Fus.; according to the Irish Guards' History, one platoon of 15 R.W. Fus was attached to each Guards company.[19] Llewelyn Wyn Griffith's company, C Company, was assigned to Blacker's battalion, 1st Coldstream Guards, and he recounted in *Up to Mametz* that Haig's orders had been received: '*We must confine our goodwill not only to fellow Christians,*' he wrote, '*but to Christians of allied nationality. We were to remain throughout possessed by the spirit of hate, answering any advances with lead*'.[20] On Christmas Eve, sounds of singing and merrymaking could be heard in the German trenches opposite C Company and the Coldstreamers, about 100 yards away, which were occupied by Catholic soldiers of the 13th Bavarian Reserve Infantry Regiment.[21] These men were reservists, dragged, probably unwillingly, from their civilian lives; they were also more easy-going as a people than the stern, Protestant Prussians. Soon, shouts of 'Merry Christmas, Tommy' were heard. These were answered with shouts of 'Merry Christmas, Fritz'.[22] Blacker confirms this account, saying that:

> ... the German breastworks were near enough for verbal exchange to be possible between the two sides... I recall someone shouting across 'What have you got for dinner today Fritz?' The reply sounded like 'a fat goose' (more Germans soke English than our people spoke German). Fritz was invited to come over, but at this stage there was no movement.[23]

The Company Sergeant Major of D Company 15 R.W. Fus was No. 22801 John Bradshaw, who had been a regular soldier in the King's Royal Rifle Corps during the South African War and who

Appendix: The *Second* Christmas Truce, 1915

had, for reasons unknown, enlisted into the Royal Welch Fusiliers in London in January 1915. His diary also survives, and it records how the company was 'brought by motors from Warne to Neuve Chapelle into the trenches with the Grenadier Guards' on 19 December. They withdrew into rest on 20th and then returned to the trenches with a different battalion on 23rd.[24] Bradshaw notes that the company was now with the Scots Guards, however the War Diary records that D Company was attached to the 2nd Battalion Irish Guards.[25] According to *The Irish Guards in the Great War*, the 2nd Battalion was indeed in the line on Christmas Eve but was relieved at 20.00 hrs that night by the 1st Coldstream,[26] as Llewellyn Wyn Griffith also recounts. Bradshaw must, therefore, be mistaken. He was never able to complete his account as he died of wounds after a trench raid near Laventie in May 1916.

Another witness to the exchanges on Christmas Eve in D Company 15 R.W. Fus. was Private Bertie Felstead. Felstead died at the age of 106, in 2001, the oldest man alive in Britain and the last witness of these events.[27] In later life, Felstead remembered how the German soldiers opposite sang, in German, a hymn which shared the same tune with the Welsh hymn 'Ar Hyd y Nos'. This was probably the German version of the hymn 'Go my Children with my Blessing' (*'gehen meine Kinder mit meinem Segen'*). Their choice – probably a lucky chance – was taken as a much-appreciated acknowledgment of the nationality of the opposing company, and the Royal Welch Fusiliers responded by singing 'Good King Wenceslas' – another detail used by Robert Graves in his fictional account. After the night's carol singing, Felstead recalled that feelings of goodwill had so swelled up that at dawn, Bavarian and British soldiers clambered spontaneously out of their trenches. Shouting such greetings as 'Hello Tommy' and 'Hello Fritz' they at first shook hands in no-man's-land, and then presented one another with gifts. German beer, sausages and spiked helmets were given, or bartered, in return for bully beef, biscuits and tunic buttons. Bradshaw's diary, rather laconically, confirms that 'the Germans fraternized with our troops for fifteen minutes'.[28] Interestingly, Bradshaw's personal effects which were sent back to his family after his death include a brass Bavarian belt buckle which, one can at least speculate, he exchanged in No-Man's Land on that Christmas Day a hundred years ago.

Away in C Company's area, Wyn Griffith recounted his memories of a very similar scene:

> As soon as it was light, we saw hands and bottles being waved at us, with encouraging shouts that we could neither understand nor misunderstand A drunken German stumbled over his parapet and advanced through the barbed wire, followed by several others, and in a few moments there was a rush of men from both sides, carrying tins of meat, biscuits and other odd commodities for barter ... this was the first time I had seen No Man's Land, and it was now Every Man's Land, or nearly so. Some of our men would not go, and gave terse and bitter reasons for their refusal. The officers called our men back to the line, and in a few minutes No Man's Land was once more empty and desolate. There had been a feverish exchange of souvenirs, a suggestion for peace all day and a football match in the afternoon, and a promise of no rifle fire at night. All this came to naught.[29]

Blacker also recounted the events in this part of the line in his diary:

> Loudening noises of shouts and singing came across no-man's-land, and when there was enough daylight figures could be seen moving about between their breastworks and wire. Our people followed suit. The Germans then came out in front of their wire. Our people did the same. No shooting anywhere. Both sides then gained in boldness until there was quite a crowd in no-man's-land ... The two sides exchanged cigarettes and other souvenirs, including buttons and badges ...
>
> The conversation, which was amiable, went on for about five minutes. It was brought to an end by a burst of shrapnel overhead.[30]

Felstead, whose company was removed from Wyn Griffith's, remembered that there *was* a soccer match of sorts:

> It wasn't a game as such, more a kick-around and a free-for-all. There could have been 50 on each side for all I know. I played because I really liked football. I don't know how long it lasted, probably half an hour.[31]

Appendix: The *Second* Christmas Truce, 1915

Bradshaw's diary does not confirm this – probably because, as Company Sergeant Major, he disapproved, would have prevented it if he could, and did not wish to preserve any evidence of collaboration which might later be inconvenient.

David Jones was in B Company, which had been attached to the 3rd Battalion Grenadier Guards. He recalled that on Christmas morning he heard the Germans singing Christmas carols and the cockneys of 15 R.W. Fus. singing louder, to drown them out. The London Welsh sang 'Casey Jones', a song he particularly liked.[32] Later that morning, however, the 3rd Grenadiers went into reserve and so Jones saw no more – but he did hear of the meetings in no-man's land and wrote of it in his epic poem, 'Anathemata':

> I saw and heard their cockney song salute the happy morning; and later, this same morning ... walking in daylight, upright, through the lanes of the war-net to outside and beyond the rusted trip-belt, some with gifts, none with ported weapons, embraced him between his *fossa* and ours, exchanging tokens.[33]

Recently, another previously unknown account has surfaced. This is the personal diary of Private Robert Keating, of 4 Rectory Close, Clapham, an under-age Private of about 16 years old in 15 R.W. Fus., who later transferred to the Royal Engineers, and survived the war. He re-joined the Army in the 1920s and by 1942 was a Regimental Sergeant Major; he was afterwards commissioned as an officer in the Intelligence Corps; he died in 1967. In 1915, Keating was in A Company, assigned to the 1st Battalion Scots Guards who were opposite No. 246 Wurttemberg Reserve Infantry Regiment – Catholic soldiers again but from the Rhineland, not Bavaria, and also reservists.[34] Keating recorded what had happened after the morning stand-to and breakfast were over on Christmas Day:

> Had breakfast after which we shouted greetings to the Germans over the way. We shouted come over – they shouted come over. We stood up and saw them walking on their parapets then some of the Jocks ran across & Gordon [unidentified] and I. The officer was shouting come back! – come back! But we took no heed & went on.
> The Germans who turned out to be the Wurttemburg Reserves crowded round us & chatted about old England – one

fellow we were talking to was born in Northampton & was longing for the day when he could return. They said the war would end in a few months in our favour & that they were absolutely fed up with everything generally. Just as we were exchanging souvenirs the blooming artillery started and you should have seen us run: - Heaps of fellows we[re] caught in the barbed wire, but really there was no danger to us as the shells were dropping on the German trenches. The reason why we rushed back was because our artillery firing on the Allerman [i.e. Allemands, or Germans] might entice their snipers to fire on us. However, this was not so. Before leaving the Germans one of their officers told one of ours that they would not fire another shot for two days if we did the same, and believe me or believe me not, on our part of the line not a single shot was fired until we were relieved by the Irish Guards on Sunday evening [26 December]. Well, to revert, at 12 noon I was told off for fatigue duty with about two dozen other Scots, we had to ... get a thousand sand-bags ... Arriving back in the trench at 2.30 p.m. I dumped my load and joined a party who were burying a dead Scot in 'no-man's-land'. We intended burying a lot of fellows but owing to our artillery fire we had to abandon the attempt.[35]

The personal diary of Captain Sir Iain Colquhoun, a company commander with the Scots Guards, supports this account. Colquhoun's diary has been made available on open source through his local historical society, the Vale of Leven:[36]

Stand to at 6.30. Germans very quiet. Remained in Firing Trenches until 8.30. No sign of anything unusual. When having breakfast about 9 am a sentry reported to me that the Germans were standing up on their parapets and walking towards our barbed wire. I ran out to our firing trenches and saw our men looking over the parapet and the Germans outside our barbed wire.

A German officer came forward and asked me for a truce for Xmas. I replied that this was impossible. He then asked for ¾ hour [three-quarters of an hour] to bury his dead. I agreed. The Germans then started burying their dead and we did the same. This was finished in ½ hrs time. Our men and the

Appendix: The *Second* Christmas Truce, 1915

Germans then talked and exchanged cigars, cigarettes etc for ¼ of an hour and when the time was up I blew a whistle and both sides returned to their trenches.

For the rest of the day the Germans walked about and sat on their parapets. Our men did much the same but remained in their trenches. Not a shot was fired. At night the Germans put up Fairy lights on their parapets and their trenches were outlined for miles on either side. It was a mild looking night with clouds and a full moon and the prettiest sight I have ever seen. Our machine guns played on them and the lights were removed. Our guns shelled heavily all night at intervals of ½ an hour and the Germans retaliated on Sunken Road. I had to leave my dug-out five times during the night owing to shells.

Further attempts at peace-making were quickly stamped out. Wyn Griffith recalled an irate Brigadier, spluttering up the line, throwing out threats of courts-martial and ordering an extra dose of military action that night.[37] This was very likely to have been Brigadier-General Lord Henry Seymour, the Commander of 2 Guards Brigade. Private Harold Diffey, another soldier of C Company 15 R.W. Fus. who survived the war and who also remembered the truce, recounted the same episode in a letter home:

After about 20 to 30 minutes a Staff Officer with red tabs ... and a vociferous sergeant-major appeared yelling, 'You came out to fight the Huns, not to make friends with them.' So our lads reluctantly returned followed by a salvo from our 18-pounders which ended the episode.[38]

Keating too recorded Seymour's arrival:

The remainder of the day we spent in shouting to the Germans. Meanwhile the Brigadier General came round the trenches and told every fellow to shoot any German he saw ... no one took any notice of this order and carried on as usual ...[39]

Keating went on to record what had happened on Christmas Night:

[That evening] we were roused out by the Scots and dragged on to the parapet where we found all the Welsh fellows gathered.

> Here we were, Welsh and Scots all, clustered round the burning brazier which was placed on the outer parapet. The Germans were sending up star lights and singing – they stopped, so we cheered them & we began singing Land of Hope and Glory – Men of Harlech et cetera – we stopped and they cheered us. So we went on till the early hours of the morning.[40]

Firmer measures were clearly needed to enforce the approved martial spirit, and Keating's diary of Boxing Day recorded that after the morning routine,

> ... The Germans were not firing but no-one got on the parapet although many heads were above. Orders were issued out that if any man was seen waving or heard shouting they would be put to the wall at once [i.e. shot] – this order put an end to our fun ...
> ... at 5.30 p.m. the Irish Guards relieved us but before going we were told not to mention anything of what happened in the trenches yesterday and today.[41]

Colqhuhoun's dairy recorded what happened to him on Boxing Day:

> Fine day. No rifle firing, but no Germans showing. I went at 10 a.m. to Winchester House to explain to a Court of Inquiry my conduct on Christmas Day. The Brigadier (who came round my trenches 10 mins after my truce was over) didn't mind a bit but the Major General [Lord Cavan] is furious about it. The Coldstreams and our 2nd Batt are also implicated. Relieved by the 1st Irish Guards. Marched out by platoons down Sunken Road and Sign Post line to Rouge Choistre. Dropped the R.W.F. and marched via Rouge Bailleul to La Gorgue at 7 p.m. and billeted there.[42]

Later, both Colquhoun and the acting commanding officer of 1 Scots Guards, Captain Miles Barne, were tried by court-martial; Barne was acquitted of all charges, Colquhoun received a reprimand but this was not confirmed by Sir Douglas Haig – possibly because Colquhoun was related by marriage to the Prime Minister, Herbert Asquith.[43]

APPENDIX: THE *SECOND* CHRISTMAS TRUCE, 1915

So ended the Christmas Truce of 1915, which unlike that of 1914 passed unrecorded in the newspapers and magazines. It was the last such event of the war, other than informal truces to bury the dead and recover the wounded which had been a feature of warfare for centuries and which lingered on in the Great War. There was little if any attempt at a truce over Christmas 1916 and none whatsoever in 1917. Fellow-feeling there might be, a degree of chivalry even, but by the end of the second year of war there was no hope of fraternization.

Notes

1. Frank Richards, *Old Soldiers Never Die* (annotated by H.J. Krijnen and D.E. Langley) (Peterborough, 2004), pp. 45–7 and voice recording in R.W.F Mus; Captain J.C. Dunne, *The War the Infantry Knew 1914–1919* (London, 1994), pp. 101–3; C.I. Stockwell's diary and letters cited in Major C.H. Dudley Ward, *Regimental Records of the Royal Welch Fusiliers, Vol. III 1914 – 1918 France and Flanders* (London, 1928), p. 112–13 and in R.W.F. Mus 2708; account by Lieutenant M.S. Richardson dated 31 December 1914 in T.N.A. WO 95/1365, 2 R.W. Fus War Dairy August – December 1914.
2. Warren Hastings, 'Descendants at site of WW1 Christmas Truce', in *Daily Mirror*, Monday, 15 December 2014.
3. 'Foes in trenches swap pies for wine', in *Daily News*, 1 January 1915.
4. 'An Historic Group', *Daily Mirror*, 1 January 1915 and Leader, 2 January 1915.
5. 'Christmas Truce at the Front', in *Manchester Guardian*, 31 December 1914; 'The Amazing Truce', 4 January 1915; and 'Christmas Day in the Trenches', 6 January 1915.
6. *I.L.N.*, 9 January 1915.
7. See, for example, Siegfried Sassoon, 'Fight to a Finish' in *Cambridge Magazine*, 27 October 1917.
8. Robert Graves, *Goodbye to All That* (London, 1929), p. 296.
9. Robert Graves, 'Christmas Truce', in *The Shout and Other Stories* (London, 1978), pp. 99–115.
10. A.J.P. Taylor, *Illustrated History of the First World War* (London, 1974), pp. 62–63.
11. Gary Sheffield and John Bourne (ed.), *Douglas Haig War Diaries and Letters 1914–1918* (London, 2005), p. 173.
12. See, for example, the signal issued by Major-General Sir Charles Barter, G.O.C. 47th Division, cited in Malcolm Brown and Shirley Seaton, *Christmas Truce* (London, 1994) p. 198.
13. Brigadier W. Thwaites, Commander 140 Infantry Brigade, for example, passed on his G.O.C.'s instructions in this way. Brown and Seaton, p. 198.
14. General Order from G.H.Q. Spa dated 12 December 1915.
15. Dudley Ward, pp. 159, 161.

16. *A Concise History of the 15th R.W.F. (1st London Welsh)* (R.W.F. Mus 3048/B), p. 4.
17. *Have You Forgotten Yet? The First World War Memoirs of C P Blacker MC GM* (ed. John Blacker), (Barnsley, 2000), p. 68.
18. T.N.A. WO 95/2556/1, 15 R.W. Fus War Diary, 1 December 1915–28 February 1918.
19. Rudyard Kipling, *The Irish Guards in the Great War, Volume II* (London, 1921), p. 41.
20. Llewelyn Wyn Griffith, *Up to Mametz and Beyond* (ed and annotated by Jonathon Riley), (Barnsley, 2010), p. 13.
21. Hermann Cron, *Imperial German Army 1914–18: Organisation, Structure, Orders-of-Battle* [first published 1937] (London, 2001), pp. 111–16.
22. Wyn Griffith, p. 14.
23. Blacker, p. 75.
24. Diary of John Bradshaw for 1915 (Permission of Mr John Griffiths), 19–23 December 1915.
25. T.N.A. WO 95/2556/1, 15 R.W.Fus War Diary, 1 December 1915–28 February 1918.
26. Rudyard Kipling, p 47.
27. 'Bertie Felstead, the last known survivor of no-man's-land football died on July 22, 2001 aged 106', in *The Economist*, 2 August 2001; 'Last Soldier recalls the Christmas truce', in *Sunday Telegraph*, 22 December 1996; 'Match of the century', in *Daily Mail*, 9 November 1999; Felstead's obituaries in *The Times*, 26, 28 July 2001; and *The Daily Telegraph*, 26 July 2001.
28. Bradshaw's Diary, 25 December 1915.
29. Wyn Griffith, pp. 14–15.
30. Blacker, pp. 75, 76.
31. Richard Alleyne, 'Veteran of 1915 soccer game dies', in *The Daily Telegraph*, 26 July 2001; Bertie Felstead, 'Football made us friends for a day', in *Western Mail*, 12 November 1999.
32. Thomas Dilworth, *David Jones in the Great War* (London, 2012), pp. 71–2.
33. David Jones, *The Anathemata* (London, 1951), p. 216.
34. *Reichsarchiv Militr-Verlag* (Berlin, 1927), S. 71, pp. 146–7.
35. Robert Keating's Diary, Vol. 1, 1 December 1915–6 July 1916, R.W.F. Mus 9203
36. Sir Iain Colquhoun's Dairy, www.valeofleven.org.uk, accessed 20 November 2015.
37. Wyn Griffith, p. 14.
38. Letter from Harold Diffey in R.W.F. Mus 7133f.
39. Keating's Diary, Vol. 1.
40. Keating's Diary, Vol. 1.
41. Keating's Diary, Vol. 1.
42. Sir Iain Colquhoun's Dairy, www.valeofleven.org.uk, accessed 20 November 2015.
43. Brown and Seaton, p. 205.

Bibliography

Primary Sources

Army List, (HMSO, London) monthly from August 1914 to September 1919.

Concise History of the 15th RWF (1st London Welsh) 1914–1924 (compiled and published by the Committee of the 15th RWF Association).

Edmonds, Brigadier General Sir James *Military Operations, France and Belgium 1917* (London, 1948).

Falls, Captain Cyril *Military Operations, France and Belgium 1918* (London, 1940).

David Jones papers in the Regimental Archives of The Royal Welch Fusiliers, Caernarfon.

Debrett's *Peerage and Baronetage* (1976).

Horne, Charles F. and Austin, Walter F. *Source Records of the Great War Volume VI, 1918* (Indianapolis, 1930).

Kirby, Major Peter MC Officers of the Royal Welch Fusiliers, 1689–1914 (Available from RWF Museum Archives and updated continuously since 1997).

Llewelyn Wyn Griffith papers, National Library of Wales GB 0210 LL WGRIF G3/10 (Army Book 136 – notebook containing a partial diary and draft poems, 1916–1917); P1/2 (letters 1914–1974); P2/2 letters to his wife 1915–1953); P3/1 (diaries 1915–1932); P4/1 (officer's record).

Roberts, Peter (ed) The Letters of Brigadier-General Price-Davies, Commanding 113 (North Wales) Brigade.

War Diary (1914–1918) of 10th (Service) Battalion Royal Welch Fusiliers (edited by Lt-Col F.N. Burton and Lt A.P. Comyns MC, Plymouth, 1926).

War Diary of the 14th (Service) Battalion Royal Welch Fusiliers 1914–1919 (printed by Gale and Polden, Aldershot).

War Diary 15 RWF 1915–1917 (RWF Archives).

Who Was Who, (various volumes, 1916–1971).

PRO WO 095.820 General Staff daily operations and intelligence summary, Headquarters VIII Corps.
PRO WO 095.827 War Diary Headquarters VIII Corps.
PRO WO 095.828 Corps Signal Company daily summary, Headquarters VIII Corps.
PRO WO 095.829 Senior Officers' diary, Headquarters VIII Corps.

Books

Adam-Smith, Patsy *The ANZACs* (Ringwood, Victoria, Australia, 1978).
Ashworth, Tony *Trench Warfare 1914–1918: The Live and Let Live System* (London, 2000).
Barne, A. *War Underground 1914–1918* (London, 1964).
Brown, Malcolm and Seaton, Shirley *Christmas Truce* (London, 1994).
Churchill, Winston S. *The World Crisis 1916–1918 Parts I and II* (London, 1927).
Coombs, Rose E.B. *Before Endeavours Fade. A Guide to the Battlefields of the First World War* (London, 1983).
Davies, Emlyn *Taffy Went to War* (Knutsford, 1976).
Dudley Ward, C.H. *Regimental Records of The Royal Welch Fusiliers, Volume III 1914–1918, France and Flanders* (Wrexham, 1991).
Dunn, Captain J.C. *The War the Infantry Knew* (London, 1989).
French, David and Holden Reid, Brian (ed) *The British General Staff. Reform and Innovation 1890–1939* (London, 2002).
Fuller, J.F.C. *Generalship: Its Diseases and Their Cure*, (Harrisburg, Pennsylvania, 1936).
Harrington, General Sir Charles *Plumer of Messines* (London, 1935).
Hill, Greg *Llewellyn Wyn Griffith* (Writers of Wales Series, University of Wales Press, 1984).
Hughes, Colin Anfield *Mametz: Lloyd George's 'Welsh Army' at the Battle of the Somme* (London, 1985).
Hyne, Anthony *David Jones, A Fusilier at the Front* (Bridgend, 1995).
James, E.A. *British Regiments, 1914–1918* (London, 1978).
James, Robert Rhodes *Anthony Eden* (London, 1986).
Jones, David *In Parenthesis* (London, 1937).
Jones, David *The Sleeping Lord and other fragments* (London, 1974).
Langley, David *Duty Done. Second Battalion The Royal Welch Fusiliers in the Great War* (Privately Published, 2002).
Liddell Hart, B.H. *History of the First World War* (London, 1970).
Lock, Nick *The Histories and Literature of The Royal Welch Fusiliers* (Available from RWF Museum Archives and updated continuously since 1998).
Lucas, Sir Charles *The Empire at War*, Volume III (London, 1924).
Macdonald, Lyn *Somme* (London, 1983).

Bibliography

Masters, John *The Road Past Mandalay* (Watford, 1961).
Middlebrook, Martin *The Kaiser's Battle* (London, 1978).
Munby, Lt-Col J.E. CMG DSO, *A History of the 38th (Welsh) Division by the GSO1s of the Division* (London, 1920).
Powell, Geoffrey *Plumer – The Soldiers' General* (Barnsley, 1990).
Richards, Frank *Old Soldiers Never Die* (annotated by H.J. Krinjen and D.E. Langley, Peterborough, 2004).
Richards, J. *Wales on the Western Front* (Cardiff University Press, 1994).
Sheffield, Gary *The Somme: Forgotten Victory* (London 2001).
Terraine, John *The Western Front 1914–1918* (London, 1964).
Tucker, W.A. *The Lousier War* (London, 1974).
Windsor, HRH The Duke of *A King's Story* (London, 1951).
Wyn Griffith, Llewelyn *Up To Mametz* (London, 1931, republished 1981, 1988).
Wyrall, Everard *History of the 62nd (West Riding) Division 1914–1919*, Volume I (London, nd).
Wyn Griffith, Llewelyn *Hiraeth* (Privately Printed, 1929).
Wyn Griffith, Llewelyn *Spring of Youth* (London, 1935).
Wyn Griffith, Llewelyn *The Wooden Spoon* (London, 1937).
Wyn Griffith, Llewelyn *The Way Lies West* (London, 1945).
Wyn Griffith, Llewelyn *The Barren Tree And Other Poems*. (Penmark Press: Cardiff, nd [1947]).

Articles in Books and Journals

Crocker, Lieutenant Colonel P.A. 'Some Thoughts on The Royal Welch Fusiliers in the Great War' in *Y Ddraig Goch*, Journal of The Royal Welch Fusiliers, September 2002.
Wheldon, W.P. 'The Canal Bank at Ypres' in *The Welsh Outlook*, Volume VI, March 1919.
Wyn Griffith, Llewellyn 'The Pattern of One Man's Remembering' in *Promise of Greatness*, ed George A Panchiras (London, 1968).

Military Pamphlets and Publications

Field Service Regulations, Volume I (Organisation and Administration). WO 26/Regs/1849.
Field Service Pocket Book. WO 26/863.

Index

Abricci, Conte de 174
Aire 38, 39, 40, 43, 44
Alabaster, E.O. 164, 170fn
Amiens 169, 170fn, 185fn
Armentières 166
Armies (British)
  First 179, 180
  Second 153, 156, 158, 159fn, 161fn, 162fn, 171fn, 179
  Fourth 34
  Fifth 147fn, 162fn, 170fn
Armies (French)
  Fourth 175
  Fifth 175, 177, 184fn
  Seventh 173
  Tenth 175
Armistice 178–9
Arras 80, 145fn
Artillery. Types of; effects of, barrages 14, 15, 19, 20, 28, 33fn, 39, 42, 56–7, 58, 59, 85fn, 103, 104, 106, 114, 115, 212fn, 132–3, 146fn, 156, 159fn, 162fn, 174–5, 176, 194
Aubers 9, 26
Auchel 86

Bailleul 80, 143, 150, 153, 160fn, 163fn, 164, 165, 166, 171fn, 196
Bantam battalions 29, 30, 31, 32, 33fn, 42

Barne, M. 196
Bazentin 104, 109, 113, 119
Bell, R.C. 62, 70fn, 147fn
Bentinck, Lord C.C. 156, 162fn
Bently, R. 65, 71fn
Berthelot, H.M. 177–8
Béthune 21–2, 31fn, 38
Beauval 130
Billets, billeting 6, 16, 22, 39–41, 42, 53fn, 63, 64, 65, 68, 77, 78, 86, 88, 90, 91, 130, 138, 154, 180, 186
Blacker, C. (Pip) 189–90, 192
Blendecques 16
Bloor, D.W. 70fn
Boesinghe 139
Bollezelle 169
Boulogne 48, 49, 50, 51, 56, 169
Bradshaw, H.C. 153, 160fn
Bradshaw, J. 190–3
Brandhoek 168
Brigades
  4 New Zealand Infantry 152
  113 Infantry 4, 16, 17fn, 121fn, 132, 137, 145fn, 199fn
  114 Infantry 121, 139
  115 Infantry 17fn, 94, 120fn, 122fn, 130, 139, 145fn
Broodseinde 155, 162fn, 167
Brown, Cpl 67
Brussels 181

Index

Caesar's Nose Trench 140
Calons-en-Champagne 173
Carden, R.J.W. 120, 121fn
Cassel 153, 156, 160fn, 161fn, 167, 171fn
Castello 173, 180
Caterpillar Wood 104, 105
Chelers 90
Churchill, Sir W.S. 168, 169, 170fn
Coigneux 122fn
Collard, A.M. 167, 171fn
Colne Valley Trench 140
Colquhoun, Sir Iain, 194, 196
Contalmaison 101, 102, 103
Cookery, rations and messing 7, 10, 12, 14, 23–5, 33fn, 58, 64, 97, 137, 140, 166, 179, 180–1
Corps (British and Empire)
  II 159fn, 184fn
  IV 17fn, 145fn
  VIII 128, 130, 131, 132, 135, 145fn, 146fn, 147fn, 159fn
  IX 136, 151
  XI 54, 69fn
  XIV 119fn, 147fn
  XXII 159fn, 167–85
  I ANZAC 146, 158, 158fn
  II ANZAC 144, 150–63
  Canadian 146fn, 158, 179, 180, 186fn
Corps (French)
  II Cavalry 167, 169
  XX 175
  XXX 175
Corps (Italian)
  II 185
Cranborne, Viscount 178
Crest Farm 158
Cundall, H.J. 138, 147fn

Dabell, A.H. 164, 170fn
Davies, E.H. ('Taylor') 100, 101, 102, 111, 112, 113, 115, 119fn
Davies, Emlyn, 120fn
Davies, J.H. 131, 145fn
Delaforce, E.F. 151, 159fn
Delivett, G. 77, 78, 79, 84fn

Derry, A. 131, 132, 137, 145fn
Dickebusch 169
Dieppe 170
Diffey, F, 195
Divisions (British)
  Guards 5–8, 16, 17fn
  6th 168, 171fn
  9th (Scottish) 168, 171fn
  11th 179
  15th (Scottish) 169, 175
  17th 120fn
  21st 122fn, 168, 169, 171fn
  25th 153, 159fn, 168, 169, 171fn
  29th 131, 14, 155
  31st 146
  34th 169, 175
  38th (Welsh) 70, 94fn, 103, 107, 108, 112, 115, 116, 119, 120, 130, 139, 146fn, 148fn
  48th 122fn
  49th (West Riding) 157, 158, 168, 169, 171fn
  51st (Highland) 175, 179, 181, 184fn
  52nd (Lowland) 179
  56th (London) 145fn, 179
  62nd (2nd West Riding) 169, 171fn, 172fn, 174, 175, 184
  63rd 177, 179
  66th (2nd East Lancashire) 158, 162fn
Divisions (ANZAC)
  1st Australian 158, 160fn
  2nd Australian 158
  3rd Australian 157, 158, 166
  4th Australian 158, 159fn, 160fn, 166
  5th Australian 152, 158
  New Zealand 150, 152, 157, 158, 159fn, 160fn, 166
Divisions (French)
  3rd Cavalry 167–9
Dodd, A.H.R. 169, 172fn
Downs, Pte 81
Downes, G.P. 70fn
Dress and equipment in trenches 5, 6, 7, 58, 59, 66

203

Duck's Bill Crater 67, 74
Dunkirk 169

Eden, Sir A (Lord Avon) 156, 161fn
Edward, HRH, Prince of Wales
 later King Edward VIII 153, 178, 186fn
Ellington, Sir L. 135, 136, 147fn
Eltham, Earl of 178, 186fn
Elverdinge 132, 133
Épernay 174
Espilly 176
Estaires 6, 44
Evans, H.J. (Brigadier-General) 90, 91, 92, 95fn, 100, 101, 102, 104, 105, 106, 107, 108, 110, 111, 112, 113, 114, 115, 116, 117, 130, 131
Evans, H.J. (Lieutenant-Colonel) 164, 170fn
Evans, L.N.V. 33fn
Evans, Padre (Peter Jones Roberts) 99–100

Fargate Trench 140
Felsted, B. 191
Festubert 29, 30, 38, 68
Ffordd y boedal 164
Flêtre 153
Floringhem 88
Flower, O.S. 120, 121fn
Foch, F. 116, 169, 170fn, 175
Forêt de Nieppe 16
Fort Erith 9, 12, 14
Fortifications and field defences, trenches, breastworks 5–7, 9–10, 16, 19–20, 44–5, 60, 61
Foss, C.C. 154, 161fn
Foulsham, Sir C. 182, 186fn
Fricourt 99
Fusilier House 140

George V, King 147fn, 153, 166
Givenchy 29, 34, 35, 36, 38, 39, 42, 52, 75, 84fn, 94fn
Godley, Sir A.J. 150, 152, 155, 159fn, 162fn, 166, 167, 168, 171fn, 174, 175, 177, 178, 180, 181

Gommecourt 121, 122fn, 145fn
Gonnehem 86
Goraud, H.J.E. 174, 185fn
Gorre 30, 31, 39
Gort, Lord 169, 171fn
Gough, Sir H. 156, 161fn, 162fn
Graves, Robert, 188–9
Green, Pte 16, 38, 39, 40, 41
Griffith, Watcyn 71fn, 100, 114, 120fn
Griffith, Winfred (Wyn) née Frimston 11, 17fn, 43, 47, 49, 50, 51, 52, 53, 55, 134, 154, 157, 164, 177, 182, 183
Griffiths, John 198
Grogan, Ewart 160fn
Grogan, G. 150, 152, 159fn, 168, 169, 173
Gwynn, Sir W 158, 160fn, 164

Haking, Sir C. 56, 69fn
Hansen, P.H. 154, 161fn, 164, 168, 177
Harington, Sir Charles 156, 161fn
Hazebrouck 158, 164
Hébuterne 122fn, 130, 166
Headingley Trench 140
Heeson, S. 71fn
Heffernan 182
Heywood, M.B. 158, 163fn
Hickie, C.J. 132, 136, 145fn
Hickie, W.B. 132, 137, 145fn
Hill Top Trench 140
Hingette 43
Hodson, H.V.R. 87, 94fn
Hoograaf 168
Horne, Sir H. 112, 119fn, 180
Howells, W.A. 14, 17fn, 22
Huddersfield Trench 140
Hunter-Weston, Sir A. 130, 131, 135, 136, 137, 138, 145fn

Irish Farm 139

Jackson, Cpl 82
Jacob, Sir C. 118, 119fn
Jones, D. 193

204

INDEX

Keating, R. 193–4, 195–6
Kemmel 151, 166, 168, 171

La Bassée 7, 28, 166
La Belle Alliance 140
La Brique 140
Lacouture 18
La Gorgue 47, 48, 196
Lancashire Farm 139, 140
Laventie 44, 56, 63, 70fn, 85fn, 166, 189, 191
Leave 27, 41, 43, 44, 47, 48–53, 55, 88, 132, 140, 154, 157, 158, 164, 177
Les Haies 176
Le Sart 16, 17fn
Liddell, D.E. 154, 156, 161fn, 175, 181
Llandudno 157
Lovie Château 135, 146, 147fn

Machonochie stew 6, 17fn
Maistre, General 173
Mametz village 97, 100
Mametz Wood 96, 100, 101–22, 125, 126
Man, H.W. 164, 170fn
Marfaux 176
Marne, Second battle of 174–8
Mason 154
Merville 18, 56, 85fn, 86
Messines 150, 151, 152, 154, 155, 157, 159fn, 160fn, 161fn, 166, 171fn, 179
Meteren 168
Mines, mining 38, 39, 46, 52, 74, 75, 76, 77, 80, 84fn, 160fn
Monk 135, 147fn
Mons 178–80, 181
Montaigne de Rheims 174, 176
Mont Noir 164, 167, 169, 170fn
Mont Rouge 167, 169, 171fn
Mortars 16fn, 20, 32fn, 69fn, 85fn, 116, 132, 140, 147fn, 156

Nappes 176
No Man's Land 13–15, 20, 26, 28, 34, 46, 53fn, 59, 60, 73, 192
Norman, C.C. 142, 148fn

Oosttaverne 152, 160fn
Organisation of brigades and divisions 4, 16, 89, 90
Osbourne Jones, N. 59, 70fn
Owen, G. 56, 69fn, 70fn

Panet, A.E. 151
Parkinson (Parkington) 27, 33fn
Passchendaele 157, 158–9, 162fn, 179, 183, 184
Patrols, patrolling 19, 27, 34, 59, 60, 73–4, 76, 114, 146fn, 156
Pile, Sir F.A. (Tim) 179
Platt, Sir W. 154, 161fn, 169
Ploegsteert 152
Plumer, Sir H. 153, 156, 159fn, 161fn, 162fn, 166, 171fn, 179, 182
Pommiers Redoubt 99, 100, 101, 102, 104, 106, 107
Pope, S.B. 150, 159fn
Poperinghe 134, 146fn, 147fn, 167, 168
Powell, E.W.M. 151, 156–7, 159fn, 175, 176
Price-Davies, Ll. A.E. 4, 25, 132, 143, 144, 145fn
Proven 147fn

Queen's Nullah 113, 114

Raids, raiding, raiding parties 15, 33fn, 34, 56, 58–60, 69–70, 147
Railways, troop trains 48–50, 51, 146fn, 160fn
Rees, W.J. 21, 32
Rheims 173, 174, 175, 177
Rhiw 17fn, 154, 161fn
Richebourg St Vaast 18
Riez Bailleul 65, 80
Road marches 6, 8, 9, 13, 18, 30, 63, 80, 86, 87, 90, 117, 123, 124, 125, 130, 157–8, 175, 178, 196
Robillot, F. 167, 171fn, 173, 177
Routine in trenches 5–7, 28, 38, 62, 132, 140–1, 142
Rubrouek 167

St Omer 4, 134, 161fn, 163fn, 167
Serre 19fn, 130, 132
Seymour, Lord Henry, 195
Signals, signallers 47, 58, 59, 69, 78, 79, 96, 98, 102, 111, 113, 116, 119, 120fn, 147fn, 168
Skipton Trench 140
Smith, F.W. 137, 147
Somme, Battles of 86, 96–118, 130, 135, 166
Songs, music, music-hall 22, 61, 63, 77, 79, 80, 81, 82, 154
Staff duties 55, 62, 64, 87, 90, 92, 95, 107, 128–9, 130, 135, 147, 150, 157, 164, 167, 168
Staff uniform, distinguishing badges 113, 121, 131, 152
Steenvoorde 166
Stranack C.E. 154, 164

Taggart, H. 59, 70fn
Taylor *see* Davies, E.H.
Tennant, Hon E.W. 63, 70fn
Thomas, O. 17fn, 146fn
Town Major 39, 40, 41, 42, 43
Tracey, W. 30, 33fn
Truces, ceasefires, live-and-let live 14–15, 17fn, 54fn, 179, 187–98
Tunnelling companies R.E. *see* mines, mining
Turco Farm 139, 140

Units
  16th Lancers 179
  3 Gren Gds 7, 191, 193
  1 Colm Gds 7, 17fn, 189, 190, 191, 196
  1 Scots Gds 7, 17fn, 192, 193, 196
  2 Irish Gds 7, 16, 17fn, 191, 194, 196

13 R.W.F. 16, 71fn, 85fn, 90, 121fn, 144fn
14 R.W.F. 16, 84fn, 94fn, 144fn
16 R.W.F. 16fn, 121fn, 144fn
17 R.W.F. 120, 144fn
10 S.W.B. 120, 121fn
16 Welch 120, 122fn, 147
19 Welch 16fn
119 Bde R.F.A. 16
124 Fd Coy R.E. 16
113 M.G. Coy 16, 46
113 Lt Trench Mortar Bty 16

Valenciennes 178
Veal, C.L. 91, 94fn, 99, 100, 103, 108, 112, 130, 145fn
Vertus 174
Vielle Chapelle 18
Vitry-le-François 173, 184fn

Walton, S. 81, 85fn
Warne 16fn, 40, 191
Welsh Harp Trench 140
Welsh language 17fn, 98, 116, 134, 137, 141, 148fn, 189, 191
Wheldon, W.P. 139, 141, 148fn, 189
Williams, J.O. 132, 146fn
Witten, P.F. 70fn
Woods, Pte 177
Working parties in trenches 7, 19, 20, 26, 60, 61, 140–1

Ypres 38, 80, 132, 139, 146, 156, 168, 169
Yser Canal 139–44

Zeppelins 38
Zillebeke 168
Zuytpeene 167
Zwanhof 139, 140